The
Champs
'81

Sports editor, Bob Hammel
Photo editor, Larry Crewell

With contributions
from The Herald-Telephone's
sports and photography staffs

Cover designed by Mel Miller

The Champs '81

Published by The Herald-Telephone
and Indiana University Press

Manufactured in the United States of America

LC 81-47625
ISBN 0-253-22700-3 pbk.

Indiana University basketball, 1980-81

Contents

Foreword

March!

It was a 35-game voyage unlike any ever taken by a college basketball team. But so are they all, all Indiana University basketball adventures, in the remarkable coaching era of Robert Montgomery Knight.

In parts, they're a rapids shoot. In the main, they wind up in the tranquility of exceptional, sometimes unimaginable, accomplishment.

Our purpose is to preserve — and to recreate, as faithfully as possible, exactly how it ran in the daily pages of *The Herald-Telephone* — a log of a journey unique even at IU: the 1980-81 season in which the *S.S. Indiana* was fired on and hit more times than any that ever completed a championship trip and yet sailed into the final harbor as elegantly as the least-nicked of its predecessors.

Five years ago, Knight and IU went into basketball's record book by winning a national championship and going 32-0, equalling the best record ever for an NCAA winner (North Carolina also went 32-0 in 1957).

This time, when a second championship came to Knight and a fourth to Indiana, the Hoosiers were 26-9, the worst record a champion has had in the 43 years the NCAA has been picking basketball winners.

First and 43rd: that's where the two Knight-IU championship teams rank on the won-lost list. On the floor — appropriately, on a floor common to both teams, each of them winning tournaments that wound up at The Spectrum in Philadelphia, the only two times the place has been the NCAA finals site — there was no visible gap at all between No. 1 and No. 43, between the all-conquering 1976 team and the one that achieved every bit as predominant a position among its peers in 1981.

Indeed, it would have made a fascinating match-up, Indiana '76 vs. Indiana '81, if each could be brought back at its finest. They were teams crafted by the same hand, yet totally different in strengths. The '81 team developed into an extraordinarily effective defensive team inside, where the big men prowl and where the '76 team got its offense. Ray Tolbert and Landon Turner became skilled enough, at 6-9 and 6-10, to take on highly mobile forwards, and Ted Kitchel showed against Maryland star Buck Williams he could handle post defense while the big men were roaming. And never was there a better pair of defensive guards than Quinn Buckner and Bobby Wilkerson of the '76 team, a combination that destroyed many an offense before it ever got set up. The prospect of 6-1 Isiah Thomas operating against the quick, engulfing hands and arms of the 6-7 "Spiderman" Wilkerson is as interesting in contemplation as the collision of strengths up front.

But how could the No. 1 team on the won-lost record list conceivably be comparable to the 43rd?

The development of invincibility simply happened so much later in '81. In the 1975-76 season, the Hoosiers showed on opening night they were clearly No. 1 in the land by swamping the reigning champion, UCLA, 84-64, on a neutral court. They were No. 1 every week the rest of the way, most of the time unanimously backed by the diverse — and sometimes perverse — electorates that do the rating for the two wire services.

In pre-season, 1980-81, the Hoosiers got one first-place vote in United Press International's coaches' poll. Jud Heathcote of Michigan State cast it, confessing that he respected his league so much he began with defending league champion Indiana, 1980 Big Ten runnerup Ohio State and a 1980 Final Four team, Iowa, 1-2-3 on his ballot.

The Hoosiers were ranked fourth in the pre-season poll. Not

until they lost their last two December games and slid to 7-5 did they finally lose enough stock with the nation's coaches to drop out of the Top 20. And they were out for only one week then. When they opened their Big Ten season by beating Michigan State and Illinois, the Hoosiers reappeared among the pollsters' elite — 19th, though their 9-5 record stood out in a list of four teams that were unbeaten, six that had lost just once, eight that had lost twice and just one other that had such a legacy of success that its four defeats didn't fool the voting coaches. Prophetically, the other multiple loser in the Jan. 13 poll was North Carolina, the classy, ever-contending program that Dean Smith put into operation long ago in the rabid Atlantic Coast Conference and the team that proved the pollsters' point by lining up opposite Indiana in the national championship game at Philadelphia March 30.

Knight and Smith didn't have the look of two coaches on a national championship collision course when, by the wildest of coincidences, travel patterns plunked the two of them into the same area of the Kansas City airport at a nadir hour for both: Dec. 31, hours after Smith's Tar Heels had taken an unaccustomed 16-point drubbing from Minnesota in a Los Angeles tournament and Knight's Hoosiers, for the first time in his 10 Indiana seasons, had lost on two straight nights (to Clemson and

Bob Knight — Philly has a familiar ring

7

Bob Knight — Lucky blue coat and tie 5-for-5 in tourney

Pan American) in a tournament at Honolulu. It was as if the fall of the armada and Waterloo had come on the same afternoon and Spain's King Phillip and France's Napoleon had happened on each other the next day in downtown Rome.

There isn't a lot of flying done, of the airport-type, on New Year's Eve. Knight and Smith, two of the most recognized men in collegiate athletics, had no problem finding privacy in the middle of the vast airport. Commiseration flowed. Three months later, almost to the day, they met again in Philadelphia, their zenith hour in a dipsy-doodle year.

For Knight, it was the year of "Jack," the mule he brought on-to his weekly TV show as the enduring symbol of a breach historic even in the bitter athletic relationship between Indiana and Purdue.

For Knight, it was the year of "Tiger Bait," the Louisiana State taunt that proved as pejorative when flung back as it is intended to be when tossed out.

Those were the rapids that passed under the Hoosier team like ripples in a placid pond. Concentration is the forte of the best Knight teams, and the team that emerged in March, 1981, certainly was one of those.

March. It was at once a time of year and a command. When March came, it was time to move, and the 1981 Hoosiers double-timed their way through the month with a brilliance that was as unexpected as it was undeniable.

From halftime of their first March game — at Illinois, on a night when all facts seemed to favor the excellent team Lou Henson put together in Champaign — through the net-cutting at Philadelphia, Knight's 1980-81 Hoosiers were college basketball's best.

Theirs was the peaking to top all peaks. Among all of the college game's late-bloomers, of all time, they are *The Champs.*

THE *Indiana* IMAGE

There are little eyes upon you
And they're watching night and day
There are little ears that quickly
Take in every word you say;
There are little hands all eager
To do anything you do;
And a little boy who's dreaming
Of the day he'll be like you.

You're the little fellow's idol;
You're the wisest of the wise,
In his little mind about you,
No suspicions ever rise;
He believes in you devoutly,
Holds that all you say and do,
He will say and do, in your way
When he's a grown-up like you.

There's a wide-eyed little fellow,
Who believes you're always right,
And his ears are always open,
And he watches day and night;
You are setting an example
Every day in all you do,
For the little boy who's waiting
To grow up to be like you.

'Walking history book'
Clair Bee meets Hoosiers

BLOOMINGTON, NOV. 26, 1980

He seemed out of place, old and tiny, sitting on a chair in the middle of the Indiana basketball dressing room, his audience the lively and strapping youngsters who make up the 1980-81 Hoosiers. The four oldest among them barely equal the 85 years Clair Bee has been on the planet. He is blind. He has an additional problem or two. But he *is* 85. "I haven't been cheated," Bee laughed.

He laughed a lot, and so did his audience in a brisk hour and a half that exposed a new generation to all the older ones that came along in basketball ahead of them. All of those. When the inventor of the game, James Naismith, wrote a book on the sport, the foreword was by Clair Bee.

He coached at Rider College for three years, then for 18 at Long Island University, during which LIU became the titan of the sport. He left the college game with a better winning percentage than any other retiring master before or since. Clair Bee won 82.7 percent of the time (410-86) in those 21 college years. Adolph Rupp's percentage was 82.1; John Wooden's, 80.6; Phog Allen's, 76.8.

Bee also coached football and baseball most of those years. He also was the leading sports author of his time, including in his works the Chip Hilton series that set standards of sportsmanship and competitiveness for generations up to today's.

His topic, four days before the Hoosiers open their season against Ball State, was basketball, contemporary basketball. He lectured, and he fielded questions. He made his years an asset, not any sort of liability, in bridging the 60-plus years between him and his audience.

"It was like talking to a walking history book," Isiah Thomas said.

"He was even *quick*," Hoosier senior Phil Isenbarger said.

Quick of mind, surely. And even quick of foot.

Though blind, he didn't hesitate to leap to his feet on occasion and illustrate the quick hand moves, the quick foot moves, the passing fakes that could be practiced without a basketball around. "You *can* develop quickness," he insisted. "You can practice foot quickness walking down the street. People may think you're crazy, but you can do it.

"The player himself can do so much to make himself great. A 6-11 boy can be just as quick as a 6-6 boy if he just believes he is and works at developing quickness."

Sophomore Jim Thomas asked what Bee considered the key to winning. It was like asking Billy Graham his view on the key to eternal life. Bee knows only one route.

"Determination," he said. "Team play, but above all determination, by player and by team. The desire to win is paramount. I hated to lose.

"But we had fun. I always tried to make my team have fun. I used to joke with them, some.

"But when we worked, we worked. I understand some teams now have two-hour practices. Not for me. We used to work all day Saturday and Sunday. I mean all day. We'd start at 11 in the morning and go till 8 at night.

"Oh, I'd send out for sandwiches and Cokes along the way . . . so they wouldn't think I was inhuman."

He gave his audience a feeling of being there at the dawn of creation of various phases of the modern game.

Zone defenses, for example.

"The first basketball I coached was when I was in the service in World War I," he said. "I was a boxer. A colonel asked me if I had played any other sports, and I said 'Sure.' So I coached the basketball team.

"We played a game against another camp team. Terrible conditions. Two pot-bellied stoves; the playing surface was so slick you couldn't stand up.

"And that's where the zone began. The other coach, a fellow named Cam Henderson who was later a great coach at Marshall, came out the second half and didn't have his men pick us up man-to-man, because of the slick floor."

Bee's fertile mind saw some immediate advantages in the Henderson move. "I devised the 1-3-1 zone — I was a zone coach," he said, aware he was talking to a team that never plays one.

It was inevitable he was asked how he would coach today.

"I would use the offense I started with, the give-and-go," he said. "There is a lot you can do out of that, with so much screening and movement.

"And when it was to my advantage, I'd use some of the four-corner offense which I gave to Dean Smith down at North Carolina.

"On defense, I would go man-to-man, mainly, and switch sometimes into my 1-3-1."

Bee recalled his first meeting with Knight.

"I had retired and I was living in Cornwall, near West Point," he said. "The West Point coaches used to come up and see me occasionally — three or four of them before Bob. And I would go to see their practices. The first time I saw him was at a practice, and he was an assistant. I noticed that he was doing more coaching than the head coach that day, and I said to myself, 'There's going to be a great coach some day.' And he is a great coach.

"Oh, he worries too much. He hollers well. And he has a pretty good command of the language. He has two or three good things going for him."

Each line came with deft timing. His listeners exploded in laughter after each of the last three.

Obviously, they didn't feel cheated, either.

Conference time for Isiah Thomas, Bob Knight

Indiana 75, Ball State 69

The tendency to associate Indiana basketball excellence with Isiah Thomas didn't exactly get a setback in the new Hoosiers' season opener, without him.

Unless Thomas carries with him the secret to making lay-ups, the man whose forte is creating them would have had as frustrating an afternoon on court as he no doubt did sitting alongside it, idled by a groin injury. The Hoosiers missed both: Thomas and lay-ups, the latter by the batch.

IU did win, beating Ball State, 75-69, at Assembly Hall. Actually, the score was 75-63 with 0:00 left on the scoreboard. A lot of things happened in that last fraction of a second.

Landon Turner's three-point play with five seconds left seemed to wrap up a two-figure victory margin. Ball State, a plucky team that fell back in a few decisive spurts but otherwise played the Hoosiers about even, went for a final basket with sub Mark Thurston on a one-on-two drive.

Thurston collided with Steve Bouchie as the Cardinal guard put up an eight-foot shot. Turner leaped from behind Bouchie to slap the ball out of the air. Foul, said one official. Goaltending, said another. What? said IU coach Bob Knight, twice, explicitly enough that he drew two technical fouls.

Chuck Franz — scored 6 in Hoosiers' opening victory

Suddenly, Ball State was looking at a potential seven-point play, and the Cardinals harvested six of them. Ray McCallum, a 5-foot-9 dynamo who looked forward to taking on Thomas and then frankly and honestly enjoyed his absence, came off the bench to hit three of the four technical free throws to round out a 25-point game for him and shrink the margin a bit.

The last half-tick ran out on the Cards' 26th turnover, a long pass that Turner intercepted.

"I was looking forward to playing Thomas," McCallum said. When word reached Ball State coach Steve Yoder the day before that Thomas probably was going to sit out the game, that wasn't exactly disappointment that crept into McCallum.

"No," he said. "I felt we had a better chance to win the game."

Ball State didn't let Indiana lead until Ray Tolbert took a pass from Randy Wittman and crammed home a dunk with 16:40 left in the first half — the perfect shot to carry crowd favorite Tolbert over the 1,000-point mark for his career. He entered the game and his senior year with 999, and he became the 19th Hoosier to make it — the first since 2,000-pointer Mike Woodson reached 1,000 late in his sophomore year, 1977-78.

That made the score 6-4, but Ball State kept matching points till Wittman shot over the Cards' two-three zone defense to tie the game, 12-12; Steve Bouchie hit the first of a two-shot foul to break the tie; Jim Thomas rebounded the missed second one for a lay-up that made it 15-12, and Thomas swiped the ball from Ball State's John Williams in midcourt for a lay-up that jumped the lead to 17-12.

It was 31-25 in the last minute of the half when Yoder called for his team to stall 30 seconds and wait for a last shot.

McCallum obviously works better without a leash. He tried to drive the middle, lost the ball and drew a charging foul, too.

"That play really hurt us," Yoder said. "We should have gone in down four. Instead, they get the ball, a more patient club, and Wittman knocks down a shot at the gun to go eight up.

"If we're down four, we come out the second half in a press. I didn't feel we could do that down eight."

The Cardinals never got the margin under eight until the last-second flurry. Tony Brown and Jim Thomas alternated on McCallum and allowed him only two free throws in the first 10 minutes of the second half, while IU was opening a 55-37 lead.

Knight pulled Wittman after he drew his fourth foul with seven minutes left and didn't reinsert him. Tolbert came out for good after a mid-court steal and crowd-awakening dunk that made the Hoosier lead 65-49 with 3:36 left. It was 70-54 with IU reserves in charge with a minute and a half left, and in that brief span Ball State ran in 15 points.

Eleven Hoosiers scored and five made double figures, Tolbert the leader with 14. Thomas had 12 points, Turner 11, and Wittman and Brown 10 each.

I think there are three awesome teams in the league — Indiana, Ohio State and Iowa. And in my first preseason poll, I had those three 1-2-3. Illinois and Minnesota were also in my Top 15. Michigan was not. I thought maybe it would look like I was slightly biased if I had six in there.

Jud Heathcote
Michigan State coach

BALL STATE 69									
	M	FG	FT	R	A	BS	St	PF	TP
Gooden, f	13	2- 3	0- 0	1	0	0	0	2	4
Albertson, f	34	2- 7	4- 7	10	2	0	0	5	8
Bradley, c	23	2- 6	0- 2	2	1	1	2	2	4
McCallum, g	39	7-14	11-13	1	0	0	1	2	25
Jn.Williams, g	35	3-11	0- 0	7	7	1	1	2	6
Fullove	27	6- 9	0- 0	8	0	0	1	2	12
Jf.Williams	5	1- 3	1- 3	1	0	0	0	1	3
Murrell	14	2- 2	0- 1	3	0	0	0	4	4
Parker	7	0- 0	0- 0	0	0	1	0	2	0
Thurston	1	1- 2	1- 1	0	0	0	0	3	3
Furlin	1	0- 0	0- 0	0	0	0	0	0	0
Hampton	1	0- 0	0- 0	0	0	0	0	0	0
Team				10					
Totals		26-57	17-27	43	10	3	5	25	69

INDIANA 75									
	M	FG	FT	R	A	BS	St	PF	TP
Risley, f	10	1- 4	2- 3	2	0	0	0	0	4
Wittman, f	31	5- 9	0- 0	5	4	0	2	4	10
Tolbert, c	28	6-13	2- 2	5	1	2	1	2	14
JThomas, g	33	6-13	0- 0	6	2	0	2	2	12
Brown, g	25	5- 8	0- 0	4	2	0	2	0	10
Grunwald	14	1- 2	0- 0	1	5	0	1	3	2
Franz	12	1- 1	4- 4	1	2	0	1	4	6
Bouchie	15	0- 3	1- 2	2	0	0	1	3	1
Turner	19	5-12	1- 3	8	0	1	1	2	11
Kitchel	4	1- 2	0- 0	0	0	1	0	1	2
Isenbarger	5	0- 0	3- 4	1	0	0	0	0	3
LaFave	2	0- 0	0- 2	0	0	0	0	0	0
Bardo	2	0- 0	0- 1	1	0	0	0	2	0
Team				4					
Totals		31-67	13-21	40	16	4	11	23	75

SCORE BY HALVES

Ball State	25	44—	69
Indiana	33	42—	75

Turnovers—Ball State 26, Indiana 16.
Technical fouls—Knight 2.

SHOOTING

	FG	Pct.	FT	Pct.
Ball State	26-57	.456	17-27	.630
Indiana	31-67	.463	13-21	.619

Officials—Art White, Marty Burdette, Gil Haggart.
Attendance—14,682.

Jim Thomas drives by Ball State's John Williams

McCallum said Thomas and Brown "both did a good job. They did let me get the ball pretty easily. I was surprised about that. But they're still the best defensive players I've played against and probably the best I will play all year.

"We were really psyched up. We talked all week about coming down here and winning. We were ready to go from the start."

Yoder said, "We've got to be careful of a letdown. Our players really felt confident.

"I think in the end we will look back on this game as being a very valuable game for us. But playing at Indiana is a tough way to come out of the chute."

A tribute to a friend

It was not Bob Knight's favorite season opener.

It really didn't have much chance. It came at the end of a sad week for the Hoosier coach. The day before in Lincoln, Neb., they buried one of his closest coaching friends: Nebraska's Joe Cipriano, victim of cancer at 49.

Knight's feelings for Cipriano were reflected in a rare tribute just ahead of the tip-off. Knight asked the crowd of 14,682 to stand for a moment of silence in memory of the thin and fun-loving little man who brought his Nebraska team into the first Indiana Classic and did as well as any visiting coach has: he finished second.

In a letter that ran in the Lincoln, Neb., *Star* the day before the game, Knight noted:

"There was always an exuberance and vitality about Joe that was seldom found anywhere, let alone in the mercurial roller-coaster world of college coaching. His enthusiasm for life and living was infectious. . . .

"Never have I been with him that he didn't capitalize on circumstances or devise situations that enabled everyone to have a good time. He was an outstanding coach, and I, along with many others, have received great benefit from his knowledge of the game. . . ."

Knight's pre-game talk to the Hoosier crowd also included presentation of a red-and-white checked sport coat to outgoing Gov. Otis Bowen. Yoder joined in the recognition — the colors appropriate for both state schools.

But Yoder knew the governor wasn't pretending neutrality. "I think I speak for everyone here, Steve," Bowen said, "in saying we're for you in every game but one — and that's this one."

Indiana 59, Murray State 41

Indiana's 59-41 victory margin looks conclusive enough, but Murray State's aptly named Racers may still be wondering just what happened about the time they were getting ready for a stretch run.

Maybe it was the dunks.

Murray State led 39-38 early in the second half when Isiah Thomas missed a shot and his Hoosier teammate, Ray Tolbert, leaped high to spear the rebound, then leaped higher to dunk the ball home.

Crowds always are electrified by dunks. This one, and the change of lead it provided, introduced Murray State to the rolling effect that can come from Assembly Hall's stands when the mood is right. It's a powerful thing that intrudes on play, continuing and building long after the basket in a conscious and concerted effort to rev up one team and rattle the other.

Whether it worked, only the Murray players may really know, but when Tolbert's lead-providing dunk was followed by a mid-court interception by the 6-foot-9 senior, open court ahead of him, everybody in The Hall knew what was coming. This dunk Tolbert powered home two-handed, and the lead was 42-39.

When Murray State followed with a carelessly lofted pass, Thomas brought out the "oooooooohs" with a leap and one-handed spear, and he challenged the Tolbert volume with a drive between two Murray defenders for the 6-1 guard's first college dunk — a three-point play by the time he bounced up after a slam to the floor.

Suddenly it was 45-39, and the Hoosiers were moving out to deafening accompaniment.

And just as suddenly the crowd was quieted. Thomas drew his fourth foul and went to the bench, 14 minutes still to play.

So maybe it was the stall.

It was 47-41 with 12:07 left when Murray State picked up its sixth foul of the half. That made IU eligible for one-and-one free-throw possibilities with each future foul.

The one-and-one vulnerability and Thomas's seat on the sidelines "were both mitigating circumstances," Knight said, in his decision to back his offense away and attempt to pull Murray State out of its 2-3 zone defense.

Murray State coach Ron Greene declined. A minute, two minutes, five minutes passed with IU playing pitch-and-catch — five non-Thomas minutes burned off the clock at no penalty to the burner. Burned was Greene, who gambled that the Hoosiers would throw the ball away before their slowdown went too long — "make a mistake, travel or something," Greene said.

"I thought if we could keep it close, within six, we had a chance with about five or six minutes left to win it."

Thomas returned with 5:35 left, the lead that had been 45-39 when he left actually grown a bit to 48-41.

By then, panic had gripped the Racers. The smoothness that had produced a series of good shots in the first half vanished. Indiscreet shots were fired from all over, and not one fell.

Indiana scored the next 12 points, and the score blinked "blowout," even though the Racers and Hoosiers and 16,278 live watchers knew better.

What happened in that second half was hard to realize even in the midst of it. Murray State, scoring almost at will in the first half when Racerj quickness left a lot of bodies strewn along trails leading to the basket, scored just two points in the last 18 minutes. IU scored 23. Murray State scored just eight in the entire second half, to Indiana's 29.

Before that, Indiana watched the Racers do a lot of cutting, faking and driving. "We gave up nine lay-ups in the first half," Knight said. Those were at least part of the reason Murray led at the half.

So maybe it was the halftime talk.

"We came right back out and made two awfully bad plays to start the second half," Knight scoffed. There weren't too many of those chargeable to the Hoosiers the rest of the way.

Thomas, taking advantage of deployment invitations to shoot over the Murray State two-three zone defense frequently, started his season with a 21-point performance. He missed the opener because of a groin pull.

Only one other player in the game managed 10 or more points: Murray junior Kenney Hammonds, who beat the Hoosiers downcourt on a couple fast breaks and totaled 14.

IU shot .553; Murray lost with .625. Those figures didn't leave many rebounds, but Indiana got 25 to Murray's 15. Once the break came, it was total.

First big role for 'other' Thomas

IU's "other Thomas" played a big role in the victory.

Jim Thomas squared off with Murray's Lamont Sleets, one of only a few 1979-80 freshmen to make an all-conference team.

MURRAY STATE 41

	M	FG	FT	R	A	BS	St	PF	TP
Wittman, f	35	2- 6	2- 3	2	3	0	0	2	6
Risley, f	7	0- 2	0- 0	2	0	0	0	1	0
Tolbert, c	34	4- 4	1- 2	4	0	2	2	2	9
IThomas, g	23	10-15	1- 1	3	2	0	1	5	21
JThomas, g	34	2- 6	2- 3	2	4	2	1	6	6
Grunwald	18	4- 6	0- 0	3	1	0	1	4	8
Kitchel	3	0- 1	0- 0	0	0	0	0	0	0
Turner	10	2- 2	0- 0	2	1	0	0	1	4
Franz	17	0- 2	1- 2	1	2	0	0	0	1
Brown	5	1- 1	0- 0	1	0	0	0	1	2
Isenbarger	14	1- 2	0- 0	2	1	0	1	0	2
Team				3					
Totals		26-47	7-11	25	14	2	7	17	59

INDIANA 59

	M	FG	FT	R	A	BS	St	PF	TP
Hammonds, f	39	7- 9	0- 0	3	1	1	1	3	14
Green, f	32	3- 6	0- 2	4	0	0	0	1	6
Montgomery, c	27	0- 1	0- 0	2	0	0	0	3	0
Sleets, g	33	3- 6	1- 2	1	3	0	2	3	7
Slaughter, g	20	1- 2	0- 0	1	0	0	0	1	2
Stewart	12	2- 2	0- 0	0	0	0	0	2	4
Davis	15	3- 5	0- 1	3	0	0	0	1	6
Smith	15	1- 1	0- 0	0	0	0	0	1	2
McKinney	7	0- 0	0- 0	0	0	0	0	0	0
Team				1					
Totals		20-32	1- 5	15	4	1	3	15	41

SCORE BY HALVES

Murray State	33	8— 41
Indiana	30	29— 59

Turnovers—Murray State 17, Indiana 11.

SHOOTING

	FG	Pct.	FT	Pct.
Murray State	20-32	.625	1- 5	.200
Indiana	26-47	.553	7-11	.636

Officials—George Solomon, Tom Rucker, Don Edwards.
Attendance—16,278.

Sleets is quick, strong and accurate from long range. But he also is 5-foot-10, so he gave away five inches in height to Thomas and regretted it — particularly in the second half when he didn't score a point. He closed with seven. He averaged 16.8 as a freshman.

"Jimmy did an excellent job," Knight said. "We told him just to stick with him, not to worry about switching or helping out."

Jim Thomas also delivered a couple scoring plays that were simple lay-ups but every bit as devastating as dunks, Tolbert insisted.

Early in the second half, Thomas got a hand on a pass, Glen Grunwald completed the steal, and Grunwald lofted a pass to Thomas for a lay-up that became a three-point play and teetered IU into a 36-35 lead.

The Hoosiers were mopping up against the Racers late in the game when Thomas intercepted a pass and converted the theft into another three-point play.

Tolbert dunked a couple in between. Isiah Thomas, who hadn't publicly tried one since misfiring on an attempt in the Pan-American Games, exploded over the top of a couple would-be defenders to deliver another — the three coming consecutively, surely a Hoosier record.

All of those were off steals. "I like to dunk," Tolbert said. "It gets the adrenalin going a little bit. But the two lay-ups by Jimmy Thomas did, too. The most important thing when you do get a steal is that you go on and convert it. So his lay-ups were just as good as dunks."

Isiah Thomas fouled out in just 23 minutes. "The last two were the kind he is going to get," Knight said. "The first three were the ones that he can't afford to get."

Thomas was called for a charge and a grab in the first 2½ minutes. "When I got the first two," he said, "the first thing I thought was, 'Don't get the third.' And then I did" — with 6:51 left in the half.

Thomas credited Murray State with causing some of the problems. "They were so quick," he said. "As a team, they're the quickest I've played against since I've been at Indiana."

That dictated some of Indiana's strategy. "We decided at the half we were going to come off the bench with only Tony Brown, Chuck Franz and Phil Isenbarger, because it wasn't a game for our bigger guys like Ted Kitchel and Steve Bouchie," Knight said.

"It really pleased me that both Isenbarger and Grunwald played very well. Grunwald kept us in the game with his shooting in the first half, and down the stretch, Isenbarger handled the ball well and made some excellent plays on defense."

Murray wrestled with the cause for the radical switch from its 33-30 halftime lead to the eight-point second half.

Sleets said the Racers quit executing. "We were all pepped up at halftime and I tried to tell everyone we had to have another half and coach did, too," he said. "They just really played good defense and we didn't execute on offense."

Greene didn't second-guess his decision to let Indiana kill time late in the game, with Isiah Thomas bench-ridden by fouls.

"I went along because I thought we looked a little fatigued," said Greene, who played high school ball at Terre Haute Gerstmeyer. "It was a good chance to give some of our players a rest and Indiana had the momentum at that time, I thought, anyway.

"I hate to see the score get kicked out there like that but their defense and our lack of execution caused it."

Phil Isenbarger covers Murray's Ken Hammonds

Isiah Thomas — A leader for a long, long time

Ever since fourth grade, Isiah has been a leader

BLOOMINGTON, DEC. 3, 1980

To a degree, it is pre-ordained, the leadership that is thrust upon Isiah Thomas as a sophomore on the Indiana basketball team. He had it, just as inevitably, on last year's Hoosier team. Isiah has the basketball. From there, leadership is unavoidable.

It's a role that settles on him naturally — more comfortably that way than when he steps back to think about it.

"It was tough — it still is," Thomas said after stepping back into the IU picture and — is there any better word? — leading the Hoosiers to a 59-41 victory over Murray State.

"You're a freshman or a sophomore," he went on in explanation of his dilemma. "Other guys are in their last year. Some people just don't like for a younger guy to be telling them where to go. It can be kinda touchy."

But leadership is something that, for him, goes a long way back — as far as the No. 11 he wears as a Hoosier.

Thomas was the seventh and last son in his family. The six brothers ahead of him played everything but specialized in basketball.

"They got me started when I was 3," Thomas said.

In kindergarten, he suited up regularly with the seventh and eighth-grade team at Our Lady of Sorrows grammar school. "I was like the water boy," he said.

But he did play. The coach, Brother Alexis, "has a picture of me shooting a lay-up when I was in kindergarten. I was really a little pee-wee then."

In fourth grade, Thomas "made the team — I had always been on it, but now I was playing.

"We got new uniforms, and Brother Alexis asked me what number I wanted. I took 11, because of Sammy Puckett."

Puckett was a star at the school in Thomas's pee-wee days. Later, Puckett made high school all-America and was recruited by Notre Dame.

The 11 stayed on Thomas, who, as a fourth grader, bossed eighth graders; as a sophomore at Westchester St. Joseph's, seniors; and, as a freshman at IU, juniors and seniors.

The only time he wore any other number was in the summer of 1979 when he became one of the youngest players ever to represent the U.S. in international competition — a high school senior playing on the team of college stars Knight took to the Pan-American Games in San Juan. Thomas wore No. 12 on that team.

But even there — as the next-last player named to the squad, moving up from alternate when Darnell Valentine of Kansas elected not to play after winning a spot in the trials at IU — Thomas's leadership showed through.

At San Juan, in the tensest moment of an indescribably electric championship game — U.S. vs. Puerto Rico, 10,000-seat Roberto Clemente Coliseum crammed with 13,000 spectators, a 54-39 U.S. halftime lead down to 73-70 with less than 10 minutes to go and the rabid crowd spurring on the Puerto Rico charge — it was the kid, Thomas, who delivered the biggest play of the game. He took an in-bounds pass on the fly, drove into the thicket of big men around the basket and delivered a back-breaking three-point play. The U.S. pulled out to win, 113-94, as Thomas finished with 21 points, five steals, four assists and perhaps the most humble squelch ever delivered. He told the wowed Latin American reporters who massed around him after the performance: "Players with my size and talent are a dime a dozen in America." His American and IU teammate, Mike Woodson, was more accurate: "Isiah played his butt off."

He was back in No. 11 with the U.S. Olympic team last summer, when he again was one of the youngest players on the team and *was* the smallest — but still unquestionably led.

Only Brother Alexis knows if there was ever anything more than sheer coincidence to the association of Isiah Thomas and that number.

One of the most familiar passages in The Bible says:

" . . . and a little child shall lead them."

It can be found in Isaiah 11.

14

Kentucky 68, Indiana 66

Charles Hurt, averaging 4.7 points a game, became an early leader in Kentucky's Most Valuable Player race.

Hurt, a 6-foot-6 sophomore buried on a roster of giants and high school all-Americans, delivered two late plays that made Kentucky a 68-66 winner in the Wildcats' annual December collision with Indiana.

Four days earlier, his midcourt steal and dunk in the last minute and a half broke a 64-64 tie and propelled Kentucky to a 70-64 victory over Ohio State. All of which, at the very least, made him all-Big Ten at the moment.

His contributions against IU were an offensive rebound basket that teetered the Wildcats on top, 64-62, with 2:05 left and a steal that pulled the ball out of Landon Turner's hands and delivered it to Kentucky with 20 seconds left and the 'Cats ahead, 66-64. Free throws kept Kentucky out of reach after that in a game that was Kentucky's for 20 minutes, Indiana's for 10, and anybody's down the stretch.

It swung when Indiana had the ball after a time out, the score 62-62, 3:27 remaining and Kentucky in a 1-3-1 zone defense.

The thought of backing off then and playing for a last shot or drawing Kentucky out of the zone "crossed my mind," IU coach Bob Knight said.

"But they're a very aggressive, quick team. That kind of thing can backfire on you."

So the Hoosiers worked patiently for a shot that figured to be pivotal, whether it came over the zone ("we had three good shooters in there — Isiah Thomas, Randy Wittman and Ted Kitchel," Knight noted) or inside it. Wittman and Kitchel cocked a couple times but didn't have quite the daylight they wanted. The ball kept moving. A full minute ticked away.

With 2:20 left, Turner broke into the middle and 7-1 Kentucky center Sam Bowie moved up to cover him. Ray Tolbert raced down the baseline from the corner, and Thomas looped him an "Alley Oop" pass high above all the giants.

Tolbert got up, got it, and his two-handed dunk attempt rimmed out, into Kentucky hands.

Seconds later, Hurt was standing in front of the Kentucky basket when Dirk Minniefield's miss bounced into his hands for a gift basket that gave the Wildcats a chance to play from ahead or even the rest of the way.

Kitchel, who came off the bench to hit five of six shots, tied the game, 64-64, with an 18-foot shot from straight out front, 1:32 left.

Kentucky was looking for a high-percentage shot when Thomas tried to trap Minniefield along the baseline and was charged with a foul. Minniefield hit both free throws with 48 seconds left for a 66-64 lead.

That was the score when IU came down, worked for an opening, got the ball to Kitchel in the left corner, and his pass had just settled in Turner's hands in the low post when Hurt knifed in from a wing on the zone, flicked the ball loose, caught it just before stepping out of bounds and dealt off a saving pass to Minniefield in the corner.

The Hoosiers had to foul after that. Bowie hit one of two chances at 0:14 for a 67-64 lead. After Thomas drove the middle and was permitted an uncontested lay-up, IU took time out

Isiah Thomas looks for an opening bringing the ball up-court against Jim Master

The B. is for bemused as Joe B. Hall watches Darwin Brown signal a foul

at 0:05, but the 'Cats got the ball in bounds and Minniefield was fouled again with two seconds left.

He hit the first, and his miss on the second was retrieved by Tolbert, whose 70-foot hope shot missed at the buzzer.

Hurt's key basket symbolized Hoosier problems. Kentucky scored 17 of its points after retrieving its own misses. "They hurt us so badly on the boards," Knight said. "That's the thing that hurt us right from the beginning through the end."

Ironically, 13 of those points came in the first half when Kentucky took a 37-33 lead. The 'Cats dashed out 6-1 and led 21-11 when Turner and Kitchel sparked a rally that cut the lead to a point a couple times before seven-foot back-up center Melvin Turpin scored five late points that opened the four-point halftime lead.

Indiana shocked the Wildcats by beating them downcourt with a fast-paced game opening the second half.

It didn't represent a change in strategy. "We did get the ball up court a little quicker," Knight said, "but in that stretch we also did a better job of controlling the defensive backboard."

"That was the whole key," said Thomas, who was at least the item of second-most importance in the IU flurry opening the second half.

Thomas snatched up a deflected pass and beat Kentucky's defense with a pass to Turner for a lay-up that started the charge. Then he:

• Stole the ball and drove to a lay-up that tied the game, 37-37;

• Rebounded Verderber's missed shot and rushed the ball up-court for a Tolbert lay-up that put Indiana ahead, 39-37;

• Drove the baseline for a shot on which Bowie was charged with goaltending, boosting the IU lead to 41-37;

• Followed a three-point play by Bowie with a soft 6-foot jump shot that put IU up, 43-40;

• Followed another Bowie basket with a pass to Tolbert breaking down the baseline for a lay-up and a 45-42 lead;

• Stole the ball again, centered a fast break and lost an assist when Tolbert's lay-up rolled off, but the Hoosiers still came out with a basket and a 47-42 lead on Kitchel's rebound basket.

The Hoosiers were up 54-48 after Wittman's jump shot with 10:27 left. "Our best stretch was the first 10 minutes of the se-

cond half," Knight said. "I think that was obvious. We were playing from behind the whole first half, and yet we stayed in position to make a move."

KENTUCKY 68

	M	FG	FT	R	A	BS	St	PF	TP
Cowan, f	34	6-15	2- 4	5	1	0	0	2	14
Verderber, f	19	3- 6	2- 2	4	2	0	0	2	8
Bowie, c	19	5- 9	4- 5	4	1	1	0	4	14
Minniefield, g	16	1- 3	3- 4	1	2	0	0	2	5
Hord, g	28	3- 6	0- 0	2	4	0	0	2	6
Turpin	21	2- 7	1- 2	5	0	0	0	4	5
Beal	14	1- 3	0- 0	1	2	0	1	4	2
Master	21	4- 9	2- 2	0	2	0	0	0	10
Hurt	26	2- 3	0- 0	4	1	0	2	1	4
Bearup	1	0- 0	0- 0	0	0	0	0	0	0
Lanter	1	0- 0	0- 0	0	0	0	0	0	0
Team				11					
Totals		27-61	14-19	37	15	1	3	21	68

INDIANA 66

	M	FG	FT	R	A	BS	St	PF	TP
Wittman, f	40	2- 2	2- 2	1	2	0	0	2	6
Risley, f	12	0- 0	0- 0	0	0	1	1	1	0
Tolbert, c	34	5-16	1- 3	4	1	1	0	3	11
IThomas, g	37	8-10	4- 6	5	5	0	2	3	20
JThomas, g	10	0- 1	0- 0	0	2	0	0	0	0
Grunwald	4	1- 1	0- 0	1	0	0	0	0	2
Bouchie	5	0- 2	0- 0	2	1	0	0	3	0
Turner	28	5-11	5- 6	4	0	0	0	4	15
Kitchel	26	5- 6	2- 2	5	0	0	1	3	12
Franz	3	0- 0	0- 0	0	1	0	0	0	0
Isenbarger	1	0- 0	0- 0	0	0	0	0	1	0
Team				6					
Totals		26-49	14-19	28	12	1	4	20	66

SCORE BY HALVES

Kentucky	37	31— 68
Indiana	33	33— 66

Turnovers—Kentucky 10, Indiana 9.

SHOOTING

	FG	Pct.	FT	Pct.
Kentucky	27-61	.443	14-19	.737
Indiana	26-49	.531	14-19	.737

Officials—Rich Weiler, Darwin Brown, Dale Kelley.
Attendance—17,254.

A quick way to grow old

It's highly debatable whether, as polls insisted, those really were two of the five best college basketball teams in the nation that met. If so, wait a couple years. In the last 4½ minutes, when the game truly was on the line, there were seven sophomores on the court. IU-UK strife likely will go on quite actively and prominently for a while.

The mental replays started with the buzzer and will continue for months and years in the basketball-loving country split by the Ohio River. Most centered on the Alley Oop that went oops: the Thomas lob pass that caught Tolbert behind the Kentucky defense with the score 62-62 and 2:20 left.

Tolbert's try to redirect the pass from above the rim, via a two-handed dunk, missed, and it was Kentucky that took the lead at a pivotal time, not IU.

"It was . . . unfortunate," Thomas said. "You can't say he should have made the shot. You can't say I shouldn't have thrown the pass. I threw it right and he shot it right. It just missed."

The play "was there and we took advantage of it," Knight said. "You can't get much better than a two-inch shot."

The dunk wasn't *the* play that beat the Hoosiers. There was a mystifying series of them — rebounds and loose balls that Kentucky monopolized and fumbles that time and again popped out of Hoosier clutches.

Even Kentucky's 37-28 edge in rebounds wasn't really a product of the enormous size the 'Cats put on the court. The floor was full of players 6-6 through 7-1, most of them wearing Kentucky blue, but nobody got more rebounds than the 6-1 Thomas (five). It was the rebounds snapped up off the floor, not the ones from basket high, that made the real difference for Kentucky.

"They got 80 to 90 percent of the loose balls," Knight said. "It was something that really hurt us."

The Hurt interception that snuffed out Indiana's last chance to tie came on a play choice as acceptable to Knight as the Alley Oop attempt.

Kitchel had the ball in the deep left corner, and when the defense converged on him, he threw a pass to Turner, posted about 10 feet from the basket. Before Turner could clamp a hold on the ball and look for a shot, Hurt cut through to make the steal.

"Kitchel saw him open and slipped him the ball," Knight said. "If we go inside, we've got two things going for us: a foul or a shot. If we take the outside shot, we've only got one thing going. I can't at all fault him for going inside at that time. Hurt made a really good defensive play.

"I thought Kitchel came off the bench and played extremely well. He helped us on the boards, and at about four different points he scored very important baskets.

"Both Landon and Ted really gave us a lift."

The game the Hoosiers intended to play was the one that made Kentucky appear slow and ponderous opening the second half. It was the one stretch in which Kentucky was getting one shot or no shots, and the Hoosiers were beating them to

Ray Tolbert's hand blocks the way for Freddie Cowan

the other end with regularity — thanks to the attacking skills of the darting Thomas.

"Whenever we got the ball in Isiah's hands, we were able to run," Kitchel said. "When we get it to him and get out, he can make things happen."

The success with a running game early in the second half came with a Hoosier team on the floor not really associated with speed. The accent was opposite the Murray State game, when countering quickness was the primary Hoosier problem.

Kitchel barely got in that game. James Thomas played most of it. This time, Thomas gave way to size.

"We're a team that's got a lot of developing to do," Knight said. "We're going to have to work hard to be a good team."

Kentucky went in the No. 1-ranked team, according to United Press International's coaches, No. 2 in the view of the Associated Press media selectors. Indiana was fourth or fifth.

"I thought we would beat them," Thomas said frankly. "I still think we should have."

Hall, Master 'cherish' win

"It took the play of our young and new players to pull this win out," Kentucky coach Joe Hall said. "When you bring a young club to a place like Indiana you expect a lot of turnovers. We only had 10, that's exceptional.

"I'll cherish this the rest of my life."

Master, Indiana's 1980 "Mr. Basketball" from Harding, said, "I'm on Cloud 9.

"Everybody said I was making a mistake going to Kentucky. I think I proved 'em wrong today."

Cheerleaders Val Gatson, Bill Patterson, Sonnie Sicklesmith, Jerry Lacey rouse IU crowd

Notre Dame 68, Indiana 64

John Paxson didn't quite neutralize Isiah Thomas, but he did occupy the little Indiana backcourt star and that made Paxson a significant contributor to Notre Dame's 68-64 victory over IU before the usual full house of 11,345 at Notre Dame's Athletic and Convocation Center.

Paxson is a 6-foot-2 Dayton, Ohio, sophomore who was the key man in a Notre Dame game plan that went at Thomas from the start.

The game was 43 seconds along when Irish senior Kelly Tripucka stepped in front of Thomas on a drive to the basket by the IU sophomore. The play brought Thomas his first personal foul, for charging.

Only three minutes and 12 seconds had been played when Thomas was called for a second foul when he tried to block a shot by Notre Dame's Tracy Jackson from behind.

The fouls put Thomas in jeopardy, and Paxson kept the pressure on him the rest of the night by driving at him one-on-one, forcing Thomas to play perfect position defense or give up close-in shots that Paxson has mastered well.

Thomas never did foul out, but he finished with only a 22-18 point edge over his Irish counterpart.

"I think John showed tonight he could play against anybody in the country," Irish coach Digger Phelps said. "Isiah Thomas is probably as good a guard as we're going to hit all year.

"This was John's chance to get some recognition for himself. If you were out there as a spectator, you would have to think those were two pretty good basketball players."

IU coach Bob Knight called it "a very good match-up. Paxson is an excellent player. He and Thomas obviously are two of the better guards in the country, and both played pretty well."

Landon Turner, making his first start of the season, was the hub of the Hoosier offense with 23 points, his high in three seasons at IU.

Steve Bouchie bounces a pass past Tom Sluby

Four times early in the second half, Turner hit shots that edged IU into a one-point lead, the last at 49-48 with 11:40 to play. Thomas followed with a driving basket that opened a 51-48 lead, and Ted Kitchel's rebound basket offset two Paxson free throws to keep the margin intact, 53-50, with 10:10 to play.

The game was tied at 54 when Irish senior Orlando Woolridge spotted daylight in the IU defense, broke to the basket and rammed home a dunk that put the Irish ahead for good and gave a noisy start to a seven-point Notre Dame spurt.

The points were like the Irish offense of the period: well spread. Once Woolridge's basket had provided the lead, the Irish patiently awaited easy shots. Kelly Tripucka, who finished with 16 points after perturbing Phelps with a 1-for-7 shooting start, drove 'round the Hoosiers for a bank shot that made it 58-54 with 7:08 left, and he drew the defense to him with another drive before passing to sophomore Bill Varner for a lay-up that made it 60-54 with 6:15 left.

In the same span, IU missed five straight shots and threw the ball away once. "They got control of the game at a time where we also had a chance to," Knight said. "When that happens, you have a real problem coming back. We almost did, but we didn't quite make it, and that's the way it usually works out."

Notre Dame took a 65-58 lead into the last minute, but the Hoosiers had it down to 66-64 when, to stop the clock with time running out, they had to volunteer for a technical foul. They took a sixth time out — one over the permissible number. Paxson cashed in the two free throws awarded for the technical foul the extra time out produced, wrapping up the victory.

Notre Dame won with a 22-10 edge in free throws, overcoming a 27-23 IU margin in field goals. "I think this was a good basketball game — very well officiated," Knight said. Fouls were 26-16, IU, but Knight said, "A lot of those (five) came at the end when we had to foul."

Seniors Tripucka (16 points) and Woolridge (14) joined Paxson in leading Notre Dame. The three barely beat the combined 45 points by Turner and Thomas, but Notre Dame reserves topped IU's, 15-4.

Digger, Knight both optimistic

Since his team had just lost by a 94-84 score to Indiana back in December, 1974, Notre Dame basketball coach Digger Phelps sounded like an overly gracious loser when he was the first to pin a No. 1 ranking on an IU team that turned out to be everything Digger said.

As a conqueror of this Hoosier team, Phelps could have been dismissed as an overly gracious winner when, as he did, he warned the Big Ten to watch out for IU.

And then a funny thing happened. Knight agreed with him. "We're going to be pretty good before it's all over," Knight said.

The team that opened for the Hoosiers — senior Ray Tolbert and sophomore Steve Bouchie at the forwards, junior Landon Turner at center, and sophomores Isiah Thomas and Randy Wittman at the guards — is the product of seven weeks of practice-floor work. But, for various reasons — among them a groin injury that kept Thomas from practicing for most of the last two weeks and a series of injuries that kept Bouchie out most of the pre-season period — that particular combination had worked together just one hour before going against Notre Dame.

It's always tough when you beat somebody you like. I think Bobby would feel the same way. I think we each have a lot of respect for the other's program.

Digger Phelps
Notre Dame coach

Isiah Thomas drives by Orlando Woolridge

Knight's goal clearly is to stay on an upswing through the pre-conference schedule and be ready by Big Ten time in January.

The Notre Dame game helped, he said, "because any time you play against a good team that plays well and works hard, it helps you.

"This whole December has been set up with that in mind. That's why we played Kentucky and Notre Dame back-to-back, and why we have North Carolina and Kansas State back-to-back on the road. We've always tried to do things like that to get us ready for the conference season, but this year I think we've set it up better than ever before.

"Notre Dame played very well. They moved back and forth (between zone and man-to-man defenses) and played both defenses well. They were probably as effective in one defense as the other."

Phelps spread his praise around to include both clubs.

"We played a very good basketball team," he said. "They were coming off a hard loss to Kentucky. I know how hard Bobby works and how hard his players work, so that game made it difficult for them."

There was ample room for improvement in the first competitive effort by the combination. Better scoring balance is needed (Turner had 23 points, Thomas 22 and the other three starters 15). Better defense is a must, since Notre Dame had some success driving the ball inside against the Hoosiers. Better rebounding is essential from the biggest front line IU has had in Knight's 10 seasons.

But since the key to the new combination, Turner, began to assume his role in the Kentucky game, the Hoosiers have done some things extraordinarily well. "The last two games, we've turned the ball over nine and eight times," Knight noted. "I'm not sure if we've ever had two games back-to-back under 10 turnovers since I've been here."

Knight isn't ready to say he's found his five and he's going with it forever and ever. "I would like to be able to settle on a lineup," he said, "but it has been difficult."

Turner could have been in the 30s with better shooting luck. Notre Dame is a good basketball team that is weak inside, perhaps the fatal flaw for a team deep in forwards and guards, unless Phelps can find a fast cure.

The situation makes it advisable to wait a little while longer before assessing how fast and how far Turner has come of late. "He has played two really good games in a row," Knight said. "His problem since he has been here has been inconsistency. We'll have to see where he goes from here."

The Hoosiers' loss was evidence that they can't get by with two primary scorers. At least a third is needed, Knight agrees. "It has to be Wittman," he said flatly.

INDIANA 64

	M	FG	FT	R	A	BS	St	PF	TP
Tolbert, f	31	2- 3	4- 4	8	3	0	0	1	8
Bouchie, f	21	1- 4	0- 0	1	1	0	0	3	2
Turner, c	39	10-19	3- 9	3	1	1	0	2	23
IThomas, g	38	10-18	2- 4	2	5	0	4	4	22
Wittman, g	21	2- 5	1- 2	0	1	0	1	5	5
JThomas	19	0- 0	0- 0	1	2	0	0	3	0
Kitchel	9	1- 1	0- 0	1	0	0	0	1	2
Isenbarger	15	1- 3	0- 0	2	2	0	2	4	2
Franz	1	0- 0	0- 0	0	0	0	0	1	0
Grunwald	3	0- 1	0- 0	0	0	0	0	2	0
Brown	3	0- 0	0- 0	0	0	0	0	0	0
Team				8					
Totals		27-54	10-19	26	15	1	7	26	64

NOTRE DAME 68

	M	FG	FT	R	A	BS	St	PF	TP
Tripucka, f	31	6-14	4- 6	8	2	0	2	3	16
Woolridge, f	40	5- 9	4- 8	6	2	1	0	1	14
Kleine, c	8	0- 0	0- 0	1	0	0	0	1	0
Paxson, g	39	5- 7	8- 9	0	2	0	0	2	18
Jackson, g	35	2- 4	1- 2	6	2	0	0	3	5
Sluby	18	2- 2	2- 3	2	0	0	1	3	6
Varner	20	2- 2	3- 4	3	1	0	0	1	7
Andree	6	1- 2	0- 0	2	0	0	0	2	2
Salinas	2	0- 0	0- 0	0	0	0	0	0	0
Wilcox	1	0- 0	0- 0	0	0	0	0	0	0
Team				5					
Totals		23-40	22-32	33	9	1	3	16	68

SCORE BY HALVES

Indiana	32	32— 64
Notre Dame	35	33— 68

Turnovers—Indiana 8, Notre Dame 16.
Technical foul—Indiana (called 6 timeouts).

SHOOTING

	FG	Pct.	FT	Pct.
Indiana	27-54	.500	10-19	.526
Notre Dame	23-40	.575	22-32	.688

Officials—Jim Bain, Verl Sell, Ralph Rosser.
Attendance—11,345 (capacity).

"But at the same time I think we had a lot to prove ourselves, after losing to UCLA (94-81 10 days earlier). I think what it shows is there are just a lot of good basketball teams in the country this year. I think there are going to be a lot of teams with seven, eight and nine losses.

"Tonight, we did the right things at the end of the game to be able to win it. I'm sure as Bobby gets his team going, they will do very well in the Big Ten and will be as good as anybody in the country by tournament time."

Phelps called it "a controlled physical game" and implied the Ohio State-Kentucky and IU-Kentucky games were rougher because of Kentucky's playing style. "Kentucky really comes at you — they just run through you," he said. "You can put Notre Dame-Indiana or Ohio State-Indiana together and the game will be physical but just like this. Kentucky just runs right over you.

"I'm sure if (Kentucky football coach Fran) Curci had some of those players, he'd probably be going to a bowl."

Tripucka sees red against IU

Wave a little Indiana Red in front of Tripucka and he becomes downright bullish.

"I get psyched up every time I see an IU uniform," said the Irish senior. "Just seeing them gets me charged up. I like playing against them and coach Knight.

"I didn't make the Pan Am team (Knight coached it and ran the tryouts in 1979) and that gives me an added incentive. I know coach Knight was not the only one who picked the team, but not making it helped get me motivated."

Tripucka may have been too motivated in the first half. At one point, he heaved a 15-foot brick that threatened to shatter the glass blackboard, then followed with an underneath layup attempt that failed to draw iron.

It was almost enough to flush his face with a little IU crimson, but he figured the second half would be his.

"It was just one of those things," Tripucka said. "At halftime I just tried to forget about it; it's still a 40-minute ball game. My shooting was a little strong for some reason, so I tried to do other things — rebound, pass the ball."

Phelps said Tripucka "didn't have a good game, but he hit some big shots at the end." In the first half, after Tripucka misfired on a 20-footer, a displeased Phelps yanked him. When Tripucka trotted to the Irish bench to find a seat, there were words between the two.

"Digger had a point but I was trying to make a point, too," Tripucka said. "Of course, my point doesn't count. But I had just come off a double pick, was squared up and had a full two seconds to shoot. I told him that, listened to what he said, and then said 'Yes, Sir' and sat down on the bench."

When the Irish were protecting a lead in the final minutes with a four-corner delay, Phelps tabbed Tripucka as the main ball handler. Knight used two of his quicker defenders — Phil Isenbarger and Tony Brown — to go after Tripucka, without success.

"My ball handling has improved," Tripucka said. "I was really confident at the end. I didn't feel they had anyone quick

Landon Turner challenges Orlando Woolridge

enough to stay with me. So I went to the basket and I either had the shot or passed off."

When Tripucka was starring for Bloomfield High School in Essex Falls, N.J., he said he gave some serious consideration to attending IU.

"Yes, I thought about it," he said.

"Coach Knight is a very good coach and a very good recruiter. And IU has a great tradition, with Scott May and Kent Benson and the rest, but Notre Dame is not quite as big a school. This is the right place for me.

"He came to see me play in the state tourney and had to stand the whole game because there weren't any seats. Then he came to our home and my mother — as she does with everyone — kept insisting he have something to eat. But he kept saying he wasn't hungry.

"Finally, she brought out some of those chocolate-covered ice cream bars. He started eating them and didn't stop till he had finished the whole box. I'm one of the few people that knows coach Knight's weakness. It's ice cream."

Bobby Knight has transformed Big Ten basketball by winning big with combative defense and disciplined offense in a league once hooked on runnin' and gunnin'.

Dave Kindred
Inside Sports

Indiana 94, California 58

California had every reason to expect the Indiana basketball explosion that left the Golden Bears withered, 94-58. It happens every Indiana Classic. Something about the Hoosiers' own tournament inspires classic basketball from them.

What the Bears couldn't have anticipated was a 22-point contribution by Hoosier sophomore Ted Kitchel, who crammed all that into just a 19-minute appearance.

At 6-1, Isiah Thomas can rebound

Kitchel's time on stage almost was considerably briefer. Summoned when starter Steve Bouchie picked up three early fouls, Kitchel had been in the game only two minutes and had one missed shot as his box score total when he got the ball on an out-of-bounds play, turned to pass the ball to the top of the foul circle, and plans went awry.

The man at the top of the circle when Kitchel looked was center Landon Turner. "He knew he wasn't supposed to be out there," Kitchel said. "So he took off for the low post. And I knew I wasn't supposed to throw it to him out there, but just as he left I threw it, anyway."

The ball went into the backcourt, IU lost possession, and from the sidelines, IU coach Bob Knight let Kitchel know his displeasure. Next time downcourt, Kitchel fired from the deep corner, hit, and he was off to his best collegiate night.

Kitchel wasn't indulging any postgame curiosity about what would have happened if that corner shot had missed. "It doesn't bother me when he gets on me," he said. "He was right. I made a mistake and I knew it.

"It used to be I'd probably have come out then. He's got some confidence in me."

Kitchel rewarded that confidence and no doubt added to it with 8-for-10 firing and six straight free throws, easily his best collegiate performance.

"It hasn't come around all at once," he said. "It's like Landon (Turner) — people probably think he came around all at once. But we've all worked hard."

Turner, who had 23 points in his first start at Notre Dame, picked up from there by hitting his first three shots to help the Hoosiers to a quick 15-7 lead. That was down to 15-11 after the errant Kitchel pass, but by halftime Kitchel had scored 10 points and IU had a 44-27 lead.

He started the second half, scored the Hoosiers' first six points, and the Bears were down 50-29 and dead.

"I thought Kitchel played well tonight," Knight said. "He did a good job at the defensive end, and he scored in a variety of ways.

"He gave us the kind of scoring we have to get out of our forwards. It was reminiscent of the way Steve Green used to score for us. Kitchel is a player very similar to Green in speed, or lack of."

The game plan was to play Bouchie for five minutes, Kitchel for five, then alternate them that way the rest of the night, Knight said. "Tonight was sort of an unfair opportunity to evaluate Bouchie, because of all the foul trouble he had.

"We were going to do it that way because both in practice have played essentially the same. Maybe we'll do it again. You've got to keep in mind that Bouchie is still out of shape. That makes him a half-step late on defense, and on offense he turns and bangs into somebody."

Kitchel wasn't the only Hoosier who waded into the Bears with zeal born out of losses to Kentucky and Notre Dame the last two times out.

"We lost two games we never should have lost," said Randy Wittman, the Hoosiers' sophomore guard who operated for a second straight game under orders to find shots.

Wittman found eight of them and hit only one in the first half. "I think he is playing under a lot of pressure," Knight said. "But I told him I don't care if it goes in or not, I just want him to shoot the ball."

Wittman has been a consistent 60 percent shooter in Hoosier workouts, so 1-for-8 was an unaccustomed plight for him. "I've

Cal's Wes Howell thwarts Steve Risley

got great confidence in my shot," Wittman said. "I think I'm a good shooter, and I don't think I'm being cocky in saying that.

"If I didn't have confidence, I probably would have stopped shooting when I was 0-for-3."

There is, of course, that matter of being ordered to shoot, regardless. "That's true," Wittman said, laughing. "I guess I wouldn't have stopped after all.

"I think the whole thing goes back to my freshman year. I was really running the offense and not particularly looking for my shot. That kind of thinking might have carried right into this year."

Wittman finished 4-for-13 for nine points. Besides Kitchel's 22, the Hoosiers got 15 points from Isiah Thomas — plus seven assists and five steals — and 12 points each from Turner and Ray Tolbert.

"Tolbert rebounded really well," Knight said. He had 11, as IU whipped the tall Californians in rebounding, 42-34.

Turner also helped to keep 6-11 Cal center Mark McNamara in harness. McNamara had 11 points and 7 rebounds, but he also committed seven turnovers in trying to get loose from the sagging Hoosier defense.

"Indiana's a great team," Cal coach Dick Kuchen said.

"I'm disappointed with the way we played. But they have a good half-court pressure defense. They can take you out of your offense, but there's no excuse for a team playing as poorly as we did."

After confusion, an early exit

Knight's first expulsion from a game at Assembly Hall came after a call that angered nobody but wound up costing both coaches technical fouls.

With three minutes left and IU ahead 86-53, Hoosier Chuck Franz made a lunging deflection to avert a Cal layup and tumbled heavily onto the floor. Shaken for a minute, Franz ultimately got back up and was ready to play, but official Bob Burson said rules required him to be removed for at least a play.

Knight, who drew an earlier technical foul from Burson, tarried in making a substitution. He was in the process of sending starter Randy Wittman back in when Burson signaled a technical foul for the delay. Burson appeared to rescind the technical signal, which brought a roaring reaction from Kuchen. Burson then signaled two technical fouls, one on each coach, and Knight stepped onto the court to get an explanation of the apparent change of mind. That's illegal territory for a coach. Burson signaled a third technical, on Knight, and that means expulsion.

Knight made no comments about the sequence, focusing his complaint on vagaries in the assessment of fouls for blocking or charging. "That blocking-charging call (the key to his first technical, in the first half, and to his chattering evening on the sidelines) destroys basketball," he said. "Tonight, you saw that call made four different ways — and it's not the officials' fault. It's in the way the rule is interpreted."

Kuchen said his complaint was with the change of mind he thought Burson had made regarding the Knight technical. "They called the technical and then they didn't," he said, "and that irritated me. You have to play within the framework of the game."

Assistant coach Roy Bates coached the last three minutes in Knight's third expulsion in 10 seasons as Hoosier coach — and first in more than six years. He previously drew three technicals and departed from a game with Texas-El Paso in the 1972 Sun Bowl finals at El Paso and from the championship game (with Southern California) in the Collegiate Commissioners Assn. tournament at St. Louis in 1974.

CALIFORNIA 58

	M	FG	FT	R	A	BS	St	PF	TP
Pitts, f	17	0- 4	0- 0	3	0	0	0	4	0
Singleton, f	32	8-12	0- 0	3	3	0	2	4	16
McNamara, c	31	4- 8	3- 9	7	0	1	0	1	11
Howell, g	15	0- 3	0- 0	2	3	0	0	1	0
Chavez, g	26	4- 9	2- 3	0	3	0	0	2	10
Hays	24	2- 6	1- 6	0	3	0	2	2	5
Potter	26	5- 9	0- 2	10	2	1	0	4	10
Owen	9	2- 2	2- 4	1	0	0	0	0	6
Haley	11	0- 1	0- 0	0	0	1	0	3	0
Ritchie	7	0- 2	0- 0	2	0	0	0	1	0
Lord	2	0- 0	0- 0	0	0	0	0	0	0
Team				6					
Totals		25-56	8-24	34	14	3	4	22	58

INDIANA 94

	M	FG	FT	R	A	BS	St	PF	TP
Tolbert, f	30	6- 9	0- 1	11	1	0	3	3	12
Bouchie, f	6	0- 0	2- 2	0	0	0	0	5	2
Turner, c	26	5-10	2- 2	6	1	3	0	3	12
IThomas, g	27	7-10	1- 1	1	7	0	5	2	15
Wittman, g	32	4-13	1- 3	3	3	0	2	0	9
Kitchel	19	8-10	6- 6	4	0	0	2	1	22
Brown	15	2- 5	1- 3	4	3	0	1	0	5
Grunwald	7	0- 1	0- 0	2	1	0	1	0	0
Risley	5	0- 2	0- 0	0	0	0	0	0	0
Isenbarger	5	0- 0	2- 2	3	1	0	0	0	2
JThomas	9	3- 5	0- 0	1	1	0	3	1	6
LaFave	8	1- 2	3- 4	0	2	0	1	1	5
Franz	6	1- 2	0- 0	2	1	0	0	1	2
Bardo	5	1- 2	0- 0	0	0	0	0	2	2
Team				5					
Totals		38-71	18-24	42	21	3	18	19	94

SCORE BY HALVES

California		27	31— 58
Indiana		44	50— 94

Turnovers—California 25, Indiana 16.
Technical fouls—Knight 3, Tolbert (grabbed rim), Kuchen.

SHOOTING

	FG	Pct.	FT	Pct.
California	25-56	.446	8-24	.333
Indiana	38-71	.535	18-24	.750

Officials—Bob Burson, Fred Jaspers, Malcolm Hemphill.

Knight didn't seem ruffled by the departure. While the last three minutes was being played, he said, "I had a Coke and read a little bit of a book I've been reading. I was at a real interesting point and I got that point finished.

"We did win, didn't we?"

Mixed reviews from Cal guards

California guards Butch Hays and Michael Chavez did some reading from the Book of Isiah, and both came away with migraines.

Six minutes into the game, Chavez tried to toss a pass over Thomas's head. Isiah leaped straight up, grabbed the ball with both hands and sped downcourt for a breakaway layup.

Three minutes later, Thomas pickpocketed Hays near midcourt, raced toward the layup despite a hack from Hays. Isiah hit the free throw to complete a 3-point play.

"Coming into the game I knew I would be matched up with probably the best guard in the nation," Chavez said. "He's so fast that I just wanted to go out and try to contain, in a way, and force him to where I could get help from other defenders. He's definitely one of the best I've ever played against."

Hays, a rookie playing in his second collegiate game, allowed, "I would say he's pretty good. He's one of the better guards I've played against. But I wasn't coming into the game looking at him like some god. He's just another player."

McNamara, a two-year starter at San Jose State before transferring and sitting out last season, was frustrated by the sea of swarming Hoosiers.

"There was a lot of double- and triple-teaming going on," he said. "They were collapsing every time the ball would come in — just as it was arriving in my hands."

Chavez found solace. "For us, nothing but good can come from this game," he said. "We've just played two games now and playing a team like Indiana shows us we still have a lot to learn."

We start assessing the potential of a player in high school. What kind of kid is he? What kind of athletic ability does he have? Then, after we get him, if he isn't playing as well as he can, why isn't he? It's a constant evaluation and re-evaluation to see where we are. Are we, as coaches and players, going down the same road?

Bob Knight

A Classic scene at Indiana's Assembly Hall

Indiana 83, Baylor 47

Landon Turner and Ted Kitchel, the newest men in Indiana's starting lineup, did the scoring for a second straight night as the Hoosiers overwhelmed Baylor, 83-47, to continue their domination of the seven-year old Indiana Classic.

Turner scored 23 points and Kitchel 17 as Indiana exploded early and never let the Southwest Conference Bears (4-2) get any kind of momentum going.

Turner, who has scored 58 points in three games since winning a starting job with 15 points in relief against Kentucky, was named the tournament's Most Valuable Player.

Kitchel, who won his way into the starting group with a 22-point game against California, went 8-for-10 for the second straight night in just missing 1975 all-American Scott May's tournament shooting record (19-for-23 for two games, .826, compared to Kitchel's 16-for-20 for .800).

Kitchel made the all-tournament team, along with teammates Turner and Isiah Thomas (though scoreless for the first time — ever, he said), plus Terry Teagle of Baylor and Mark McNamara of California.

Indiana's defense had Baylor churning out turnovers as fast as points in taking a 41-20 halftime lead.

"That first half was the best we've ever had anybody play against us," Baylor coach Jim Haller said.

"I didn't think Turner missed a shot."

Turner did hit his first six jump shots to lead IU to quick 8-2, 14-4, and 28-8 leads.

Through that point, almost 12 minutes into the half, the Hoosiers had forced 10 turnovers without committing a foul.

Kitchel carried the offense the rest of the way to intermission. Kitchel was 5-for-5 in the half in carrying on the sizzling streak that began for him with 5-for-6 firing against Kentucky.

Knight used 10 men in the half, pulling Thomas with 7:21 to go and IU ahead, 28-10. The lead topped out in the half at 25 points, 41-16, after seven straight points by Kitchel. By then, the Bears had their first-half total of 16 turnovers.

IU's lead never dipped under 19 in the second half. The Hoosiers went up by more than 30 for the first time when Tolbert hit two shots in a row, the second a rebound dunk that put IU up 69-36.

The lead peaked at 37 (79-42 with 4:25 left). That's a magic number in the tournament, which has had a total Hoosier domination. The record winning margin in any Classic game is 37, achieved four times by past IU teams. Both Hoosier victories this year were by 36.

Baylor's Teagle, who brought a 24.5 scoring average into the tournament, was the opening assignment of Ray Tolbert, with Phil Isenbarger and Glen Grunwald sharing later in the duty. The 1980 Southwest Conference player of the year finished with 17 in providing most of Baylor's offense.

Indiana closed with a .585 shooting percentage. Turner was 11-for-14 and Randy Wittman, taking the ball to the basket most of the night, was 8-for-11 in scoring 17.

IU also had a 41-30 rebounding edge, Tolbert and Turner leading with seven apiece. Turner played 28 minutes, the most of any Hoosier. Among the starters, Tolbert (who had 10 points) was low with 20 minutes.

Haller was proud of the zero in Thomas's point column. "Our guys did a tremendous defensive job on him," he said, "but it didn't make any difference."

Two-week stretch a corner-Turner?

For MVP Turner, the last week has had the earmarks of one in which he turned a long-sought corner. He came off the bench to score 15 points against Kentucky's big front line. That earned him a start against Norte Dame, and he was most of the Hoosier offense with 23 on a night when, if makable shots had dropped at an outrageous rate, 35 points was within reach. He had 12 in a brief playing stint against California and 23 more against Baylor as IU won its seventh straight Indiana Classic — a 73-point week.

But it really wasn't a one-week matter at all, Turner and Knight agreed.

Several weeks ago, Knight felt the concepts of the Hoosier passing game hadn't been fully picked up by Turner in his two IU seasons, and, ever a teacher, Knight sat down with Turner and told a story.

"I told him when I was a kid I took my wife to a dance," Knight said. "When it was over, she told me I was the absolute worst dancer she had ever seen, and she said, 'You really just don't have a grasp of music, do you?'

"And I have to agree that's pretty much true. I'm afraid if they played the 'Star Spangled Banner' without the words, I might not recognize it. I just don't have a feel for music.

"I told him that's the way he seemed to be to me in basketball. It's not a matter of being dumb. I don't consider myself dumb because I can't grasp music.

"I told him we were just going to restrict the things we wanted him to worry about doing, and to do those as well as he can. What we did was confine him basically to an area around the basket, very much the way we did Kent Benson his freshman year."

Knight told the tale long before Turner started expanding his

Randy Wittman, Baylor's Pat Nunley face off

An MVP smile for Landon Turner, named tops in the Indiana Classic

role. Suddenly, he's playing a big man's game that has reshaped the whole Hoosier outlook.

"He has really played pretty well for six straight games now," Knight said, "and that's the longest stretch of pretty good basketball he has played since he has been here.

"What he has done to date is a credit to three people — Joby Wright, Steve Downing and Jimmy Crews. They have worked with him almost since practice started, and Landon has taken the things they have worked on and really done them well these last few games."

Turner radiated his own happiness when the MVP announcement was made. He beamed widely and took hand slaps and grasps from Hoosier teammates who looked equally happy about the selection.

"I do feel pretty confident right now," he said. "I've been working harder, doing everything they want me to do. I've got more confidence in myself that I can do those things."

Turner came out of Indianapolis Tech with the sort of high school recruiting raves that have been more than some "can't-miss" prospects could handle. "I went through a lot of things," he said. "But I kept my head, and a lot of people have helped me.

"I'm stronger right now, and Coach Knight does have me concentrating on the low post right now, and that's helping.

"I know what I can do. I try to do what I can do best and stay away from what I can't do.

"After the Notre Dame game, he told me he thought I had been playing pretty well and to keep it up.

"Really, I didn't think I played well in that game. I scored a lot of points, but I didn't rebound well and I didn't do some other things I should do. Scoring isn't the whole game.

"Even before, I really didn't lose confidence. I was just kinda scared of making mistakes.

"Now if I make a mistake, I feel I can forget about it and try to get the ball back at the other end."

Knight also came out of the tournament pleased with the play of the other two men on the current Hoosier front line: Tolbert and Kitchel.

"Tolbert has done some really good things the last three games," Knight said. "He has done an excellent job on the boards, and he has played well on defense.

"Kitchel the last two games in particular has made a lot of positive contributions.

"He has always been a player who could shoot the basketball. I remember the first time I saw him play in high school (for Lewis Cass High, near Logansport), he impressed me as kind of a combination of Steve Green and Tommy Abernethy.

"Right now, he's playing an awful lot like Steve Green."

Knight considered Hoosier play in the tournament encouraging. "I saw some good things we're doing defensively," he said.

Haller called the Hoosiers "the best defensive team we've seen in the last three or four years. They're just physically stronger than we are. They manhandled us.

"In the first half, we were very shaky and way too tense — plus they were near-perfect. I thought our defense was very good throughout the first half but they just put the ball through the hoop."

We had 5,000 people at our banquet when Bobby spoke. He was the greatest thing that happened to us since one of those things from Mars fell on our campus.

Dave Whitney
Alcorn State coach

Hoosiers always play classy in Classic, MSA

BLOOMINGTON, DEC. 15, 1980

There may be no single factor that stands up as the reason why Indiana has had such an easy time winning seven straight Indiana Classic championships and, to almost as consistent and overwhelming an extent, six straight games on its "second home" court at Market Square Arena, where the Hoosiers play Oral Roberts tonight.

The first cause always raised after the two-night Hoosier tournament is "bad field." The consensus after the 83-47 final-game cruise past Baylor was that this year's group was the weakest ever. That also was the consensus last year, and two or three other times since the weak-field charge first was applied to the first-year Classic group.

Teams booked into Market Square haven't always been awe-inspiring, either. But the thing that stands out in looking at the 20 teams that have been whipped by IU in past Classic or Market Square Arena games is that some teams that had outstanding seasons were made to look amazingly inept.

Four of the Hoosiers' 12 previous Indiana Classic victims went on to 20-victory seasons. Three of the previous six teams the Hoosiers played at Market Square went on to win 20 games. All seven of those teams took their worst beating of the season at IU or Market Square:

• Creighton (which finished 20-7), 71-53 in the first Indiana Classic game in December, 1974;

• Texas A&M (20-7), 90-55 in the first MSA game that same year;

• Florida State (21-6), 83-59 at Market Square in December, 1975;

• Virginia Tech (21-7), 101-74 in the Classic in December, 1975;

• Miami (20-6), 76-55 in the 1977 Classic;

• Texas-El Paso (20-8), 75-43 in last year's Classic finals;

• Toledo (23-6), 80-54 last year at Market Square.

That's an average losing margin of 26.1 points for seven teams that had notably successful years.

For virtually all the teams, the game represented an introduction to Knight's IU-style defense. It has become the primary influence on the game in the Big Ten and, to a lesser degree, in the rest of the nation.

Big Ten teams and regular opponents like Kentucky and

I think our '75 team was maybe the best college team I've ever seen play. They played pretty good defense and they coupled it at times with an incredible ability to score points. Steve Green was an extremely good shooter. John Laskowski could have been an outstanding player for most teams and we were able to use him as our sixth man. Scott May was as good an all-round basketball player as I've seen in the Big Ten. The combination of Green, Laskowski and May made it very easy for Kent Benson to operate in the middle . . . and he was pretty good. And Bobby Wilkerson and Quinn Buckner were the best pair of defensive guards I've ever seen on one team.

Bob Knight

BAYLOR 47

	M	FG	FT	R	A	BS	St	PF	TP
Teagle, f	34	6-12	5- 5	3	0	0	2	1	17
Sears, f	18	1- 4	1- 2	1	1	0	0	2	3
Hall, c	19	2- 5	0- 0	2	1	1	0	1	4
Nunley, g	29	3- 9	0- 0	4	3	0	3	1	6
Shakir, g	24	1- 5	3- 7	7	8	0	0	1	5
Blake	10	1- 2	0- 0	0	0	0	0	1	2
Temaat	22	1- 1	2- 4	1	0	0	0	3	4
Battle	20	3- 7	0- 2	4	0	0	0	3	6
Copeland	12	0- 4	0- 0	4	0	0	0	2	0
Jackson	2	0- 0	0- 0	0	0	0	0	0	0
Team				4					
Totals		18-49	11-20	30	13	1	5	15	47

INDIANA 83

	M	FG	FT	R	A	BS	St	PF	TP
Tolbert, f	20	5- 7	0- 0	7	1	0	0	0	10
Kitchel, f	24	8-10	1- 2	5	2	0	2	3	17
Turner, c	28	11-14	1- 2	7	3	2	3	3	23
IThomas, g	22	0- 4	0- 0	2	5	0	1	1	0
Wittman, g	27	8-11	1- 1	1	2	0	0	1	17
Brown	12	0- 2	2- 4	1	2	0	1	0	2
Bouchie	15	1- 4	0- 0	4	0	0	2	5	2
Isenbarger	11	2- 3	0- 0	3	3	0	1	2	4
JThomas	18	1- 2	0- 0	3	4	0	1	2	2
Grunwald	9	1- 2	0- 2	2	0	0	0	2	2
Risley	6	1- 3	2- 2	1	0	0	1	0	4
Bardo	4	0- 1	0- 0	0	0	0	0	1	0
LaFave	4	0- 2	0- 0	2	0	0	0	1	0
Team				3					
Totals		38-65	7-13	41	22	2	12	21	83

SCORE BY HALVES

Baylor		20	27— 47
Indiana		41	42— 83

Turnovers—Baylor 23, Indiana 13.

SHOOTING

	FG	Pct.	FT	Pct.
Baylor	18-49	.367	11-20	.550
Indiana	38-65	.585	7-13	.538

Officials—Bob Burson, Fred Jaspers, Malcolm Hemphill.
Attendance—13,612.

Notre Dame have learned what to expect and produced their own aggressive versions.

But there has been an obvious effect on some teams running into it for the first time. Florida State's 1975-76 team was an example. The Seminoles ranked with the nation's best clubs as the season unrolled, but they were down by a humiliating 47-20 score at halftime against IU.

Defense was the factor that both California and Baylor coaches mentioned first after last weekend's games. It remains the constant in the outstanding Hoosier performances each year — and the variable that usually has broken down when the Hoosiers have struggled.

Florida State is the only team of the six the Hoosiers have played at Market Square that shot .400 or better. The Seminoles got up to .433 against IU reserves; the five other teams have ranged between .352 (Texas A&M) and .392 (Toledo). The composite is .388 — almost 100 points below the average all NCAA schools maintained last year (.479).

In the Classic, the same figure jumps out — opponents' field goal percentage for seven years, 14 games and 14 different teams, .388.

When IU's defense is working that well, the offense customarily benefits.

But the fascinating thing in defensive performances is the tiny bit of collective sharpness that separates the outstanding team efforts from mediocre ones: milliseconds in reaction times, involving more than just the player guarding the man with the ball.

It's in that millisecond that the usual Hoosier edge comes.

Indiana 65, Oral Roberts 56

Roommates Ted Kitchel and Randy Wittman did the shooting and a blend of defense and good fortune provided enough else as the Hoosiers won for the seventh straight year at Market Square Arena, 65-56, over Oral Roberts.

Indiana was playing its third game in four days. So was Oral Roberts. Each school has final exams this week. Each team might have been better off at home, studying. If the exam had been given in basketball, the curve would have been low.

Indiana survived its 22 turnovers because Oral Roberts committed 25. Indiana survived .444 shooting because Oral Roberts shot .429. Indiana survived, period, because Kitchel continues to be the biggest thing out of a corner since Little Jack Horner.

"I'd never heard of Ted Kitchel until we came to Indiana," Oral Roberts guard Steve Bontrager said. "Then I read where he made all-tournament. I can see why."

The 6-foot-8 junior with two years of eligibility left — the same class standing Wittman, a 6-5 guard, has — followed his two 8-for-10 shooting shows in the Indiana Classic with 8-for-12 firing. It's questionable if any Hoosier ever went 24-for-32 in a four-night span before.

Cat Johnson (10) finds Isiah Thomas a tall barrier

The one who did it this time fouled up a skimpy but effective game plan.

Oral Roberts sat all night in a 1-2-2 zone defense. "The biggest thing we wanted to do was keep Isiah Thomas from penetrating," ORU's 7-foot junior center, Tom Prusator, said. "Our point man (guard Gary Johnson, the only starter back from last year's 18-10 Titan team) did a good job of that, and our two wing men closed the gap whenever he needed help.

"And the other thing we wanted to do was jam them up inside. Usually on defense, I'm supposed to front my man (6-10 Landon Turner, author of 23 points in two of his previous three games), but I played behind him, and it seemed like he had a difficult time shooting over me.

"But if I play back there, the wing man on our zone has to drop down and cover the corners till I get out there."

Repeatedly, the drop-down theory failed. Kitchel stood in the corner as open as he was in pre-game warm-ups.

"He was shooting from areas you wouldn't guard anyway," Oral Roberts coach Ken Hayes said.

Hayes *wanted* Kitchel covered. He watched Kitchel hit his first three shots from long range to fuel an 11-6 Hoosier take-off. Then, Kitchel missed one, came back to bank in another side shot and the Hoosiers led, 13-6.

"Obviously, we wanted to get him covered," Hayes said. "Obviously, our 7-footer couldn't get there quick enough."

Obviously, the attempt to drop the wing down in Kitchel's area opened up shooting room for Wittman, who hit two in a row to check an Oral Roberts spurt and give IU a 17-10 lead.

Things got messy from there for IU. The Hoosiers went four minutes and eight possessions without scoring. In the process,

A talk 'tween Thomases, Isiah (11) and Jim (20)

they gave up a 10-point run to Oral Roberts to fall behind, 20-17, and lost Kitchel and Ray Tolbert along the way with three fouls each.

Reserves Glen Grunwald and Phil Isenbarger delivered the jump shots that reclaimed the lead for the Hoosiers, 21-20, and their aggressive board work was equally valuable to IU in opening a 29-22 halftime lead.

"The thing that pleased me most about our ball club was the poise we showed the second half," Hayes said.

The Titans got within 36-34 on Prusator's basket with 14:10 to play, but Kitchel shot 'em down again with four in a row — two from behind screens set by Tolbert to make it all the tougher for the back men in the zone to reach him.

The Hoosiers rushed on up to 58-42 with 5:45 left, and normally, that would be a time for a wave of the hands from the sidelines, a retreat to backcourt and a possession game to bleed the clock and force the trailing team to do what it obviously didn't want to do: chase the Hoosiers man-to-man. The wave didn't come. Oral Roberts scored seven in a row to cut the lead to 58-49 with 3:25 left.

Isiah Thomas, whose shooting chills carried over from his 0-for-4 Baylor game to a 1-for-11 start, came off the bench with 3:16 left, hit a baseline jump shot from Kitchel's operating area with 2:55 to go for a 60-49 lead, committed the Hoosiers' 20th turnover of the night with a traveling violation, and then, with the lead at 60-52 and a bare minute and a half left, backed off and began the stall. An uninspiring victory had an inelegant ending for the Hoosiers. They committed two more turnovers in the last 18 seconds.

Kitchel's two spurts gave him game scoring honors with 16 points, although he played only 25 minutes because of foul problems that eventually removed him with 5:04 left.

Wittman went most of the way and scored 15, responding to his orders to shoot by launching 10 shots, hitting five, and going 5-for-5 at the free-throw line.

The twin objects of the ORU defense, Turner and Thomas, had just eight points apiece. Mission accomplished, battle lost.

Freshman forward Jeff Acres had 14 points for Oral Roberts. Johnson — a 5-10 guard nicknamed Cat — had 10 points, six assists, three steals and 13 turnovers. Thomas had a similarly mixed bag, 12 assists and three steals brightening it and his final 4-for-14 shooting mark deglamorizing things.

ORAL ROBERTS 56

	M	FG	FT	R	A	BS	St	PF	TP
Acres, f	38	4-11	6- 8	9	4	0	2	2	14
Gd.Johnson, f	12	0- 2	2- 2	2	0	0	0	0	2
Prusator, c	35	5- 9	1- 3	8	0	0	0	1	11
Gy.Johnson, g	32	4- 8	2- 2	1	6	0	3	4	10
Bontrager, g	32	2- 6	0- 0	2	2	0	1	4	4
Showman	14	1- 5	0- 0	2	1	0	0	1	2
Clement	12	1- 2	2- 2	0	1	0	0	2	4
Williams	24	4- 6	1- 2	1	1	0	3	1	9
McGee	1	0- 0	0- 0	0	0	0	0	0	0
Team				7					
Totals		21-49	14-19	32	15	0	9	15	56

INDIANA 65

	M	FG	FT	R	A	BS	St	PF	TP
Tolbert, f	24	1- 3	1- 1	4	0	2	0	4	3
Kitchel, f	25	8-12	0- 0	4	1	0	0	5	16
Turner, c	26	4-11	0- 0	7	1	0	3	4	8
IThomas, g	33	4-14	0- 1	1	12	0	3	2	8
Wittman, g	39	5-10	5- 5	3	2	1	0	2	15
Bouchie	4	0- 0	0- 0	1	0	0	0	0	0
Grunwald	16	3- 5	0- 0	4	2	0	0	3	6
Isenbarger	10	1- 2	1- 2	6	0	0	1	0	3
JThomas	13	2- 5	0- 0	4	3	0	0	0	4
Risley	7	0- 0	0- 0	2	1	0	0	0	0
Brown	2	0- 1	0- 0	0	0	0	0	0	0
Bardo	1	0- 0	2- 2	0	0	0	0	0	2
LaFave	1	0- 0	0- 0	0	0	0	0	0	0
Team				2					
Totals		28-63	9-11	38	22	3	7	20	65

SCORE BY HALVES

Oral Roberts		22	34— 56
Indiana		29	36— 65

Turnovers—Oral Roberts 25, Indiana 22.

SHOOTING

	FG	Pct.	FT	Pct.
Oral Roberts	21-49	.429	14-19	.737
Indiana	28-63	.444	9-11	.818

Officials—Art White, Gil Haggart, Darryl Lamps.
Attendance—13,616.

'Hide-burning' rallied Titans

Prusator was a sophomore consigned to a distant spot on the Bradley bench when Indiana clouted the Braves at Market Square Arena two years ago, 80-64.

That made him something unique: the first two-time participant on a visiting club in the annual Hoosier appearances at Market Square. "All I could tell them was 'I've been here before,' " Prusator said of his sudden elder statesman role on his new club.

"I had a little bit more fun this time."

The fun didn't extend to the scoreboard, but Prusator was on the court at least for most of the action and contributed 11 points and eight rebounds.

"We played one of our better games," he said.

"We're a young team and Indiana's ranked. I think we were loose — a young team with nothing to lose. We just went out and tried to get after 'em.

"If we could have cut down our turnovers, we might even have beaten them."

Since there were 25 turnovers by the Titans, he may well be right.

"Obviously, we made way too many mistakes to beat a good ball club like Indiana," Hayes said.

"We were probably pretty fortunate to have caught Indiana a little flat after their great effort in their tournament. But I don't want to take anything away from our players. I thought they played hard."

He had the feeling Indiana's defensive reputation paid dividends for the Hoosiers early in the game, while the Titans were getting used to their first basketball battling with the Hoosiers.

"I thought Indiana intimidated us," Hayes said. "We're a pretty good shooting club and we go to the half shooting 30 percent (8-for-26, for .308).

"I did some hide-burning at the half. We had to see what we're made of."

The Titans found the basket, singed hide and all. They hit 13 of 23 second-half shots (.565), but their other two first-half headaches — turnovers and the hole in their zone that Kitchel kept exploiting — hung on even after the intermission.

The scouting gap that left the Titans oblivious to Kitchel's long-range threat — "I didn't know he could hit from the corner like that," Prusator said — was not a factor by the time the second half rolled around. Hayes had made some zone adjustments, strictly for Kitchel.

"Our guy from that side (Prusator) was filling in behind," Hayes said, "but the guy he was behind (Turner) wasn't hurting us.

"At all costs, we had to get there to guard Kitchel. You need to know the difference between Abdul-Jabbar and . . . the worst basketball player I know of is me, so, between Abdul-Jabbar and Ken Hayes."

Prusator didn't ascribe any sort of greatness to the Indiana team he met Monday. The Titans were whomped by Kansas earlier this year, 90-66, and by Georgia on the Oral Roberts court, 81-65. "Georgia was awful tough," he said. "Georgia and Kansas were probably our two toughest games."

He admitted he came in expecting more from the Hoosier defense. "I thought they'd deny the ball more than they did," he said. "I thought their denial of the passing lanes would be a lot tougher than it was.

"But they were like us, playing their third game in four days. It's been a hectic two weeks. It takes its toll."

Glen Grunwald — Ready reserve

North Carolina 65, Indiana 56

Al Wood, the dominant senior on this year's North Carolina basketball team, came into the game in a shooting slump. He promptly prolonged it by hitting just one of his first seven shots, running into the early moments of the second half.

Then, the 1980 U.S. Olympian sank his last six to lead a second-half charge that gave the Tar Heels a 65-56 victory over Indiana and a sweep of their two-year, nationally televised series with the Hoosiers.

The key was patience, Wood said.

"The second half, Coach (Dean) Smith told us to move the ball around more and make the defense work," Wood said. "And that's what we did."

Guard Jimmy Black, blanked in the first half before contributing 11 second-half points, gave the same explanation. "We weren't rushing our shots the second half," Black said. "We were making four or five passes to loosen the defense up."

Everything came loose for the Hoosiers in the second half, after Indiana had stopped the Tar Heels the first half and bordered on blowing the Carolinians out of the game.

Indiana surged from a 7-6 hole to an 18-9 lead in the first eight minutes of the game. North Carolina turned the ball over four times and got only one shot its five other possessions during that stretch.

The Hoosiers had a couple chances to take the lead on up from there, and they still had the nine-point margin at 24-15 after Randy Wittman's rebound basket with 7:20 left in the half.

North Carolina managed to get within 30-24 at halftime, and after dropping back to 34-26 on baskets by Ted Kitchel and Isiah Thomas early in the second half, reversed the game's control with an 11-point burst that included five points by Wood.

Still, IU came back to take the lead, 48-47, on consecutive baskets by Glen Grunwald and Ray Tolbert. The Hoosiers lost the lead to two free throws by Wood, then teetered on top two more times (50-49 and 52-51) before Black tied the game with a free throw at 4:58.

And that's when the lights went out for IU.

Thomas's long, high pass aimed for Turner didn't fool Carolina freshman Sam Perkins, who picked it off easily and got the ball upcourt to Wood for a driving lay-up that gave North Carolina the lead for good.

Indiana missed its next two shots, and Black scored after the first to open the lead to 56-52 with 4:20 to go. The second Hoosier miss gave Smith the opportunity to employ his four-corner possession game — his team up by four, the game in the last four minutes, IU already into one-and-one foul vulnerability.

The Tar Heels turned the ball over once, after killing only 30 seconds, then got the ball back; missed a one-and-one, but got the ball back on a long rebound, and broke Perkins free for a lay-up that made the score 58-52 with 2:40 to go. IU couldn't get the margin under four again.

Wood closed with 18 points and nine rebounds, leading Carolina's crushing 35-21 control of the backboards.

After shooting .379 in its first 20-minute look at Indiana's defense, North Carolina jumped the figure to .679 (16-for-23) in outscoring the Hoosiers in the second half, 41-26.

"We were just so impatient the first half," Smith said. "I couldn't believe it.

"I thought it was a great defensive game the first half. There were a lot of turnovers (15 by North Carolina, which added only five the second half; nine by IU each half), but a lot of those were forced.

"The second half, we were more more poised and patient. We got the ball where we wanted to get it and we were able to score."

Indiana got 20 points from Thomas, but his day's marks were blotched by a season-high six turnovers and the second-half defensive problems against Black. Kitchel was the only other Hoosier to score in double figures, with 10. He also had the defensive assignment against Wood during the Tar Heel veteran's rocky first half, and during his scorching take-off in the second.

INDIANA 56

	M	FG	FT	R	A	BS	St	PF	TP
Tolbert, f	40	4- 9	0- 0	1	2	1	3	2	8
Kitchel, f	24	4- 6	2- 2	1	2	0	2	2	10
Turner, c	39	4-12	0- 0	6	2	3	1	3	8
IThomas, g	29	10-19	0- 1	3	2	0	3	4	20
Wittman, g	40	4- 8	0- 0	5	4	1	1	3	8
JThomas	11	0- 0	0- 0	0	0	0	0	0	0
Isenbarger	9	0- 1	0- 0	1	1	0	0	3	0
Grunwald	9	1- 2	0- 0	2	0	0	0	1	2
Bouchie	1	0- 0	0- 0	0	0	0	0	0	0
Brown	1	0- 0	0- 0	0	0	0	0	0	0
Team				2					
Totals		27-57	2- 3	21	13	5	10	18	56

NORTH CAROLINA 65

	M	FG	FT	R	A	BS	St	PF	TP
Worthy, f	36	5-14	0- 0	8	4	3	1	2	10
Wood, f	37	7-13	4- 6	9	3	0	0	2	18
Budko, c	21	3- 5	0- 0	7	0	2	1	0	6
Black, g	32	3- 5	5- 6	0	6	0	3	3	11
Pepper, g	33	4- 4	1- 2	3	1	0	1	1	9
Perkins	26	5- 8	1- 3	4	1	1	1	0	11
Braddock	6	0- 2	0- 0	0	1	0	0	1	0
Kenny	3	0- 0	0- 0	1	0	0	0	1	0
Exum	1	0- 1	0- 0	0	0	0	0	0	0
Barlow	1	0- 0	0- 0	0	0	0	0	0	0
Brust	4	0- 0	0- 0	3	0	0	0	0	0
Team				0					
Totals		27-52	11-17	35	16	6	7	10	65

SCORE BY HALVES

Indiana	30	26— 56
North Carolina	24	41— 65

Turnovers—Indiana 18, North Carolina 20.

SHOOTING

	FG	Pct.	FT	Pct.
Indiana	27-57	.474	2- 3	.667
North Carolina	27-52	.519	11-17	.647

Officials—Hank Nichols, Bob Forte, George Solomon.
Attendance—10,000 (capacity).

Loss makes Hoosiers 0-3 against good teams

The pattern isn't pretty for Indiana:

A 64-64 tie with Kentucky with a minute and a half left became a 68-66 Wildcat victory.

A 54-54 tie with Notre Dame with 8½ minutes to go broke open for the Irish, who held on to win, 68-64.

And a 52-52 tie with North Carolina in the last five minutes became a 65-56 Tar Heel victory.

Three highly regarded teams, met amidst the tension and excitement of a collegiate rivalry, three straight losses for a

Dean Smith, Bob Knight — Just a preliminary

Hoosier team that North Carolina's Smith touted highly before the game. He left it a little more guarded in his appraisal.

"I *think* Indiana has a great team," Smith said. "Time will tell."

He thought back 52 weeks, to a day in IU's Assembly Hall when North Carolina expected to meet an Indiana team that had been ranked No. 1 in early season — and probably deserved it. Instead, the Tar Heels were the first team to take on IU without Mike Woodson, who had back surgery a few days later, and the Hoosiers also were just beginning to adjust to the loss — for the season, it turned out — of starter Randy Wittman.

North Carolina won that day, 61-57, in large part because freshman Worthy came of age as a collegian with an 18-point, nine-rebound effort.

"This time last year we thought we were in pretty good shape," Smith mused, "and then we lost James (to a broken ankle in the Tar Heels' 14th game) and Indiana went on to win the Big Ten. You just never know."

Worthy is a sophomore now, playing with a pin in the ankle that he shattered with a fast-break move against Maryland.

"It bothers him some," Smith said. "He says he feels it when he lands on the foot.

"The pin will come out when the season is over, and he should have no more trouble with it."

Meanwhile, he continues to play rather well for a man with a limp: 14 points, 11 rebounds, four assists a week ago against former Purdue coach Lee Rose's South Florida team; 10 points, eight rebounds, four assists, three blocks and a steal in another strong showing against IU — successful although Tolbert's defensive work helped to check him with 5-for-14 shooting.

"James is the best player we've ever recruited," Smith said flatly. That spans a lot of standouts, including two straight players who became the NBA's rookie of the year: Walter Davis (1977-78) and Phil Ford (1978-79).

"Walter and Phil became great players," Smith said. "But James was better as a recruit. Walter especially just kept getting better and better every year."

Wood shot .572 as a sophomore to lead the ACC and came back with .571 last year. His 1-for-7 game-opening stretch, as a follow-up to shooting problems in some games before, had him down to .461 for this year before he boosted that 30 points by going 6-for-6 the last half.

Wood gave some credit to the Hoosiers ("they're known for their defense") but said the slump was of long duration. "The shots just didn't seem to come to me," he said, "and when you hunt for them, most of the time you mess up. The second half, I felt like I had my rhythm back."

Wood said he and IU's Thomas became "tight" as teammates on the U.S. Olympic team this summer. "I like to win," he said, "but I don't like to see Isiah lose.

"I did tell our guys some things about him. I said he loves to drive and set up the other guys. You definitely don't want to go out and try to steal it from him, the way Jimmy did the first half when he got three fouls. You just want to try to counter him and keep him from penetrating — make him shoot the long outside jumper. He hit a few of them, but not enough. I thought Jimmy did a great job on him the second half. He played him straight-up and he couldn't take the ball to the basket. That was a big difference."

'ACC!' chant booms, but Smith denies differences

Ahead 62-56 with 26 seconds left and Perkins at the free-throw line shooting a one-and-one, the full house at North Carolina's Carmichael Auditorium erupted with a booming chant: "ACC! ACC!"

Atlantic Coast Conference backers have had to swallow national acceptance of Big Ten superiority the last couple years, and in North Carolina, two straight victories over Indiana have amounted to a declaration of ended deference.

Smith, a native Kansan, declined the chance to trumpet his adopted section's victory.

"We're really more similar to Indiana and Indiana is more similar to us than all that stuff you hear about a finesse league vs. a power league," Smith said. "That's TV talk. I don't believe in that at all. I think every team is what its coach wants it to be, and Bobby and I have a lot of the same ideas about what we want."

Indiana 51, Kansas State 44

Indiana's basketball team did just what college students are supposed to do when a tough test comes up.

The Hoosiers passed.

And they passed.

And they passed on and on and on till they found the openings that let them whip Kansas State, 51-44.

Both defenses made points come hard, but the dominant factor in the game was the IU offense, the one called "the passing game." Kansas State now knows why.

Bob Knight's cardinal rule since he went to the passing-game offense in 1974 has been "four passes before a shot." Knight searched through films of the Hoosiers' 65-56 loss at North Carolina and claimed he found only one sequence all day when the Hoosiers used as many as four passes. The cardinal rule came back with emphasis.

Most of the time, the Hoosiers played it straight on offense: 6-9 Ray Tolbert and 6-10 Landon Turner working for openings inside Kansas State's 1-2-2 zone defense, shooters Randy Wittman and Ted Kitchel looking for openings on the sides, and Isiah Thomas directing things from out front.

For a stretch of the second half, Indiana came out in something new: Thomas atop the foul circle and the other four along the baseline in a one-four alignment.

Whatever positioning the Hoosiers used, they swung the ball back and forth, side-to-side, making the Wildcat zone scramble to cover new territory.

"They moved the ball well," Kansas State coach Jack Hartman said. "It was tiring chasing the ball that way, and we paid the price."

Kansas State did the early dictating, delighting a full house of 11,220 by rushing to a 6-0 lead before Indiana got a shot away.

The game was barely 15 seconds old when Kansas State's all-America candidate, 6-foot-6 guard Rolando Blackman, lured Wittman out high on the court and then cut behind him to take a pass for a wide-open lay-up.

"That was my fault," Wittman said. "I knew that's what they wanted to do, but I just got out too far.

"I was just glad it happened then rather than late in the game. Their whole team came out really pumped up, and so were we."

The play started Kansas State's 6-0 charge, but it was the last easy score Blackman managed all night. Wittman hounded him for 35 minutes, giving up only 12 points.

At the other end of the court, Wittman was providing some leadership, too. He hit six of eight shots, most of them over the zone, to total 14 points.

In the one-four offense, he was in one corner and Kitchel was in the other. Kitchel went 4-for-6 for 10 points.

"They hit every shot they had to hit," Hartman said.

"It looked like we might be able to make some moves on them, but they hit some shots, tough shots.

"Did Wittman ever miss?"

It wasn't till the second half that Indiana's shooting settled mainly into the hands of Wittman and Kitchel. When the Hoosiers scrambled out of the 6-0 hole to go up 16-12, they did it with seven field goals by seven different players.

Wittman's second basket made it 18-12 with 5:11 left in the half. Kansas State had the Hoosier lead down to a point when Wittman banked in a shot four seconds ahead of the halftime buzzer for a 22-19 Indiana edge.

Kansas State never got the margin under that again. Wittman opened the second half with a shot from the deep left corner as Knight unveiled the one-four offense.

After Blackman worked loose for a jump shot at the K-State end, Indiana worked the ball around and over the Wildcat zone till Kitchel hit a shot from the deep right corner.

That was the pattern of attack that opened the lead to 38-27 with 10 minutes left and forced Hartman to abandon the zone and go after the Hoosiers man-to-man.

The switch worked some temporary wonders for Kansas State, which had the lead down to 42-37 with 5:43 left when Wittman left the corner to drive up the baseline, found himself in traffic between two big K-State defenders and went up with a shot intended to draw a foul.

No whistle came.

The shot went through.

"That was a bad shot, really," Wittman said. "I went out of the offense a little. I'm glad it went in, but it was a bad shot.

"Their big guy (6-7, 215-pound Randy Reed) jumped out on me, so I went up to draw the foul. But they didn't call it."

It was a vital basket for the Hoosiers, but it wasn't a backbreaker for Kansas State. The Wildcats kept clawing, pressuring Tolbert into two straight ball-handling errors and edging within 44-40 with 3:11 left.

"We felt he was the worst ball-handler of the five they had out there at the time," K-State forward Ed Nealy said. "We let him catch it and then tried to shut him off with pressure."

However, with 2:52 to go, Nealy tried to steal the ball and bumped Tolbert, whose one-and-one conversion widened the Hoosier lead to 46-40.

INDIANA 51

	M	FG	FT	R	A	BS	St	PF	TP
Tolbert, f	40	2- 4	4- 4	9	0	1	0	3	8
Kitchel, f	26	4- 6	2- 2	3	2	1	0	1	10
Turner, c	27	2- 2	0- 0	1	1	1	0	3	4
I.Thomas, g	40	3- 6	3- 5	3	10	0	2	3	9
Wittman, g	40	6- 8	2- 2	3	1	1	2	4	14
Isenbarger	5	0- 0	0- 0	0	0	0	0	1	0
Grunwald	8	1- 4	0- 0	0	0	0	0	1	2
Bouchie	14	2- 3	0- 0	2	0	0	0	1	4
Team				1					
Totals		20-33	11-13	22	14	4	4	16	51

KANSAS STATE 44

	M	FG	FT	R	A	BS	St	PF	TP
Adams, f	40	3- 8	3- 3	5	1	0	0	3	9
Nealy, f	40	5-10	0- 1	7	1	0	3	3	10
Craft, c	29	4- 8	0- 0	2	0	1	0	3	8
Blackman, g	40	6-12	3- 6	1	7	0	1	1	15
Jankovich, g	17	0- 4	0- 0	1	2	0	0	1	0
Reed	11	0- 2	0- 0	1	1	0	0	0	0
Barton	23	1- 2	0- 0	2	2	0	1	3	2
Team				5					
Totals		19-46	6-10	24	14	1	5	14	44

SCORE BY HALVES

Indiana		22	29— 51
Kansas State		19	25— 44

Turnovers—Indiana 10, Kansas State 11.

SHOOTING

	FG	Pct.	FT	Pct.
Indiana	20-33	.606	11-13	.846
Kansas State	19-46	.413	6-10	.600

Officials—Jim Bain, Rich Weiler.
Attendance—11,220 (sellout).

Wittman gave possession back to IU by rebounding Tyrone Adams's miss with 2:20 to play. Tolbert was above the free-throw circle, ball in hand, when Nealy slapped at it.

"When he made a swipe at the ball, I took off," Tolbert said. "Landon (Turner, IU's center) saw me coming and got out of the way."

In a couple quick strides and one long, high bound, Tolbert got in dunking range. It was authoritative, Nealy agreed. "You did know it was going down."

That play gave IU 48-40 command with barely a minute and half to go. Kansas State got within four but no closer.

Indiana took only 33 shots and hit 20 for a .606 shooting percentage. Besides the double-figure scoring from Wittman and Kitchel, the Hoosiers also got eight points and nine rebounds from Tolbert and nine points and 10 assists from Thomas.

Blackman's 15 points led Kansas State.

North Carolina game warning for Hartman

Hartman had a feeling when he watched Indiana lose to North Carolina it wasn't good news for his team.

And when he sat at courtside and watched Indiana set up on offense and go to work with the basketball seeking to find shots without regard for how long it took, he knew exactly what was happening.

"I thought after that North Carolina game, Bobby would be disappointed," Hartman said, "and he might come in here and try to grind one out.

"He did, and they did a great job.

"At the same time, we were not very smooth offensively. We were a little anxious."

That, too, may have been a spin-off of the Hoosier offensive patience, Hartman conceded. "That's the theory: keep the ball away from them and when they do get it, they'll be overanxious," he said.

Defenses sparkled at both ends of the court, and Knight enjoyed the show.

"That's the hardest any team has played against us this year — maybe the hardest any team has played against us since I've been at Indiana," he said.

"It's also the best we've been able to sustain anything over a 40-minute period. And it's the hardest we've played defensively."

Thomas, whose greatest contributions of late have been his long-range jump shots, put those away for the most part and concentrated on getting the ball into high-percentage openings in the K-State defense.

"This is the most patient we've been all year," Thomas said. A Kansan asked if there was a particular reason for the extra patience. "Yes," Thomas said, "There's a big reason: coach Knight."

Knight passed some high grades around. "I thought Tolbert really played the game for us. I don't think I've ever seen him play better for 40 minutes."

Isiah — what a guy. He is a very, very enthusiastic ballplayer. He's a super leader . . . always laughing and smiling. There are no gimmicks to stopping him. I'm not planning on guarding him, but if I had to tell my teammates what to do, I'd say play him straight up.

Rolando Blackman
Kansas State guard

Our older people around here remember the great Indiana and Kansas State series of the past and they've been after me to get it back ever since.

Jack Hartman
Kansas State coach

"We also got excellent shooting from Wittman and Kitchel, and we got a couple good buckets from Steve Bouchie.

"I'm just glad we won a tough ball game.

"We've been in four now where in the last five minutes we could win or lose. We're 1-for-4 now. I've always felt a really good team will win 75 percent of those games and a good one will win two out of four. So we're just getting started in the right direction now."

Even in defeat, Hartman and his players had the same feeling about their team. Kansas State came into the game 5-1, the loss an 84-61 stinging at Arizona State and the victories over a string of non-entities, many of them not major colleges.

"I haven't been happy with the way we've played," Hartman said. "But they went after it tonight. They played hard. I was proud of that."

Blackman called the Indiana game "a lot tougher" than the blowout at Arizona State.

"We didn't go out and play with intensity at Arizona State, the way we did in this game," he said. "We didn't give ourselves a chance out there.

"We knew how good we were before this game, but this gives us a better idea of how we compare with the nation's other good teams."

Blackman said Wittman "played a very good game. He played me very well. But he did have a good supporting cast. They played a really good supporting defense."

Wittman said he guarded Blackman some during the U.S. Olympic Trials last summer.

"Isiah also gave me some key points," he said. "He told me he likes to spin and go to his left, and he likes to come off the dribble and shoot right away.

"So I tried to play him a little more to the right and just control him as much as I could. He's a very good player."

When Wittman drew his fourth foul with five minutes left, Knight switched the 6-1 Thomas onto Blackman.

"We've never played against each other — not even in practice," Blackman said.

"He's a very good basketball player — in any gym, against anybody," Thomas said. "Randy is 6-6. He did a good job."

Both Hartman and Blackman marveled at IU's outside shooting.

"Obviously, the way they were passing the ball made us work our tails off at the defensive end. That makes the defense adjust.

"They were watching for any time it pulled apart so they could pop the ball down in there to someone inside, but it didn't happen very often.

"Basically, the shots we gave them were low percentage, but they got every shot they had to have."

Blackman said the Wildcats "knew they were going to be patient and keep grinding it out.

"They hit the shots they needed to hit. Those long shots out of the corner were really going down for them, which was just what they needed."

Knight called Blackman "a great player, as good a player as there is in the country. We told our kids before the game he can do anything at the offensive end. He's a good defensive player, too, but it was hard to judge him off tonight's game because what they did was more of a team defense."

Indiana 55, Rutgers 50

HONOLULU, DEC. 28, 1980

When it came time to do or die for dear old Rutgers, the Rutgers basketball team darned near did before it died.

Indiana put the Scarlet Knights in a 12-0 box at the beginning of their Rainbow Classic first-round game, the best Hoosier start in recent years.

It was 49-32 with 9½ minutes left, but Rutgers, which couldn't find the basket in the first half, couldn't miss it at the finish and actually made things squirmy for the Hoosiers before falling, 55-50.

The closest Rutgers got was 53-50 with seven seconds left. Two free throws by Phil Isenbarger padded the margin with four seconds to go.

Indiana's defense plainly was new to the Knights, who turned the ball over five times and missed three shots in falling into the 12-0 hole in the game's first five minutes.

"Obviously, if you get that far behind a team like this, you're going to have a hard time catching up," Rutgers coach Tom Young said.

The lead never shrank under eight as Indiana advanced to a 30-17 halftime lead. The Hoosiers hit their first five shots of the second half to jump the lead quickly to 40-24 — a steal by Isiah Thomas and a Ray Tolbert dunk capping the early second-half burst.

Up to that point, Rutgers had hit just nine of 25 shots. "We just didn't run an offense," Young said. "You've gotta give Indiana credit for that."

The Knights got their next nine field goals with nine shots, and they followed that string with enough success to stand 13-for-17 in the last 15 minutes, .765.

"The ironic thing is we told our kids just this afternoon that they tend to shoot in streaks," IU coach Bob Knight said. "We told them Rutgers could be out of a ball game and shoot their way back into it."

Indiana's 17-point lead began to shrink when the Hoosiers, who didn't commit a turnover in the first 11 minutes of the second half, bogged down with three in a row.

Indiana didn't score a point for almost seven minutes, because of five turnovers, 0-for-3 shooting and a missed one-and-one opportunity within Rutgers' 12-0 spurt that negated the fast Hoosier takeoff.

Tolbert ended the streak with two free throws with 2:26 left, widening the Indiana lead to 51-44.

Kentucky transfer Clarence Tillman hit his last three shots — in the last 41 seconds — to lead Rutgers with 15 points.

Kelvin Troy, a 6-7 senior forward who had 28 points in a 71-54 loss to North Carolina, couldn't get a field goal against Tolbert's tight defense the first half. He came out firing with a three-point play only five seconds into the second half and finished with 13 points.

Isiah Thomas, who directed the Hoosier offense during its mutiny first 30 minutes, scored 16 points although three one-and-one chances got away from him. Thomas also had 11

assists and three steals to provide the Hoosier offensive punch.

Ted Kitchel's .729 shooting percentage shrank to .683 with his coldest mark since he became a starter (6-for-12). Still, he had 13 points and a career-high nine rebounds, leading Indiana to a 26-19 board edge.

Powers almost met in losers' bracket

Before the 17th Rainbow Classic began, Knight noted the Hoosiers' schedule could throw them against Rutgers, Clemson and Marquette on three straight nights. "I hope that's the way it does work out," he said. "I think it would be good for us to play three teams like that, just before the Big Ten season."

He wasn't so eager to get the match-up after Marquette plunged into the losers' bracket on opening night, but for a time in their own openers, it looked like both Indiana and Clemson might be in there, too. Both survived, but both Knight and Clemson's Bill Foster were wheezing a little.

"We were a pretty good basketball team for 30 minutes," Knight said. "After that, I don't think you could say we stopped them. It was a game that kinda got over before Rutgers could catch up."

The Rutgers rally didn't surprise Knight. "They were nine or 10 down against North Carolina and had a chance to tie the game in the last minute," Knight said. "They're a team that can do that."

This is where I've felt all along this team could really develop. We want these kids to relax and have a good time here, but we also want to use this time to bring everything together, if we can.

Bob Knight

INDIANA 55

	M	FG	FT	R	A	BS	St	PF	TP
Tolbert, f	33	4- 6	2- 2	4	0	0	0	3	10
Kitchel, f	36	6-11	1- 2	9	0	0	0	3	13
Turner, c	29	3- 9	0- 0	6	0	0	2	1	6
I.Thomas, g	40	6- 8	4- 9	1	11	0	3	1	16
Wittman, g	37	4- 9	0- 0	1	2	0	1	4	8
Isenbarger	7	0- 1	2- 3	0	0	0	0	1	2
Grunwald	6	0- 0	0- 0	1	0	0	0	0	0
J.Thomas	4	0- 2	0- 0	0	0	0	1	0	0
Bouchie	8	0- 0	0- 0	0	0	0	0	0	0
Team				4					
Totals		23-46	9-16	26	13	0	6	14	55

RUTGERS 50

	M	FG	FT	R	A	BS	St	PF	TP
Troy, f	34	4-11	5- 5	6	2	0	0	4	13
Tillman, f	34	7-13	1- 2	3	1	0	0	2	15
Hinson, c	28	4- 7	0- 0	4	0	1	0	2	8
Payne, g	26	2- 4	0- 0	0	3	0	0	2	4
Black, g	25	3- 4	0- 0	0	2	0	0	2	6
Nieberlein	18	0- 1	0- 0	1	1	0	1	2	0
Brunson	25	0- 0	0- 0	3	5	0	0	1	0
Griffin	10	2- 2	0- 0	1	1	0	2	5	4
Team				1					
Totals		22-42	6- 7	19	15	1	3	20	50

SCORE BY HALVES

Indiana		30	25— 55
Rutgers		17	33— 50

Turnovers—Indiana 12, Rutgers 15.

SHOOTING

	FG	Pct.	FT	Pct.
Indiana	23-46	.500	9-16	.563
Rutgers	22-42	.524	6- 7	.857

Officials—Dave Phillips, Giff Johnson.
Attendance—5,221.

Teams are not supposed to do that to Indiana, and it's certainly not supposed to happen after the Hoosiers use their lead to pull the opposition out of a zone defense, the take-off point to many a past rout.

It was a voluntary switch for the Knights. "Obviously they did a good job against our zone," Young said.

Against the man-to-man, IU had one seven-minute scoreless stretch.

"Of all the defenses they played against us," Knight said, "the toughest for us was their man-to-man.

"We haven't executed things as well as I'd like against a man-to-man lately."

There was nothing wrong with the Hoosiers' man-to-man defense.

"Their defense was very aggressive," Young said."They're aggressive and they know how to play it. It obviously chased us out of some stuff."

"That's the first time we have played a team as aggressive as they are.

I really like Bobby's team this year. I think it's the best outside shooting team he's had in a long, long time.

Lou Henson
Illinois coach

I think anybody could play here. The way we play is very simple. We do it this way and there is no other way. Maybe that's why a guy who isn't as talented as other guys can play here and do well. It's so simple that it's kind of hard to screw up. But sometimes we find a way.

Isiah Thomas

"We just didn't run an offense, and you've got to give them credit for that.

"You have to go through a game like that for your kids to realize how disciplined you have to be to stay in your offense against a team like that.

"We just basically fell too far behind.

"We were only getting one shot, and sometimes that wasn't a good one."

Foster was far more upset with his team's first Honolulu performance than either Knight or Young. Foster talked of benching half his lineup, including all-America candidate Larry Nance.

"We didn't have the respect for that team (Louisiana Tech) that we should have had," Foster said.

"I think they'll be a little more ready to play the next time.'"

Hoosiers on way to victory, hands down

Clemson 58, Indiana 57

Indiana's championship hopes in the 17th Rainbow Classic basketball tournament died with a shot and a rebound that each rolled teasingly around the basket but did not drop through.

Randy Wittman put up the 15-foot shot and Ray Tolbert got enough of a hand on the rebound to boost it back onto the rim and give the Hoosiers a second chance.

But Clemson came out a 58-57 winner, because of guard Chris Dodds's 10-foot shot from a tough angle: on the baseline, almost blocked off from the rim by the backboard.

Dodds didn't use the rim, swishing the shot that moved Clemson into the finals against Hawaii, which got by Pan American, 79-75.

The Hoosiers seemed likely to be in the championship game after Phil Isenbarger hit both halves of a one-and-one chance with 1:05 left for a 57-54 lead.

At 0:52, Clemson center Bill Ross hit a 15-foot jump shot to cut the Indiana lead to 57-56. The Hoosiers ran the clock down to 0:36 before Isenbarger was fouled again. That time, his shot bounced off the rim into Clemson hands.

The Tigers took time out with 27 seconds left, and the plotting in both huddles dealt with the same prospect.

"Our idea was to get the ball inside," Clemson coach Bill Foster aid. "We ran what we call our lopsided play with all three of our big men on the same side of the floor.

"But we couldn't drop the ball into one of them, so Dodds just ad-libbed. He's the best ad-libber on the team."

IU coach Bob Knight said the Hoosier defense "tried to jam up the middle to make them shoot over the top, but Dodds did an excellent job. He penetrated and made a difficult shot."

When the play involving Clemson's three 6-10 players didn't work, the most noted of them, Larry Nance, gave the ball to Dodds, near the right sideline, about 15 feet from the baseline.

"Isiah (Thomas) may have been shading me a little toward the middle, to make me go baseline where he had some help," Dodds said. "I went down there and he did get help. Wittman stepped up, so I pulled up and shot.

"It was a very tight angle, but I figured if their guys were coming in on me, we'd have a pretty good chance at the rebound if I did miss."

He didn't, so the strategical battling shifted to the other end of the court, after IU took a time out with seven seconds to go, the ball still at the Clemson end.

"I thought they would give the ball to Isiah for a drive," Dodds said.

Indiana lined Thomas up as the backcourt receiver, but Isenbarger's in-bounds pass instead went to Wittman near center court. Wittman drove to the left of the foul circle, pivoted and worked himself free for a straight-out, slightly off-balance shot just inside the free-throw line.

"I thought it was going in," Dodds said. "I'm sure that was the shot they wanted. It just didn't fall."

Clemson's Horace Wyatt contended with Tolbert for the rebound, but the ball still was eased back toward the goal before it fell off into Clemson hands, deciding the game.

"I don't think we could have had a better shot," Knight said. "It just didn't drop. Some do and some don't.

"When you get down to that point, that's about all you can ask. We had our chance to win it and didn't."

Dodds's shot switched the lead for the 14th time in a game that saw each team burst ahead with point flurries only to see the other come back and reverse momentum.

Ross, a junior making his first collegiate start because Foster benched three hitherto regulars for their poor play in a first-round scrape past Louisiana Tech, celebrated his new status with a three-point play only 14 seconds into the game. Indiana caught up on six straight free throws, but Clemson went ahead, 19-16, before Indiana ran in seven points in a row to lead 25-21.

Clemson had a 31-27 halftime lead, but Indiana scored the first six points of the second half to go on top again.

Tolbert's dunk with 4:07 to go gave Indiana a 55-53 lead. Dodds drew Ted Kitchel's fifth foul with a baseline drive, but he hit only one of the free throws to leave Indiana ahead, 55-54, with 3:32 to play.

Indiana worked cautiously for a shot, then backed off and kept the basketball frozen until Isenbarger was fouled at 1:05, the start of the decisive sequence.

Ross led Clemson with 13 points, and Dodds had 11. Thomas had 14 and Kitchel 12 for Indiana.

INDIANA 57

	M	FG	FT	R	A	BS	St	PF	TP
Tolbert, f	40	3-10	2- 2	6	4	0	0	1	8
Kitchel, f	25	4- 9	4- 4	3	2	0	0	5	12
Turner, c	19	3- 7	2- 2	3	0	1	0	4	8
I. Thomas, g	40	7-11	0- 1	2	2	0	1	2	14
Wittman, g	40	4- 7	1- 2	3	3	0	1	1	9
Isenbarger	4	0- 0	2- 3	0	0	0	0	0	2
Grunwald	4	0- 0	0- 0	0	1	0	0	0	0
Bouchie	21	1- 2	2- 2	3	1	0	0	4	4
Risley	7	0- 0	0- 0	1	1	0	0	0	0
Totals		22-46	13-16	21	14	1	2	17	57

CLEMSON 58

	M	FG	FT	R	A	BS	St	PF	TP
Jones, f	23	3- 7	0- 1	5	2	0	2	2	6
Wyatt, f	30	4- 7	0- 0	4	2	0	0	3	8
Ross, c	23	6-10	1- 1	4	2	0	1	2	13
Dodds, g	27	4- 6	3- 4	0	4	0	0	2	11
Hamilton, g	30	2- 5	0- 0	4	2	0	1	1	4
Nance	18	3- 6	2- 3	4	1	0	0	1	8
Bynum	10	1- 2	2- 2	0	0	0	0	0	4
Campbell	16	0- 0	0- 0	2	0	0	1	1	0
Gilliam	23	2- 6	0- 0	5	3	0	0	5	4
Team				1					
Totals		25-49	8-11	27	18	0	5	17	58

SCORE BY HALVES

Indiana	27	30— 57
Clemson	31	27— 58

Turnovers—Indiana 7, Clemson 10.

SHOOTING

	FG	Pct.	FT	Pct.
Indiana	22-46	.478	13-16	.813
Clemson	22-42	.524	6- 7	.857

Officials—Dave Phillips, Pat Tanibe.
Attendance—7,575.

Embarrassed Tigers not blushing now

Clemson was an embarrassed basketball team after a one-point first-round victory in the Rainbow Classic. One night later, the Tigers were one-point winners again and proud and pleased.

The opponent does make a difference. Indiana was a prized

scalp for the Atlantic Coast Conference team to claim.

"Indiana is a great team — with a great coach," the game's hero, Clemson guard Chris Dodds, said. "Their execution was as good as anybody we've ever seen.

"Everybody knows how good their defense is, but we felt we played pretty good defense, too. I just thought it was a great basketball game, and it's a big win for our program.

"We beat Kentucky in the NIT a couple years ago and went to the final eight in the NCAA tournament last year, but we're still fighting for recognition. This one will really help us."

It came one day after Foster was so unhappy with his team's effort that he decided to bench starters Larry Nance, Clarke Bynum and Fred Gilliam.

There was a method to his anger, Foster confessed.

"Three guys we started (center Bill Ross, forward Raymond Jones and guard Vincent Hamilton) have been playing well for a couple weeks," Foster said. "It wasn't a one-time thing. I've been looking for a chance to do something like that.

That's the worst this team can play. We really played bad as a team and as individuals.

Isiah Thomas

This team was mismatched in December, not in terms of talent but in intangible qualities.

Bob Knight

"When we won but didn't play well, the situation was perfect. I think our guys responded to it all very well.

"We still didn't shoot very well, but the best part of Indiana's game is its defense."

Clemson's first nine opponents shot a cumulative .406, and that's a defensive figure that ranks No. 1 in the nation.

"We're proud of that," Dodds said. "I think we held Indiana down again tonight."

The Hoosiers shot .478, surprising Dodds. "Well," he said, "I'd say Indiana is better than most of the teams we've played, too."

Knight felt "it was a good basketball game the second half. The first half, they outplayed us, and that was the difference."

It was a game with some extraordinary entries in the box score. Together, the teams had just 17 turnovers, 10 by Clemson. Indiana went to its last-second scoring attempt with a second-half shooting log that read 14-for-17, .824. All those figures were good only for second — partly because Indiana's first-half shooting was the Hoosiers' chilliest of the year (.297).

Bob Knight — *searching for answers after two losses in Hawaii*

Pan American 66, Indiana 60

Kenneth "Apple" Green was named the outstanding player of the 17th Rainbow Classic basketball tournament, and Indiana wasn't about to challenge the vote after meeting Green.

The 6-foot-10 Georgian who went to junior college in Texas and stayed in the state to play for Pan American led the Broncs' power attack inside with 21 points and nine rebounds in a 66-60 victory over Indiana in the tournament's third-place game.

Clemson won the championship with a 75-71 overtime victory over Hawaii.

Green ranked with the leading big men in the nation last year with his 19.6 point average and 12.0 rebound mark. It was in the Hawaiian tournament, however, that he showed he could take his game against teams like Marquette and Indiana.

"He's amazing," Pan American coach Bill White said. "Every game, 20 points, 10 rebounds. I believe we could play a YWCA team and he'd get 20 points and 10 rebounds."

Green's most painful contributions against Indiana were a couple shots he forced up while surrounded by IU defenders. Both swished, helping Pan American open a 34-25 halftime lead.

His most damaging effect, however, was his board play and inside work that drew repeated fouls from the Hoosiers.

Even with his work and complementing 20-point, seven-rebound contributions from 6-6 center Curtis Glasper, the Broncs had to beat back an IU challenge in the second half.

Jim Thomas, moved into the Hoosier starting lineup in a switch that broke up the big combination (Ray Tolbert and Landon Turner) that the Hoosiers had been starting for several games, got the Hoosiers started in the second half with a jump shot, and Turner followed with a basket that cut the Bronco lead to 34-29 and forced White to a fast time out.

Indiana kept coming, moving within 40-38 on another combination of baskets by Thomas and Turner — Turner's a midcourt steal and dunk.

In the next three minutes, Pan American scored three offensive rebound baskets — two by Glasper and one by Green — to blunt the Hoosier rush.

Still, it was 51-48 and Indiana was off on a fast break in pursuit of another basket when Pan American guard Rueben Cole stole the ball from Turner near the Indiana goal and took off to a lay-up at the other end.

Indiana got 14 points each from Isiah Thomas and Randy Wittman, and Jim Thomas scored 11. For the second straight game, Indiana had only seven offensive turnovers, but the Pan American inside domination was so total that that kind of efficiency and .500 shooting weren't enough to get the Hoosiers close.

Isiah Thomas and Green, the only players in the Classic to play all 40 minutes in each of their team's games, were among six players named to the all-tournament team.

Others on the team were the tourney's scoring leader, Oliver Lee of Marquette (68 points), guard Chris Dodds of Clemson and Rodney Jones and Rocky Sesler of runnerup Hawaii.

I'm very, very dissatisfied with the play of our inside people. We have been getting beaten very, very badly inside. If we can't improve ourselves inside, we're going to have a long 18 games.

Bob Knight

PAN AMERICAN 66

	M	FG	FT	R	A	BS	St	PF	TP
Green, f	40	7-17	7- 9	9	0	0	0	1	21
Kirby, f	28	2- 4	5- 6	8	3	2	0	3	9
Glasper, c	40	6- 7	8-10	7	0	0	0	1	20
Carroll, g	39	2- 5	0- 2	1	4	0	0	3	4
Cole, g	40	6- 9	0- 0	3	4	0	4	2	12
Owen	6	0- 0	0- 0	0	2	0	0	0	0
McGrath	7	0- 3	0- 0	1	2	0	0	3	0
Team				3					
Totals		23-45	20-27	32	15	2	4	13	66

INDIANA 60

	M	FG	FT	R	A	BS	St	PF	TP
Kitchel, f	13	1- 5	0- 0	0	0	0	0	3	2
Wittman, f	40	7-14	0- 0	3	3	0	3	2	14
Tolbert, c	14	0- 2	0- 0	3	0	1	1	3	0
I. Thomas, g	40	7-13	0- 0	0	5	0	4	4	14
J. Thomas, g	40	5- 8	1- 3	6	6	0	0	5	11
Risley	23	4- 9	1- 1	2	0	1	0	2	9
Bouchie	4	1- 3	0- 0	2	0	1	0	2	2
Turner	19	3- 3	0- 0	3	0	0	1	2	6
Isenbarger	4	0- 0	0- 0	1	1	0	0	0	0
Franz	1	1- 1	0- 0	1	1	0	0	2	2
Brown	2	0- 2	0- 0	1	0	0	0	1	0
Team				1					
Totals		29-58	2- 4	23	16	3	7	24	60

SCORE BY HALVES

Pan American		34	32— 66
Indiana		25	35— 60

Turnovers—Pan American 11, Indiana 7.

SHOOTING

	FG	Pct.	FT	Pct.
Pan American	23-45	.511	20-27	.741
Indiana	29-58	.500	2- 4	.500

Officials—Bob McKendry and Gordon Birk.
Attendance—5,818

'Lot of questions unanswered' — Knight

Knight said in advance he hoped the Hawaiian trip would be the making of the Hoosiers, getting them ready for the start of Big Ten play. A 1-2 record in the tournament and 7-5 pre-conference record left him disappointed.

"We have a lot of unanswered questions about our team that I had hoped to have answered by this time," he said.

"From our standpoint, we did not come out of this as solidly as we would have liked. There's a certain way we have to play in our league, and we're certainly not there yet."

Knight used the third-place game for some last-minute experimentation — sophomore Jim Thomas back in the starting lineup at 6-3, with 6-9 Ray Tolbert and 6-10 Landon Turner sharing a spot rather than operating together.

Tolbert started and played 14 minutes before running into foul trouble. Turner opened the second half and went most of the rest of the way. Each had three rebounds. Turner scored six points and Tolbert was blanked.

Jim Thomas went all 40 minutes and led the Hoosiers in both rebounds (six) and assists (six) in addition to scoring 11 points.

Steve Risley, who had been bothered by flu, played his longest stint in a while, 23 minutes, and had nine points with two rebounds.

Indiana 55, Michigan State 43

Indiana's collapsing defense and his own foul problems checked Michigan State scoring star Jay Vincent with 11 points, and the rest of the Spartans couldn't keep up in a 55-43 Hoosier victory that launched both teams' Big Ten season.

The Hoosiers took the lead with their quickest basket of the year: Ted Kitchel from under the basket after a pass from Isiah Thomas only five seconds into the game.

Michigan State never caught up, but the Spartans, after falling back 14-6, never let Indiana get a bigger lead in keeping things worrisome for IU until Vincent fouled out with 5:18 to go.

Vincent picked up his third foul with 2:24 left in the first half when he tried to take the ball away from IU's Isiah Thomas in the Hoosier backcourt.

Michigan State trailed at the time, 24-19, and Thomas sank two free throws while Vincent was getting comfortable in a sideline seat. The Hoosier lead was 28-20 at halftime.

Two straight baskets by MSU guard Kevin Smith cut the Indiana lead to 34-30 six minutes into the second half.

It was 43-36 with less than six minutes to go when Vincent went up for an inside shot that IU's Ray Tolbert swatted away. Michigan State sought a goaltending call, but the whistle that came exacted a far different penalty: a charging foul on Vin-

cent, his fourth. Only 23 seconds later, with 5:18 to go, Vincent got his fifth trying for a rebound.

The defending Big Ten scoring champion spent a crowded night at the Spartan offensive end, and Tolbert headed the Hoosier defensive effort. Vincent's foul trouble was "as big a factor in holding him down as anything we did," IU coach Bob Knight admitted. "But we did work hard defensively."

Michigan State departed from its gamelong zone defenses to chase IU man-to-man in the last seven minutes.

The Hoosier counter was to mix the 6-1 Thomas in with the front-court players for a while, popping him in and out of the pivot.

Thomas hit one baseline jump shot and missed a close-in shot just before Vincent's exit. But, at a time out that coincided with Vincent's departure, Knight let his displeasure with the Hoosiers' late-game offense be known.

"We had four guys standing around and Thomas moving," Knight said.

"I don't think our offensive movement has been particularly good against man-to-man defenses. Our biggest problem has been making the transition from one defense to the other.

"Any time anybody changes, you've got to react quickly to it, and that's difficult."

Thomas scored eight of his game-high 20 points after Michigan State went to the man-to-man.

Earlier, Randy Wittman had led the outside sniping against the Spartan zones. Wittman was 6-for-8 the first half and 8-for-12 for the game to total 16 points.

Tolbert also made double figures for Indiana with 11 points, and Jim Thomas, the 6-3 sophomore who started at forward for a second straight game, again led the Hoosiers in rebounding with seven.

"He goes after the ball," Knight said. "To date we just haven't had good rebounding."

The Hoosiers had a 27-25 board edge over Michigan State in the meeting of the two teams that ranked ninth and 10th among Big Ten clubs in pre-conference rebounding.

Smith's 14 points led Michigan State (6-4). "I don't feel like we lost to a great team," Spartan coach Jud Heathcote said. "We lost to a very good team . . . and they'll get better and better as the season goes along."

The Hoosiers survived a couple unusual negatives: for the first time all year, they committed more turnovers (14) than their opponent (13), and Ted Kitchel, a .700 shooter from deep regions through most of December, paid some back to the law of averages with a 2-for-10 night.

Isiah Thomas, however, shook a slump of his own, at the free-throw line. Thomas missed his first try Thursday to drop to an even .500 for the season, 15-for-30, including 2-for-9 over a four-game stretch extending into the MSU game. A .759 free-throw shooter in Big Ten play a year ago as a rookie, Thomas jumped right into the league race again by hitting his last eight in a row.

Wittman was as reluctant as the most cautious Indiana fan to read much into the victory.

MICHIGAN STATE 43

	M	FG	FT	R	A	BS	St	PF	TP
Perry, f	18	2- 2	1- 2	1	0	0	0	1	5
Brkovich, f	38	2- 4	0- 0	2	1	0	0	0	4
Vincent, c	33	4-11	3- 5	3	3	0	1	5	11
Smith, g	39	7-12	0- 2	2	2	0	3	4	14
Morrison, g	28	1- 4	0- 0	3	2	0	1	5	2
Kaye	13	1- 3	0- 0	1	2	0	0	2	2
Bostic	11	0- 2	2- 2	1	0	0	0	2	2
Tower	13	0- 0	0- 2	4	0	0	0	0	0
Cawood	3	0- 1	0- 0	0	0	1	0	0	0
Gore	2	1- 1	1- 2	1	0	0	0	1	3
Fossum	1	0- 0	0- 0	0	0	0	0	0	0
Bates	1	0- 0	0- 0	0	0	0	0	0	0
Team			0- 1	7					
Totals		18-40	7-16	25	10	1	5	20	43

INDIANA 55

	M	FG	FT	R	A	BS	St	PF	TP
Kitchel, f	31	2-10	0- 0	3	4	0	0	2	4
JThomas, f	36	1- 2	0- 0	7	4	1	2	3	2
Tolbert, c	36	4- 5	3- 5	4	0	1	0	3	11
IThomas, g	36	6-11	8- 9	2	4	0	4	2	20
Wittman, g	37	8-12	0- 0	3	1	0	2	2	16
Grunwald	14	0- 0	0- 0	2	0	0	0	1	0
Brown	3	0- 0	0- 0	1	1	0	0	0	0
Franz	3	0- 0	0- 0	1	0	0	0	0	0
Isenbarger	1	1- 1	0- 0	1	0	0	0	1	2
Risley	1	0- 0	0- 0	0	0	0	0	0	0
Turner	1	0- 1	0- 0	0	0	0	0	1	0
LaFave	1	0- 1	0- 0	0	0	0	0	0	0
Team				3					
Totals		22-43	11-14	27	14	2	8	15	55

SCORE BY HALVES

Michigan State		20 23—	43
Indiana		28 27—	55

Turnovers — Michigan State 13, Indiana 14.

SHOOTING

	FG	Pct.	FT	Pct.
Michigan State	18-40	.450	7-16	.438
Indiana	22-43	.512	11-14	.786

Officials — Bob Showalter, Bill Herzog and Ben Reilly.
Attendance — 15,624.

There is one positive thing: whenever you go to Indiana, you don't have to go there again.

Jud Heathcote
Michigan State coach

Rebound firmly in Isiah Thomas' hands, 'conversion' begins

41

"You can't turn around the way we've been playing on one night," Wittman said. "I can't say we're going to go out and win 17 in a row or anything like that. So many times this year we've got it going and let it get away. We haven't been playing hard and we haven't been playing tough.

"But we know now that if we screw up in the Big Ten, we don't have *any* chance to go to the tournament. We're looking at this as a new start."

The Hoosiers altered their defensive rules a bit in concentrating on Vincent.

"All the perimeter people had responsibility to help out on Vincent," Jim Thomas said.

"Overall," Wittman said, "we tried to stop Vincent and I thought we did a pretty good job."

Isiah Thomas spent much of his night dropping back in to swat at the ball when Vincent had it. "With a guy like Vincent, you know he's going to look to score," Thomas said. "He draws people like a magnet."

On offense, the Hoosiers waited for a chance to go into operation against a man-to-man defense.

"A couple times they came down the floor saying they were going to go into a man-to-man," Isiah Thomas said. "But then they'd set up in a zone.

"When they did go to a man-to-man (with seven minutes and IU ahead, 41-34), we were so excited about it we forgot to attack certain spots."

Wittman was the Hoosier most adept at finding and exploiting those spots against Michigan State. "They picked up high," Wittman said, "which leaves the wings and the baseline open."

"I thought tonight we played pretty well," Isiah Thomas said. "But there still were a lot of things to improve on.

"We got a lot of breaks. I thought we played hard, but certain things we were very lucky on. We could have been burned and we weren't.

"But the big thing always is that we determine how we play. This time, we played well enough to win."

IU not No. 1, but still Top 20 — Heathcote

Before the season began, Heathcote was the UPI voter who gave Indiana its lone first-place vote. He has done some re-analysis.

"I don't think Indiana is the No. 1 team in the country," he said. "I think they belong somewhere in the Top 20. Whether they belong in the Top 10 will depend on how the season goes along. They are still having some personnel problems.

"This is a typical Bobby Knight team that will get better and will be at its best at the end of the season.

"When you're as solid as they are defensively and have an Isiah Thomas to create things offensively, you're going to be a very, very good basketball team.

"But when you're consistently scoring in the 50s, then you are totally relying on defense. I think maybe they have to be a little more productive offensively."

Jim Thomas has a rebound, almost

To beat the Hoosiers, you have to almost play — not a perfect game, because there never is such a thing as a perfect game — but you have to play very well. Because Indiana never beats itself. They're always very patient, and they play the best defense of any team in college basketball.

Jud Heathcote
Michigan State coach

He attributed the Spartan loss to that Indiana defense.

"Indiana did an absolutely great job of taking us out of what we wanted to do," he said. "We couldn't get it into Jay."

Vincent called his off-day "a combination of things — they had great pressure off the ball plus they were sagging two or three men back and it was hard to get the ball in.

"I wouldn't call it a zone they used against us; I would call it a man-to-man zone, because Isiah was just running all around the floor."

Vincent offered his own prediction about the Hoosiers:

"I still think they'll be in the top two or three in the Big Ten."

Joby Wright and Steve Downing — Helped

42

Indiana 78, Illinois 61

Ted Kitchel collected records by the batch with a 40-point shooting show, but the record that pleased the 6-8 junior the most was 2-and-0: Indiana's in the Big Ten.

For the first time since the Hoosier teams swept to successive 18-0 Big Ten marks in 1975 and '76, IU closed its first week of league play unbeaten by whipping 16th-ranked Illinois, 78-61, before 17,083 at Assembly Hall.

IU coach Bob Knight reached back to those golden years to put some of the Hoosiers' long periods of excellence into perspective. "I told them at the half the first part of the game they played as well as any of our teams have played — when those teams played well, that was the way they played," Knight said.

"Those" teams were the best in the land, among the best ever. The team that clicked so well so often in this game lost five times in December and seemed to reach the start of Big Ten play in disarray.

Kitchel scored only four points in the Hoosiers' Big Ten-opening victory over Michigan State and missed his last eight shots.

Two days later, he may have been the most efficient 40-point scorer in college basketball history. From the field and the free-throw line, he put up 31 official shots and 29 of them went through.

He did it sneakily, without ever drawing special attention from either Indiana passers or Illinois defenders.

"Once they got ahead, we were just chasing," Illinois coach Lou Henson said. "There's really not much you can do then — you can't concentrate on him, regardless of what he's doing

"But he is a tremendous shooter."

"It's been a long time since I've seen a team execute like Indiana today. They had a fantastic game."

The Hoosiers hit eight shots in a row early in the game for a withering 16-2 spurt that gave them an 18-6 lead and quick control.

After 16 minutes, they:
• led, 38-19;
• were shooting .739 (17-for-23);
• had committed just 1 turnover.

Their one shaky stretch of the game came immediately after that. First Kitchel (two fouls), then Isiah Thomas (three fouls) came out, and Illinois scored the last 10 points of the half to move within 38-29.

Kitchel, who had 16 first-half points without missing from anywhere, worked free for a jump shot on IU's first possession of the second half and missed. Derek Holcomb's jump shot from the baseline kept the Illini charging, the lead down to 38-31.

Kitchel stopped them with seven points in barely more than a minute. He worked inside for a three-point play that restored a 10-point edge, beat the Illini downcourt for a fast-break lay-up, then banked a shot in from the left side and Indiana had command again, 45-31.

"We came out in the second half (down 38-29) and thought we had a good chance to get back in the ball game," Illinois coach Lou Henson said. "That was pretty demoralizing."

"We didn't have a play going for us the last three minutes of the first half," Knight said. "That's the reason I was so pleased with the way they came out in the second half."

The lead built to 62-39 with 10½ minutes to go and by then Kitchel already had 34 points. He also had begun his repetitious

trek to the free-throw line, drawing four of the six fouls that pushed Illinois into one-and-one vulnerability less than seven minutes into the second half and then leading the way as the Hoosiers capitalized on that.

Thomas left the game again after picking up his fourth foul just before the lead peaked out at 62-39. He returned with 5:28 to go, after a deft pass by Ray Tolbert gave Kitchel a lay-up against the frantically pressing Illini and widened the IU lead to 66-50.

It was down to 66-54 when Thomas was fouled with 3:39 left. "The two free throws he hit right there were very, very big," Knight said. "He has missed some, but those two stemmed the tide and started a seven-point string for us."

Kitchel's 39th and 40th points — and the free throws that gave him the Big Ten one-game accuracy record over a former Knight teammate, Larry Siegfried, who went 16-for-16 for Ohio State in a 1959 game against Purdue — came with 1:47 left to put Indiana ahead, 75-59. Knight waved in the reserves then, and the play that let them enter was Thomas's fifth foul.

"I had 40 three times in high school (at Lewis Cass, near Logansport)," Kitchel said. "But I've never shot free throws like that. I was 10-for-10 once in high school. And I shot 21 one game, but I only hit about 16.

Ted Kitchel reacts to bump by Eddie Johnson

"It feels great, but what even feels better is we're 2-and-0 in the Big Ten.

Knight said "Kitchel's shooting has definitely improved this year, but in this game he really went to the basket. That's what we haven't been getting. Those 18 free throws he had — we haven't had four guys shoot 18 free throws in very many games this year."

Tolbert also had a box score line that glistened in efficiency: 16 points on 7-for-9 shooting, 2-for-2 at the free throw line, a team-high six rebounds (as IU beat the Illini on the backboards, 30-28), three assists, only one turnover and something that didn't show up in the IU box: strong defensive work against Illinois forward Eddie Johnson. "I thought Tolbert played as well, perhaps, as I've ever seen him play," Knight said.

Johnson's 15 points led the Illini, but the four-year standout who is about to claim the Illinois career scoring record was 6-for-17 in getting the points. Craig Tucker had 14 points and Perry Range 12 for Illinois. Derek Harper, one of the nation's top-ranked freshmen, suffered through an 0-for-10 shooting day for the Illini, whose 9-1 record going in had been blotched by only Brigham Young.

"A lot of people have said 'Indiana hasn't been very good this year'," Henson said.

"They should have seen this game."

Coaches agree foes will be in contention

Neither Knight nor Henson wanted to read too much significance into the surprise blowout.

"Illinois is going to win a hell of a lot of basketball games," Knight predicted, "and when the first of March comes it's a team that is going to be in the scramble for the whole thing."

It will be March when Indiana pays its return visit to Champaign and Knight hopes if his prediction is correct there won't be just one team on the floor with championship hopes.

"If they play like this every game, they're going to be hard to beat," Henson said.

"But they can't play like this every game.

"This was just a case of playing a ball club that really played a super game. They took us out of our game. They played great defense.

"At times we think we do. We led the league in opponents' shooting going into this game — .395 I think it was." Indiana bettered that by almost 200 points to make Henson more philosophical than angry.

"We just have to remember this was only one game," he said. "It really didn't make any difference what we did today. Kitchel was tremendous. He played great. We knew he was a shooter — he was hitting 90 percent from the free-throw line, wasn't he? Randy Wittman is a great shooter. Tolbert played well. And everybody knows about Isiah."

It was a sublime time to be a Hoosier. The team in white had both good play and good fortune going for it.

The Hoosier lead had shrunk a tad, to 54-39, when Tolbert drove across the free-throw lane, felt 6-10 defender Brian Leonard's grasp on his arm when he started up with a hook shot and "went for two shots — I just kinda pushed it up there." He almost banged the backboard down with a shot that shook Leonard loose — and Knight up. He got the foul call he wanted and a basket as a bonus, because somehow the most unglamorous shot of a spiffy Hoosier afternoon bounced through.

"He made a great bad-shot basket," Knight said. "I was glad for him, and his family, and his future family, that that bank shot went in."

He also hit the free throw for a 57-39 lead. The Hoosiers got

ILLINOIS 61	M	FG	FT	R	A	BS	St	PF	TP
Johnson, f	35	6-17	3-3	9	0	0	2	3	15
Smith, f	30	4-7	0-0	2	0	1	0	5	8
Holcomb, c	12	1-1	0-0	0	0	0	0	0	2
Harper, g	34	0-10	2-2	3	7	0	1	3	2
Range, g	33	3-5	6-6	3	3	0	2	2	12
Tucker	24	5-9	4-5	1	2	0	0	2	14
Griffin	22	3-6	0-0	2	2	2	0	3	6
Leonard	5	1-1	0-0	2	0	0	0	2	2
Richardson	3	0-2	0-1	0	0	0	0	2	0
Bontemps	2	0-0	0-0	1	0	0	0	0	0
Team				4					
Totals		23-58	15-17	28	14	3	5	22	61

INDIANA 78	M	FG	FT	R	A	BS	St	PF	TP
Kitchel, f	35	11-13	18-18	5	1	0	0	2	40
J. Thomas, f	29	0-1	1-2	2	6	0	2	5	1
Tolbert, c	39	7-9	2-2	6	3	0	0	1	16
I. Thomas, g	31	5-12	2-2	3	6	0	0	5	12
Wittman, g	39	3-7	0-0	3	4	0	0	0	6
Brown	12	0-1	0-1	3	3	0	2	1	0
Turner	4	0-2	0-0	0	0	0	0	1	0
Franz	6	0-0	0-0	0	0	0	0	1	0
Isenbarger	1	0-0	1-2	3	0	0	0	0	1
Risley	1	1-1	0-0	1	0	0	0	0	2
Grunwald	1	0-0	0-0	0	0	0	0	0	0
Bouchie	1	0-0	0-0	0	0	0	0	0	0
LaFave	1	0-0	0-0	0	0	0	0	1	0
Team				4					
Totals		27-46	24-27	30	23	0	4	17	78

SCORE BY HALVES

Illinois		29	32— 61
Indiana		38	40— 78

Turnovers—Illinois 10, Indiana 12.

SHOOTING

	FG	Pct.	FT	Pct.
Illinois	23-58	.397	15-17	.882
Indiana	27-46	.587	24-27	.889

Officials—Jim Bain, Verl Sell, Ralph Rosser.
Attendance—17,083 (sellout)

the ball back and got lucky again. A careless pass brought quick Craig Tucker shooting forward like a game fish after bait, but Tucker brushed IU's Jim Thomas in his burst toward the ball. A Hoosier mistake blossomed into three points when Thomas hit a free throw, Kitchel drew two free throws that he sank.

But fortune favors teams playing as well and as hard as the Hoosiers in this one. Tolbert came back with a genuine hook shot a few minutes later, and when the Hoosiers were running out the clock with a fat lead and a delay game, Tolbert shot past Johnson on the baseline for a reverse lay-up that became a three-point play.

"Now that," Knight said, "was a hell of a play."

Kitchel third option as IU worked inside

Only a week after Knight publicly lamented his team's lack of inside punch, forward Kitchel scored 40 points.

Ironically, his big day came almost as a third Hoosier option in their attempt to go at Illinois inside.

The Hoosiers went after the Illini first with Tolbert (IU's first two baskets were Tolbert lay-ups after passes inside) and Isiah Thomas in mind.

"The way Ray can get by people with his first step, we thought we could get him wide open," Wittman said.

"And we put Isiah under because he plays so well with his back to the bucket."

So the third man in the Hoosiers' inside group scored the 40.

"Ted did end up getting a lot of points," Wittman said. "But it wasn't anything we were really going for."

Kitchel said his success had its roots in the closing minutes of the victory two nights earlier over Michigan State, when the Hoosiers also worked Thomas, Tolbert and him inside.

"Isiah told both Ray and me we were thinking too much about getting him open and not getting ourselves open," Kitchel said.

Thomas said "They (the Illini) were switching down low, so when Ted and Ray screened for me, all they had to do was step back and they'd be wide open. Ted did that several times. Randy and James (Thomas) did a good job of handling the ball on top, and it all just happened naturally.

"And there's no person who deserves 40 points more than Ted Kitchel."

Kitchel's first word of his 40-point game came from manager Steve Skoronski seconds after Knight pulled the starters with about a minute and a half left. "I didn't believe him," Kitchel said.

"I was so into the game I didn't really even think about it till I sat down. I had no idea I shot that many free throws, but I knew I did have a pretty good night.

"I was really proud just to be on the floor with these guys today. I thought Ray did a great job on the boards. I don't know how many rebounds he got (six, leading the Hoosiers), but he really was blocking out. And he did a heck of a defensive job on Johnson. He deserves as much credit for that as I do for offense."

Kitchel IU's ninth to score 40 or more

Kitchel's performance made him the ninth Hoosier to score 40 or more points in a game.

He missed the Assembly Hall record by a point. Steve Downing set it with 41, also against Illinois, in IU's drive to the 1973 Big Ten championship.

Kitchel's figure was the highest by a Hoosier, and by a Big Ten player, since Mike Woodson closed out his junior year with a 48 points at Illinois in 1979.

The Hoosier record in 56 points, set by Jimmy Rayl in an overtime game against Minnesota in 1962 and tied by Rayl against Michigan State in his senior year, 1963. Both games were in the "new" IU fieldhouse, now the site of the Hoosiers' indoor track.

The only 40-point performance at Assembly Hall in addition to Downing's was an even 40 by the late Terry Furlow of Michigan State that topped a career-high 38-point by IU's Kent Benson in the same game — an 85-70 victory that was part of a 32-0 year for IU's 1976 NCAA champions.

The NCAA record record for consecutive free throws in a game is 24-for-24, by Arlen Clark of Oklahoma State against Colorado in 1959.

Illinois senior Mark Smith, who had much of the man-to-man coverage on Kitchel, had the same unfortunate duty against Woodson in his 48-point game at Champaign in 1979.

Smith was generous in praise of Woodson then and he saluted Kitchel and the Hoosiers this time.

"Attribute it to him and poor defense — it goes both ways," Smith said.

I thought we probably played an average game. I just think Indiana played a tremendous game — one of the finest I've ever seen a team play.

Lou Henson
Illinois coach

Tony Brown ducks flying Craig Tucker

Michigan 55, Indiana 52

Michigan jerked Indiana back into a seven-way tie for the early Big Ten basketball lead by beating the Hoosiers in overtime, 55-52, before a sellout crowd of 13,609 at Crisler Arena.

A string of free throws by the Wolverines' Bodnar twins, Marty and Mark, provided the decisive overtime points on a night when Michigan scrambled out of an early hole on free-throw points and outscored the Hoosiers at the the line, 17-4. "That's probably what happens when you foul more than the other team did," Hoosier coach Bob Knight said.

It was Indiana that led going into the final minutes of both regulation time and overtime, but Michigan came up with the defensive plays each time that snatched the advantage away.

Ray Tolbert slipped away for a lay-up that gave Indiana a 47-44 lead with 4:55 left in regulation time. Michigan's Johnny Johnson scored from the left corner to slice the lead to 47-46, and Indiana went into a possession game that wasn't broken until the Wolverines' Mike McGee fouled Phil Isenbarger with 2:00 to go.

Isenbarger hit his first free chance but missed the second, and Michigan capitalized on the opening by tying the game with two free throws by Thad Garner with 1:24 left.

Indiana was working the ball for a final shot when Isenbarger lost control of a dribble with 22 seconds to go. Michigan got a shot at the gun by McGee, who missed from about 18 feet.

Isiah Thomas gave Indiana a 50-48 lead with a jump shot only 19 seconds into the five-minute overtime period. IU got the ball back when Ted Kitchel rebounded Paul Heuerman's missed free throw with 4:15 left.

But, with the Hoosiers working for a high-percentage shot or a foul, Garner deflected a Glen Grunwald pass, outran the ball to the sideline and the lefthander from Hammond Noll snaked a quick pass downcourt to McGee for a lay-up that tied the game, 50-50, with 3:41 to go.

"Thad is quick," Michigan coach Bill Frieder said. "He has some limitations, but one of them isn't guts."

Indiana worked the basketball almost a minute again before losing it when Tolbert traveled. It was Michigan that operated with patience then, passing the ball till Marty Bodnar drove toward the baseline and Thomas was called for blocking his way.

With 1:13 to go in the overtime, Bodnar hit the two free throws that put Michigan ahead for good.

Indiana went for a tying basket by freeing Kitchel for a shot from the left corner — "a fine shot for him to take," Knight said. "As I recall, he was 11-for-13 the last game. This time, it just didn't go down."

Garner fielded the miss for Michigan, and the Wolverines ran up their victory edge with two free throws by Mark Bodnar at 0:23 and, after Tolbert cut the lead back to 54-52 with a rebound basket at 0:13, another Mark Bodnar free throw with six seconds left.

Mark didn't even enter the game until the overtime was half over. Frieder said he was in the game "because he's a great

free-throw shooter," and the senior guard's status in coming off the bench cold didn't worry his coach at all. "Not Mark Bodnar," Frieder said. "A lot of kids, yes, but not him.

"I've got confidence in the Bodnars, man. They're steady and they're dependable."

Indiana's defense throttled Michigan early, and the Hoosiers jumped out to a 13-4 lead.

It was 15-8 when two straight quick breaks backfired on Indiana. Wittman and Tony Brown missed open jump shots in the two broken-floor thrusts, and each time Kitchel was called for a rebounding foul. The net result was four points for Michigan from situations that looked advantageous for IU and an accumulation of fouls (three) that removed Kitchel for the rest of the half.

Michigan followed the free-throw lift-off to complete a 10-2 spurt that gave the Wolverines their first lead, 18-17. The lead

Ray Tolbert, IU's chairman of board

I don't know how anybody in America could be happy when they're about to play Indiana.

Bill Frieder
Michigan coach

switched eight more times before Thomas looped in a jump shot from the top of the foul circle for a 33-32 Hoosier halftime lead.

There were five more lead changes in the second half before Thomas slipped inside the Michigan zone defense for a short jump shot that gave IU a 45-44 edge with 7:23 to play. Thomas stole the ball from Garner, but the Hoosiers gave the ball away once before getting it back and holding it till Tolbert's shot off a Kitchel pass that created the 47-44 margin the Hoosiers took into the last 4:55.

"I don't know if there was a turning point," Frieder said, "unless it was the way we just hung in there and played defense when they had the ball and those two-point leads at the end. We couldn't make a mistake then, and we didn't."

McGee, about to become the second Wolverine, eighth Big Ten player and 111th collegian to score 2,000 points, moved his career total to 1,993 with 21 in leading both teams. Johnson added 12 for Michigan, which is in the seven-team knot atop the Big Ten at 2-1 (IU, Purdue, Illinois, Iowa, Minnesota and Ohio State are the others).

Indiana got 18 points from Thomas and 14 from Tolbert, who also had a game-high 10 rebounds.

Overtime experience paying off for Wolves

Knight's four Indiana teams that won clear-cut Big Ten championships each got some propulsion from a victory at Michigan — the only victories IU has at Crisler Arena.

That makes the Hoosiers' loss there something of an unwelcome omen, but omens are the least of Knight's concerns in trying to build a team for the second half of a 30-game season that is 9-6 at the midpoint.

"There were two critical points that just really hurt us in this game," Knight said. "One was when we had the ball working for a last shot in regulation time and lost it, and the other was when we had the ball and a two-point lead in overtime and lost it."

Michigan muffed the first chance to win, but the Wolverines came back in the overtime to work the lead and the clock well, once they had the chance.

The game was the Wolverines' second straight Big Ten overtime, their second with IU in two years and their seventh in their last 19 Big Ten games.

They may represent an argument for experience. They lost four of their five overtime games last year (including the one at Indiana), but they're 2-0 this year, adding Indiana to a victim list that started at Minnesota last week.

"It was just a typical Big Ten game," Frieder said. "If you don't play smart and you don't play hard and you don't play well, you're not going to win.

"I said after our game with Minnesota and I'll say it again tonight: It's a shame somebody has to lose, because there was a great effort out there from two fine teams."

Frieder said the victory was big to him not because the victim was Indiana but because it was a home game.

"That made it very important," he said. "If you're going to

INDIANA 52									
	M	FG	FT	R	A	BS	St	PF	TP
Kitchel, f	33	4- 9	0- 0	2	2	0	2	4	8
J.Thomas, f	10	0- 2	0- 0	3	0	0	1	1	0
Tolbert, c	45	6-10	2- 5	10	4	0	1	2	14
I.Thomas, g	44	9-17	0- 0	2	4	0	1	4	18
Wittman, g	43	3- 8	0- 0	2	1	0	1	2	6
Brown	10	0- 2	0- 0	0	0	0	0	3	0
Bouchie	7	1- 1	1- 1	2	0	0	0	1	3
Turner	6	0- 0	0- 0	1	0	0	0	2	0
Isenbarger	16	1- 1	1- 2	2	0	0	0	3	3
Grunwald	9	0- 1	0- 0	0	0	0	0	1	0
Risley	2	0- 0	0- 0	0	0	0	0	0	0
Team				3					
Totals		24-51	4- 8	27	11	0	6	23	52

MICHIGAN 55									
	M	FG	FT	R	A	BS	St	PF	TP
McGee, f	44	9-17	3- 5	3	1	0	0	0	21
Garner, f	36	0- 1	4- 4	4	2	0	2	4	4
Heuerman, c	38	2- 4	1- 2	3	1	0	1	4	5
Johnson, g	40	6-10	0- 0	6	2	0	1	2	12
Mt.Bodnar, g	42	2- 7	2- 2	6	4	0	0	1	6
McCormick	23	0- 3	4- 4	1	1	1	0	3	4
Mk.Bodnar	2	0- 0	3- 4	0	0	0	0	0	3
Team				6					
Totals		19-42	17-21	29	11	1	4	14	55

SCORE BY HALVES

Indiana		33	15	4— 52
Michigan		32	16	7— 55

Turnovers—Indiana 12, Michigan 11.

SHOOTING

	FG	Pct.	FT	Pct.
Indiana	24-51	.471	4- 8	.500
Michigan	19-42	.452	17-21	.810

Officials—Phil Robinson, Phil Bova, Dick Bestor.
Attendance—13,609 (sellout).

have a good season in the conference, you've *got* to win your home games. Indiana proved that last year. They won every game at home and won the championship."

Frieder praised the defensive work of Marty Bodnar against IU's Isiah Thomas, although Thomas — bothered by an eye scratch much of the second half and by leg cramps that hit him late in the game — scored nine field goals.

"The second half, Marty was outta sight," Frieder said. "He's a tough, tough kid."

Thomas went home with a patch over an eye. The Hoosiers had another injury during the night at Ann Arbor — before the game. Reserve center Landon Turner got up from bed during the night and fell in his hotel room, cutting his face in two places. Turner was treated by IU trainer Bob Young and by Bloomington physician Larry Rink, who made the trip with the Hoosiers. Turner played in the game.

Indiana 67, Ohio State 60

It wasn't exactly the battle plan, but Indiana showed a national TV audience there is a great deal more to basketball than shooting in whipping Ohio State, 67-60.

The Hoosiers shot at their season low, did it against a team that specializes in rebounding, and came away with a significant and thorough road triumph.

The victory regained for the Hoosiers a share of the early Big Ten lead (tied with Illinois, Iowa and Purdue at 3-1). It should have paid off at least that well for IU. It was one the Hoosiers had to win twice.

The game was still in its first minute when Indiana's intentions were clear. Ohio State used its size to control the opening tip, but Isiah Thomas used his quickness to steal possession away before the Bucks could shoot. Swiftly and efficiently, the Hoosiers worked new starter Steve Risley open for a jump shot and a 2-0 lead.

Risley was in the game not for jump shots but for defense: against Buckeye sophomore Clark Kellogg, ultra-frisky after a 42-point showpiece three nights earlier. And when Ohio State guard Larry Huggins tried to throw an in-bounds pass to Kellogg, Risley played his role to its maximum, stealing the pass and driving to the lay-up that put IU up four — with only 45 seconds gone.

The lead became 16-8 and Risley was up on Kellogg, 8-0. Ohio State caught up a couple times but never got ahead — till a 31-26 lead that the Hoosiers took into the last 90 seconds of the first half disappeared under an avalanche of ball-handling errors, rebounding mistakes and fouls. A half-game the Hoosiers had controlled and at times dominated ended with the home team experiencing the euphoria of a dodged bullet: Ohio State up, 34-31.

Coaching legend Clair Bee used to argue that he'd rather be behind at halftime than ahead — on the theory he'd rather speak to an alarmed audience than a satisfied one. Bob Knight is a Bee-liever, but not particularly of that commandment. This game, however, could be a case in point for Bee — less from the sudden last-minute shift's effect on Indiana minds than on Ohio State.

"We did not have the defensive intensity at the start of the second half we had at the end of the first half," Buckeye coach Eldon Miller said. He didn't buy the theory his team might have have had its zeal dulled by the sudden lead. "I don't believe so," he said. "It's a 40-minute game."

However, it swung in less than six. Indiana seized control back from the Bucks by attacking them in their under-the-basket area of strength — the bitsiest of the Hoosiers, Thomas, exacting the most damage with darting forays that helped Indiana open a 47-39 lead with 14:33 left.

Certainly, by then Miller was alarmed. He took a time out. The team that came out with motors racing was from the opposite huddle.

Knight watched the Hoosiers hurry through five pointless possessions in barely more than a minute and took a time out himself. "I thought I was watching the evacuation of a burning building," Knight said.

The frenzy had let Ohio State move within 47-43 and excite the sellout crowd of 13,591. Indiana went back to its carve-and-cut game and popped Thomas loose for a short jump shot that rolled off. When the Buckeye giants sought to assert their physiological rights to the rebound, however, IU's Jim Thomas slapped the ball onto the backboard and Risley fielded it over a

Buckeye to bank in the rebound basket that checked the Buckeye charge.

"That play by Jimmy Thomas keeping the ball alive was really a big one for us," Knight said. "His quickness was a real factor in the game."

So was Ray Tolbert's.

The score was 49-45 when Tolbert worked free inside for a dunk, then came back with another 20 seconds later after stealing a Buckeye pass and roaring in on OSU defender Carter Scott one-on-one. Scott adroitly cut off Tolbert's ground access to the basket; Tolbert thwarted him with an air strike, his take-off somewhere around the free-throw line and his bomb delivered dead on-target.

Miller took another time out, for gasping and regrouping. But the game was gone. Indiana kept carving on the listless Buckeyes for a 58-45 lead with 3:15 left before Scott ended almost eight minutes of offensive silence by OSU by banking home a jump shot.

Scott, a three-year starter who lost his lineup spot last week, ran in three more late shots — but they came in a game that was over before it was over. All the Scott barrage did was shrink the margin and make him the Buckeye scoring leader with 16 points.

Risley came out of the Kellogg match-up with a 12-10 point edge. Tolbert had a 17-13 lead in the other major match-within-a-match, with Buckeye star Herb Williams. Isiah Thomas, a .554 shooter going into the game, was 5-for-16 in scoring 16 points and Ted Kitchel (.598) was 4-for-15 in scoring eight. But figures like those (and IU's season-low .419 shooting) were af-

INDIANA 67

	M	FG	FT	R	A	BS	St	PF	TP
Kitchel, f	33	4-15	0- 0	6	0	0	0	2	8
Risley, f	38	6-13	0- 0	8	4	0	1	2	12
Tolbert, c	39	7- 9	3- 5	7	2	0	0	3	17
I.Thomas, g	39	5-16	6- 6	6	3	0	1	2	16
J.Thomas, g	27	2- 3	5- 6	7	3	1	1	3	9
Wittman	16	1- 3	1- 2	0	1	0	0	2	3
Turner	7	1- 3	0- 0	1	0	0	0	1	2
Bouchie	1	0- 0	0- 0	1	0	0	0	2	0
Totals		26-62	15-19	36	13	1	3	17	67

OHIO STATE 60

	M	FG	FT	R	A	BS	St	PF	TP
Kellogg, f	39	5-16	0- 0	17	4	3	0	2	10
Smith, f	23	1- 3	3- 4	4	0	1	0	4	5
Williams, c	38	4-13	5- 5	8	1	3	0	4	13
Huggins, g	31	2- 7	0- 0	4	1	0	1	4	4
Penn, g	30	4-12	2- 4	1	2	0	1	2	10
Scott	23	7-12	2- 2	6	0	0	0	2	16
Waiters	7	0- 1	0- 0	0	0	0	1	0	0
Kirchner	5	0- 0	2- 3	1	0	0	0	0	2
Miller	4	0- 0	0- 0	0	0	0	0	2	0
Team				5					
Totals		23-64	14-18	46	8	7	3	20	60

SCORE BY HALVES

Indiana		31	36— 67
Ohio State		34	26— 60

Turnovers—Indiana 9, Ohio State 14.

SHOOTING

	FG	Pct.	FT	Pct.
Indiana	26-62	.419	15-19	.789
Ohio State	23-64	.359	14-18	.778

Officials—Richard Weiler, Darwin Brown, Eric Harmon.
Attendance—13,591 (sellout).

fordable for the Hoosiers on a day when they shrank Buckeye shooting to .359.

Kellogg did sweep off 17 rebounds to lead Ohio State to 46-36 board control. The Hoosiers partially offset that with their lowest turnover total in Big Ten play, nine — three of those in the shaky 90-second stretch that closed out the half.

Buckeyes' big men called 'frustrated'

Indiana had seven shots blocked and two of its best shooters, Isiah Thomas and Kitchel, put up several of those in hitting just nine of 31 shots, most of them from in close.

And still they were a vital part of a game plan that worked. The aggressiveness of going at the big Buckeyes in their area of strength, typified by Thomas's audacious burst penetrating the Buckeye middle for a lay-up that started the second half, obviously had its own worth.

"We were trying to drive the ball to the basket to get to the foul line," Thomas said. "We tried to go into their big people and get them into foul trouble." Thomas did wind up shooting (and hitting) six free throws, and the Hoosiers, down 12-1 on free throws in the first half, finished with a 15-14 point edge there. But fouls were not the problem for Ohio State that IU hoped they would be.

Instead, Indiana's defense was.

"We didn't get the penetration the second half we had in the first," Ohio State coach Eldon Miller said.

"You have to give them the credit. Indiana played a good defensive game all the way. They cheated back inside, and the second half in particular we didn't shoot very well so we never did pull them out.

"Outside shooting has been a problem for us all year, and usually in this league, things like that eventually are going to be exposed."

Scott said he had the feeling Williams and Kellogg became frustrated as the game went on and Miller agreed: "I think they were getting frustrated, sure."

Scott said the Buckeyes "started out kinda flat the second half. We knew it was a whole new ball game, but we weren't playing as sharp.

"And they really packed it in on defense at our end. They were giving us the jump shot and it didn't fall.

"And we didn't get the ball inside, so we never did get on the one-and-one the second half, and that hurt us."

Scott came off the bench firing, and his point total included four late baskets when defender Jim Thomas had a difficult assignment: bother him but avoid fouls.

"I just tried to keep him under control," Thomas said. "He's a great player. I just tried to anticipate where he was going to go."

Thomas said his own priorities on going into the game were "to play good defense, help out inside and help on the boards. And if I did have a shot, take it." He wound up with nine points, seven rebounds, three assists, a blocked shot and a steal in a 27-minute role that included 3-for-3 shooting on the front end of one-and-one free-throw opportunities down the stretch.

Isiah Thomas also was 4-for-4 in late one-and-one chances and 6-for-6 in the game, continuing his own turn-around from a late-December free-throw slump.

Tolbert, Risley Buckeye-killers

"I love to play against Ohio State," Tolbert admits. So, the record says, does Risley. And it's fortunate for the Indiana basketball team that the two get their kicks in such robust circles

Lynn Hays signals who's No. 1

49

Ted Kitchel rebounds over Jim Smith

because they have been vital to the 6-2 edge the Hoosiers have over the Buckeyes in the four seasons since Tolbert, Risley and a Buckeye wonder-class headed by Williams arrived in college.

Certainly, the two were monumental reasons why the Buckeyes fell in the latest meeting. They took on the Big Ten's most talented tandem of big men, Williams and Kellogg, with better results than Knight surely even hoped for.

Knight probably would have settled quite cheerfully for Risley-Tolbert neutralizing Kellogg-Williams and making it a game to be decided by the other three men on court. Instead, the figures work out to most of Hoosiers' victory margin coming from the big-man match-up and even the 29-23 game-ending figure there was altered by Buckeye points in the last two minutes when Indiana wasn't really trying to score. Williams and Kellogg had seven of their 23 in that stretch, Williams saving his streak of 83 games in double figures with two rebound baskets in those closing seconds.

Tolbert's fondness for taking on the Buckeyes reflected respect, not smugness.

"They've got great talent and they're big as heck," Tolbert said. "I know if I can play with guys like theirs, it gives me a great opportunity to be among 'em."

Ohio State's offense is considerably more oriented toward getting Williams shots than IU's is toward Tolbert — and, of course, IU's full team defensive concept is more concentrated on Williams than Ohio State's on Tolbert. But the four-year eight-game figures remain a testimony to Tolbert's response to the Williams and Ohio State challenge: the Williams edges sufficiently small that Hoosiers could offset them elsewhere (points, 122-117; rebounds, 79-75).

In the four-game Big Ten season to date, Tolbert has been the first-round NBA draft choice Knight spoke of in pre-season.

"I thought Tolbert played extremely well," Knight said. "He has played very well in all four Big Ten games." For an afternoon, at least, that put Knight on the same thought wavelength with his jocular sparmates of NBC, former coaches Al McGuire and Billy Packer, who made Tolbert their choice as player of the game.

Tolbert came out of the pre-conference season down. Knight was critical of Hoosier rebounding and general inside play.

"Coach sat me down and told me I just have to go out and play," Tolbert said. "I've just been concentrating more.

"It's like for the first time I can really see myself playing — I can see what I'm doing. I even talk to myself about what I'm doing and what I have to do. If I miss a block-out or something, I'm better at being able to put it out of my mind and make sure I make the next play.

"I really can feel like I'm playing better now. It makes me feel better, it make my teammates feel better and it makes the coach feel better."

Risley's emergence for his first start since the Kentucky game also had something to do with his Ohio State history. He has started and played most of the way against the Buckeyes three times in his four seasons now, and each time he made a solid contribution to an IU victory.

"We told him Friday he was going to start," Knight said. "He's a good, big athlete; he has good speed, quickness and strength.

"It takes a really good athlete to play Kellogg. We thought Steve was our best match-up and we had no hesitation whatsoever to go to him.

"If you had seen him in pre-season, you'd have seen he played really well over a period of several weeks. Then he kinda stumbled around when the season got going (Risley started the first three games), and this is the most we have used him in a while. He helped us not only with the defensive aspect but he also helped us get off to a good start on offense."

Risley had four of the Hoosiers' first eight baskets. That was a surprise, even to Risley.

"Basically, I was put in there to try to stop Kellogg," he said.

Time to rejoice for Ray Tolbert, Mike LaFave

Iowa 56, Indiana 53

Iowa charged when it had to and put the brakes on with equal success to slip out of Bloomington with a big 56-53 Big Ten victory over Indiana.

The Hawkeyes, ending a nine-game losing streak at IU's Assembly Hall, jumped on the Hoosiers, 10-1, in the first five minutes of the second half to move from a 29-24 hole to a 34-30 lead. "The game was decided right there," IU coach Bob Knight said.

Indiana spent the next eight minutes trying to catch up and finally did at 46-46 on two free throws by Ted Kitchel with 7:25 left.

Iowa responded to that situation by spreading the court and killing the clock, four-corners style.

Hawkeye coach Lute Olson hinted darkly that there was more to the move than sheer desire to break Hoosier momentum. "Fouls were 11-3 at that point," Olson said, reciting a second-half figure that showed Indiana as the team with only three fouls called against it and was slightly inaccurate (IU did have three, but Iowa really had eight).

"That's a tremendous discrepancy," Olson said. "If it's going to be that way, we figured we'd spread it out and make sure they (officials) saw whatever happened."

Nothing happened for four minutes. Then, Hawkeye guard Kenny Arnold cut up the middle and sank an eight-foot jump shot for a 48-46 Iowa lead with 3:19 left.

Indiana put on its own display of patience, working for the tying shot. Almost a minute after Arnold's basket, IU's Isiah Thomas drove into the middle of the Iowa zone. Hawkeye center Steve Krafcisin, eight inches taller than Thomas, stepped in his path, and when Thomas tried to slip a pass under the basket to Ray Tolbert for a lay-up, Iowa's Bob Hansen deflected the pass and Kevin Boyle intercepted it.

"I thought he was going to shoot," Hansen said. "I was trying to get in position to rebound. I just reacted to the ball and was able to hit it. It was just instinct — it just happened."

Iowa caught the Hoosiers confused on coverage on an out-of-

Lute Olson — on a night he won

Ted Kitchel, Iowa's Steve Waite jockey for spot

bounds play shortly after the steal and the Hawkeyes broke senior forward Vince Brookins free for a lay-up that made it 50-46 with 2:15 to go.

IU's Randy Wittman and Brookins exchanged baskets to keep the margin at four, but with 1:02 to go, Tolbert fought his way to a rebound basket that became a three-point play and gave the Hoosiers a chance, down 52-51.

Indiana broke up Iowa's stall once when Jim Thomas fouled with 45 seconds left — the Hoosiers' sixth foul, setting up Iowa for one-and-one free throws with any subsequent fouls.

When the Hawks came out stalling again after the Thomas foul, however, Indiana chased but didn't come close to fouling. Finally, with 10 seconds left, Isiah Thomas in desperation and frustration shoved Hansen out of bounds — an intentional (two-shot) foul call against Thomas, his fifth foul of the game.

Hansen, 0-for-9 from the field as he stepped to the free-throw line, hit both free throws, then intercepted an IU pass and hit two more with four seconds left to bury the Hoosiers.

"There was only one thing on my mind when I got to the line and that was that we *needed* those free throws," Hansen said. "I didn't even hear the crowd.

"When I hit the first one it calmed me down. I worked on my free throws last summer and really improved. Really, there's no reason to miss a free throw. You have all the time you need and no one's guarding you."

"It was great to see Bobby up at the line," Olson said.

"There's a lot of pressure when you know you're not hitting well. The first two were so critical, but they hit nothing but the bottom of the net."

For a change, free throws were life support for the Hoosiers, who forced their way inside against the Hawkeyes, drew the fouls they wanted, even outrebounded Iowa (the first time any team has done that this year), and lost.

A major reason was a breakdown in an area that has been a Hoosier strength this year. Indiana had 19 turnovers to Iowa's 11, and five of the Hoosiers' came consecutively to allow Iowa to jump from an 11-8 deficit to a 16-11 lead in the middle of the first half.

IU scrambled back, and when Ted Kitchel — 14-for-18 on free throws for the night — hit six in a row in the final minutes of the half, Indiana went into the break with a 29-24 lead.

"That was really a good stretch for us, certainly our best of the game," Knight said.

But starting the second half, Wittman and Tolbert missed connections on an under-basket lob, then Kitchel — 27-for-28 in conference play at the free-throw line up to then — missed both halves of a two-shot foul. During the same period, the Hoosiers missed three shots, one more free throw, and lost Thomas on a charging call, the sophomore guard's fourth foul.

Tolbert made an all-out effort to keep the Hoosiers afloat. His first three-point play of the night and a follow-up jump shot snapped the 10-1 downspin and returned the lead to IU, 35-34. Tolbert went on to get 14 of the Hoosiers' 24 second-half points and a season-high 18 for the game. He had two free throws and Kitchel four in a Hoosier spurt that erased a 46-40 Iowa lead and tied the game, setting up the delay game.

"This was a heck of a win for our guys," Olson said. "I think this one plus the other two road games (victories at Wisconsin and Michigan last week) makes up for our Ohio State game (a 58-56 homecourt loss for the Hawks, who are now 4-1 in league play and tied for the lead with Purdue.

Randy Wittman fires over Iowa's Bob Hansen

IOWA 56

	M	FG	FT	R	A	BS	St	PF	TP
Brookins, f	30	5-13	0- 0	1	1	0	6	3	10
Boyle, f	34	6- 7	2- 2	4	2	0	3	4	14
Krafcisin, c	31	4- 7	2- 3	2	5	3	0	4	10
Arnold, g	34	5- 8	0- 0	3	4	0	1	2	10
Hansen, g	29	0- 9	4- 4	4	0	0	2	4	4
Gannon	22	1- 4	0- 0	1	0	0	0	1	2
Carfino	9	2- 3	0- 0	0	0	0	0	0	4
Waite	9	1- 1	0- 0	1	0	0	0	0	2
Johnson	2	0- 0	0- 0	0	0	0	0	1	0
Team				5					
Totals		24-52	8- 9	21	12	3	12	19	56

INDIANA 53

	M	FG	FT	R	A	BS	St	PF	TP
Kitchel, f	38	2- 6	14-18	5	1	0	2	2	18
Risley, f	31	0- 2	0- 0	2	2	0	2	1	0
Tolbert, c	40	7-12	4- 4	5	0	5	0	4	18
I.Thomas, g	28	2- 4	2- 2	4	1	0	0	5	6
J.Thomas, g	17	0- 0	2- 2	4	0	0	0	1	2
Wittman	35	3- 6	1- 2	3	2	0	1	2	7
Brown	11	1- 2	0- 0	0	3	0	0	0	2
Team				4					
Totals		15-32	23-28	27	9	5	5	15	53

SCORE BY HALVES

Iowa		24	32— 56
Indiana		29	24— 53

Turnovers—Iowa 11, Indiana 19.

SHOOTING

	FG	Pct.	FT	Pct.
Iowa	24-52	.462	8- 9	.889
Indiana	15-32	.469	23-28	.821

Officials—Ed Maracich, Mike Stockner, Rollo Vallem.
Attendance—17,101 (sellout).

53

"This is the biggest win of my life," Boyle bubbled. "Bobby Knight is a great coach and it's always great to win one against him."

"Kevin played absolutely super," Olson said. "If there's a better clutch player in America, I want to see him."

Brookins, Iowa's scoring leader for the season, was blanked the first half. He finished with 10 points and contributed six steals to Iowa's total of 12, easily the highest theft mark against IU this year.

Kitchel matched Tolbert's 18 points as the only players in double figures for the Hoosiers, who were at the free-throw line so much (23-for-28) and turned the ball over so often they wound up charged with only 32 shots for the entire game.

Olson, Indiana fan exchange barbs

Olson never has had much of a love affair with Indiana basketball fans, and even victory did little to enhance the romance.

Late in the first half, Olson rose to protest a call and got involved in a verbal altercation with an elderly man seated behind the IU bench.

"Sit down!" the man yelled at Olson, to which the silver-haired coach pointed a threatening finger and said, "You keep your mouth shut!"

The boiling cauldron of humanity that had jammed into Assembly Hall — 17,101 strong — chimed in with a deafening chorus of boos that drowned out the rest of the two men's words.

"The guy gave me a few choice words and I told him to keep his mouth shut," Olson said later. "Then someone at the scorer's bench told me to sit down. You would think someone at the official scorer's table would have other things to worry about."

IU athletic director Ralph Floyd moved in quickly as a conciliator-policeman. Floyd walked into a position between the two benches and the sideline mood cooled.

Early in the second half, with Wittman on the foul line, a cry from the east bleachers pierced the momentary silence, "Olson, you big crybaby!" The Hoosier faithful roared with laughter. Olson didn't smile.

After his first Assembly Hall victory, Olson got a less-than-affectionate farewell from some more Indiana fans.

"I told them that I only wished they could be as gracious when they lose as they are when they win," Olson said. "The crowd here is a great crowd. They get behind their team. But they are not nearly as good losers as they are winners."

Boyle thought it was Iowa's defense that spelled the Hoosiers' doom.

"I think we rattled them with our press," he said. "And they played right into our hands against our matchup zone. They put a man in every place where we had a defender.

"They were confused out there. Several times they were asking, 'What offense are we in?' "

Steve Krafcisin, who at 6-10 and 235 was the largest specimen on the floor, testified to the physical nature of the game. Iowa's first basket of the game came when Kraficisin none too gently removed IU's Ray Tolbert from the scene and fielded an offensive rebound for a layup.

Ed Maracich gets help from Lute Olson, Bob Knight

"Personally, I like that kind of game," Krafcisin said. "I can't compete with Ray and those guys with finesse, so if I can be physical it helps me. What makes it tough is when someone gets away with a foul and then you get called for one.

"Ray would throw me on one end of the floor and I would throw him. Then one of us would get caught. We needed nine or ten officials out there to catch all the fouls."

Even after big victory, Olson sees 'dogfight'

Iowa's important road victory didn't inspire Olson to make any early championship claims.

"It's gonna be a dogfight," he said.

"There are going to be nights like this and there are going to be nights like our Ohio State game. You're going to lose some you probably should win.

"But this one will do more for us confidencewise than any other game we've had. When we got into close games now, we may feel like the pressure is on the other team."

To beat an Indiana team at Assembly Hall, as 13 teams have done now in 123 games, "takes experience and very tough kids mentally," Olson said.

"I can think back to my first year at Iowa when we were the hamburger kings in here (a 102-49 IU victory sent 17,000 ticket-clutchers out into the afternoon entitled to an all-American meal, under a hamburger chain's promotion.)

"We did not have mentally tough kids. Now, they're tough, and they also have more ability."

Knight agreed on both counts. "Iowa is an excellent basketball team,," he said. "They played very well at both ends of the court."

Indiana 93, Northwestern 56

Isiah Thomas made another triumphal return to Chicagoland, so Indiana moved back into a tie for first place by surviving the day's Big Ten upset wave.

The Hoosiers did it with 93-56 ferocity at Northwestern's McGaw Hall, behind 23 points, nine assists and "the best total game" Thomas has played.

IU coach Bob Knight offered the judgment on the 6-1 sophomore. "He was the dominant factor in the game," Knight said. "He enabled us to really get control at both ends of the floor."

With the victory, its 19th in a row over Northwestern, Indiana joined Iowa and Purdue, two of the day's upset losers, and Ohio State atop the Big Ten with 4-2 league records. Nine teams are bunched two games apart.

Indiana needed a 13-point run midway through the first half to take command.

From there on, the Hoosiers had their offense in high gear — another Chicago guard, sophomore Tony Brown, making his own sizable contribution with 16 points in his first Big Ten starting chance.

A third Chicago high school product, Glen Grunwald, also started, and Northwestern coach Rich Falk said, "I didn't know, but I suspect he started them because they were going home. He isn't settled on a lineup yet, so why not?"

Falk was partly right. Knight isn't settled on a lineup, and Brown moved in because "it was time to use him," Knight said. "I'd like to say it was a brilliant strategical move, but it was just his turn."

The Hoosiers began as if they were about to join the day's Big Ten losers.

Northwestern struck where it was supposed to be hurting, at guard. Minus starter Michael Jenkins, out with a leg injury, the Wildcats opened with little-used senior John Egan alongside four-year starter Rod Roberson, and the two combined to hit their first five shots.

Their firing enabled Northwestern to stay just ahead of Indiana's most efficient offensive play of the season for the game's first seven minutes.

Indiana finally popped on top, 17-15, when Ray Tolbert worked free inside the Northwestern zone defense for a dunk.

It was 19-19 when Isiah Thomas struck a blow back for Indiana's guards.

Thomas hit a baseline jump shot to break the game's last tie and extend a Hoosier streak through a seventh straight field shot.

Ironically, Thomas broke that streak, but he atoned by swiping the ball from Egan and driving in for a lay-up.

On IU's next possession, Tolbert missed a close-in jump shot but Thomas popped up amidst the tall people for a rebound and follow-up basket that made it 27-21.

Falk gave Egan a brief reprieve from his dueling with Thomas, sending in football safety Bobby Anderson.

Anderson was on court only 12 seconds before he had to revert to his autumnal habits. Thomas stripped him of the basketball and was on his way in for another cash-in when Anderson grabbed him. It was a one-point save; Thomas hit only one of the two free throws, ending a personal string of 20 conversions.

But the Indiana streak went on, through a lay-up by Tolbert and two free throws each by Tony Brown and Jim Thomas to open a 32-19 lead.

The margin topped out at 17 (42-25 after a gymnastics routine that got Tolbert a reverse layup with 3:50 left in the half).

The rest of the half was shoot-out basketball as it is not counseled by Robert Knight. Native Hoosier Roberson (Elkhart) did most of the Wildcat shooting, ending the half with 18 points.

From the 48-33 halftime lead, Indiana kept moving — to 58-37 just 4½ minutes into the second half and 77-47 with 5:45 left, the point when Knight removed Thomas to a roaring ovation.

Roberson finished with 26 points, but he got only one more basket — indeed, only one more shot — in the first 13 minutes of the second half.

The change was Indiana's, not anything Northwestern planned, Falk said.

"I wasn't surprised," he said. "I'm sure after he had 18 points at the half that he was three-fourths of Bobby's halftime talk."

Jim Thomas inherited Roberson in the middle of his hot streak closing out the first half and had primary duties against him in the second.

INDIANA 93

	M	FG	FT	R	A	BS	St	PF	TP
Kitchel, f	29	3- 7	0- 1	6	3	1	1	3	6
Grunwald, f	14	0- 2	1- 2	4	0	0	0	1	1
Tolbert, c	31	8-11	1- 1	6	2	2	0	3	17
I.Thomas, g	32	9-15	5- 6	3	9	1	3	3	23
Brown, g	36	7-11	2- 2	4	5	1	2	2	16
Wittman	11	4- 6	0- 0	1	2	0	1	2	8
J.Thomas	24	4- 4	2- 2	6	5	1	2	2	10
Isenbarger	3	1- 1	0- 0	0	0	0	0	0	2
Franz	6	1- 1	2- 2	1	1	0	0	0	4
Bouchie	9	1- 1	2- 2	1	2	0	0	1	4
Risley	3	1- 1	0- 0	0	1	0	2	0	2
Turner	1	0- 1	0- 0	1	0	0	0	0	0
LaFave	1	0- 0	0- 0	0	0	0	0	0	0
Team				6					
Totals		39-61	15-18	40	30	5	10	18	93

NORTHWESTERN 56

	M	FG	FT	R	A	BS	St	PF	TP
Stack, f	23	3- 9	0- 0	6	1	0	0	4	6
Rathel, f	26	1- 6	5- 6	0	3	0	2	0	7
Grady, c	26	1- 5	1- 2	1	2	1	1	3	3
Roberson, g	34	12-16	2- 2	3	2	0	1	4	26
Egan, g	34	2- 8	0- 0	0	6	0	0	3	4
Murray	14	0- 2	0- 0	3	0	1	0	1	0
Anderson	5	0- 1	0- 0	1	0	0	0	1	0
Schultz	16	4- 8	0- 0	3	0	0	0	2	8
Aaron	14	1- 3	0- 1	2	1	1	0	0	2
Blackard	6	0- 1	0- 1	0	0	0	0	0	0
Schnepp	1	0- 0	0- 0	0	0	0	0	0	0
Schner	1	0- 0	0- 0	0	0	0	0	0	0
Team				1					
Totals		24-59	8-12	20	15	3	4	15	56

SCORE BY HALVES

Indiana	48	45— 93
Northwestern	35	21— 56

Turnovers—Indiana 16, Northwestern 16.
Technical fouls—Grady (grabbing rim).

SHOOTING

	FG	Pct.	FT	Pct.
Indiana	39-61	.639	15-18	.833
Northwestern	24-59	.407	8-12	.667

Officials—Bob Burson, Fred Jaspers, Malcolm Hemphill.
Attendance—6,453 (sellout).

"I think I did a little better job against him the second half," Thomas said, "and I got a lot of help.

"I tried to make it hard for them to get the ball to him, but after he got it, I played him straight-up. The first half, I think I played up too high on him, and he made some excellent plays."

Roberson's 26-point total was the highest against IU this year, topping 25 by Ball State's Ray McCallum in the Hoosier opener.

"I thought Rod played extremely well," Falk said. "One of their goals is that nobody scores 20 against them. It's got to build his confidence that he played so well against Indiana. He's been struggling a little bit of late."

Roberson was virtually all of the Northwestern offense. The Wildcats shot .407 — on 12-of-16 (.750) by Roberson and 12-of-43 (.279) by everyone else.

Indiana posted its season high with a .639 shooting mark. Besides the 39 points from starting guards Thomas and Brown, IU got 17 from Tolbert and 10 from Jim Thomas. Indiana also had a 40-20 rebounding edge.

Happy homecoming for Thomas, Brown

Westchester St. Joseph's High School turned out another huge gathering to salute returning son Isiah Thomas.

Tony Brown had his own crowd. "My whole family was here," said Brown, who includes 12 brothers and sisters and his parents in his assessment.

Brown made a bid to keep his starting spot with 16 points and five assists.

"I thought he was very good," Knight said. "He scored some points, but the big thing to me was I don't think he turned the ball over at all — maybe once." Brown was charged with one turnover.

"He maintained control of the basketball fairly well," Knight said.

Brown also was pleased — both at the starting chance and the results. "I wouldn't say I was surprised (to start)," he said. "I was just trying to be prepared. I had a little inkling Friday it might happen."

The former Chicago DeLaSalle High star said he didn't think the return to homeland was a factor in the game. "I knew in the past some people had tried extra hard for something like that and it didn't work out so well," he said. "Things just fell into place for me."

From amidst his crowd of well-wishers, Thomas was uncertain if there was anything more than coincidence to his season-high 23-point performance coming in the same arena where he reached his regular-season high as a freshman, with 28 points.

"I don't know," he said. "Maybe it is the people here who excite me so much. I know I felt a lot different up here.

"I wish I had felt that way after the Iowa game."

Knight said IU's loss to Iowa may have been the primary factor in Thomas's play. "He made a couple mistakes in that game, and I think he tried to correct that," Knight said.

Thomas and Tolbert said the Hoosiers were fully aware of what had happened elsewhere in the Big Ten Saturday, opening the door to IU to a return to first place.

Tolbert said he read the afternoon results as "an opportunity," not a warning.

"We were aware of the situation. We were definitely trying to go out and regain the lead."

Thomas said the Iowa loss left the Hoosiers "all down, till this afternoon. When we heard all those teams lost, we knew we had a chance to get back in first place. It's a bad feeling when you're not in first place."

Randy Wittman — Long-range shooting beats Gophers

Falk called Indiana "a quality basketball team and they really haven't found their identity yet. Bobby's still playing a lot of people.

"I have great respect for Indiana and a Bobby Knight-coached team, because they always do so many fundamental things so well. To beat them is not an easy task, to say the least."

Falk admitted the afternoon results "may have been an extra motivation for them."

Knight discounted that. "I didn't even know the scores," he said. "That kind of thinking loses you more games than it wins.

"I wasn't surprised we played well. I'd have been surprised if we wouldn't have."

Tony Brown — A winner before home folks

Indiana 56, Minnesota 53

Indiana broke a couple habits to maintain its share of the Big Ten basketball lead.

And Randy Wittman broke a drought.

The Hoosiers, scoring almost as many points in a five-minute overtime as they did in the 20-minute first half, got by Minnesota, 56-53 — the first Indiana victory in five years at Williams Arena.

The game also ended a streak of near misses that was beginning to build its own frustrations. It was the first close game the Hoosiers have won.

It appeared to be repeating the recent Hoosier performances in Gopherland when Minnesota edged out in the last few minutes of the half for a 26-18 lead, then widened it to 30-18 in the first minute of the second half.

Ray Tolbert's inside squirm around 7-foot-2 Randy Breuer for a basket got Indiana's comeback started, but its main propulsion came from three straight long-range baskets by Wittman over the Gophers' 2-3 zone defense.

They were Wittman's first points of an eventual 14-point total in his return to the starting lineup after three games of reserve duty.

"Wittman's shooting was definitely the reason he started the ball game," IU coach Bob Knight said, "and it was almost why he didn't start the second half.

"I told Randy and Ted Kitchel at the half that they had scored zero baskets against their zone, and they're our best shooters. We can't win with that."

All three shots that got Wittman and the Hoosiers rolling came from the left side of the court, near the out-of-bounds line. They came from any zone's outer limits, but Gopher coach Jim Dutcher thought they should have been covered better. "They weren't really attacking our zone from on top," Dutcher said, "so we could sag our wing men a little wider. Darryl Mitchell tried, but he just didn't get out there soon enough."

The three came within a minute span to pull Indiana within 32-26. When Tolbert followed with a steal that blossomed into a three-point play by Isiah Thomas, the lead that had been at 12 only a couple minutes earlier was down to 32-29. "From there on, it was a ball game," Dutcher said.

IU finally got around the Gophers on a picture play that tied in four Hoosiers — ironically, all but Wittman.

Tolbert, 6-9, leaped high to block a Breuer shot. Tony Brown, starting for the second game in a row, outran the rejection to grab the ball just before it went over the sideline, flipping it back in-bounds over his head. Thomas fielded the save, wheeled downcourt and got the ball to Steve Risley for a lay-up that put Indiana ahead, 37-36, with 11:15 to play.

Minnesota never led again, but the Gophers caught up when two Hoosier turnovers broke up a possession game in the last five minutes and it was Minnesota that had the ball for a last-second shot in regulation time, the score tied 43-43.

Dutcher took a time out with 10 seconds left to set up a play. "We tried to get the ball into Breuer," he said. That didn't surprise any of the 16,972 in the sellout crowd or Knight, who pulled 6-10 Landon Turner off the bench to use him with Tolbert for double-teaming designed to discourage Gopher access to Breuer.

It worked. Trent Tucker took the last shot, from about 20 feet, and it wasn't close. "Darryl thought he was covered," Dutcher said. "So he reversed the ball to Tucker. We didn't really get a good shot."

Indiana came out blazing in the overtime. Wittman fired from the deep left corner and had the ball dip deep into the basket but spin out. Minnesota rebounded and was in the midst of a play aimed at getting guard Mark Hall open when Brown slapped away a Breuer pass aimed for Hall, beat Breuer to the loose basketball and streaked downcourt toward a lay-up.

"Their guy (Ben Coleman) was trying to foul me," Brown said. "He bumped me a couple times, and when I went up for the shot, I was off-balance but I was going for the three-point play." No call came and the shot missed, but Tolbert came along behind for a tip-in and a 47-45 lead.

Breuer offset that with a close-in basket, but Wittman got loose in the same spot where he had barely missed before. "I thought for sure the first one was in," Wittman said. "It felt so good when I shot it I didn't let what happened bother me. I was just happy to be open a second time."

That one swished, and Indiana had a lead (47-45) it never again lost. Wittman doubled the margin with a driving basket off an inside screen and pass from Thomas, putting IU up 49-45 wih 2:25 to go in the overtime.

It was 51-47 with 1:15 to go when Hall — one of the league's best percentage shooters all three of his collegiate seasons — drove on Brown to get a 10-foot baseline jump shot. Thomas swooped in to help, smothering Hall's shot just as he launched it and retrieving the block from behind the Gopher guard.

INDIANA 56

	M	FG	FT	R	A	BS	St	PF	TP
Kitchel, f	21	1- 7	0- 0	2	2	0	0	2	2
Wittman, f	39	6-10	2- 2	0	0	0	0	1	14
Tolbert, c	45	8-10	1- 3	10	0	2	2	4	17
I.Thomas, g	43	4-11	5- 6	7	4	1	1	2	13
Brown, g	41	2- 7	0- 0	1	0	0	1	0	4
Turner	3	1- 1	0- 0	1	0	0	0	3	2
J.Thomas	2	0- 0	0- 0	0	0	0	0	0	0
Risley	28	1- 2	2- 2	1	1	0	0	4	4
Franz	2	0- 0	0- 0	0	0	0	0	0	0
Bouchie	1	0- 0	0- 0	1	0	0	0	0	0
Team				6					
Totals		23-48	10-13	29	7	3	4	16	56

MINNESOTA 53

	M	FG	FT	R	A	BS	St	PF	TP
Holmes, f	42	2- 6	0- 0	4	0	0	1	3	4
Tucker, f	41	2- 8	0- 0	2	1	1	3	2	4
Breuer, c	32	7-11	7- 8	5	2	1	0	2	21
Hall, g	34	5-10	0- 0	3	2	0	1	4	10
Mitchell, g	34	1- 5	2- 2	2	0	0	0	0	4
Coleman	20	2- 3	3- 4	4	0	1	0	2	7
Howell	17	1- 1	0- 0	1	0	0	0	2	2
Peterson	3	0- 1	0- 0	0	0	0	0	0	0
Kaupa	1	0- 0	1- 2	0	0	0	0	0	1
Wiley	3	0- 0	0- 0	1	0	0	0	1	0
Team				3					
Totals		20-46	13-16	24	6	3	5	16	53

SCORE BY HALVES

Indiana	18	25	13—	56
Minnesota	26	17	10—	53

Turnovers—Indiana 18, Minnesota 13.
Technical fouls—Indiana bench, Minnesota (6 timeouts).

SHOOTING

	FG	Pct.	FT	Pct.
Indiana	23-48	.479	10-13	.769
Minnesota	20-46	.435	13-16	.813

Officials—George Solomon, Tom Rucker, Don Edwards.
Attendance—16,972 (sellout).

Ray Tolbert's big, but not beside 7-2 Randy Breuer

With 34 seconds left, Brown slipped away from the gambling Gophers to score a lay-up that widened the lead to 53-47. Breuer cut it with a basket at 0:22, but when Minnesota called time out to stop the clock before IU's pass-in, it was the Gophers' seventh — one too many. Thomas cashed in one point on the resultant technical foul and two more when he was fouled after receiving the pass-in, making two Breuer baskets in the final seconds moot.

Tolbert had 17 points and led both teams with 10 rebounds, while Thomas added 13 points and seven rebounds as IU enjoyed a 29-24 rebounding edge over the Gophers. Breuer's 21 points led Minnesota.

Flurry of worries early for Tolbert

All ended well, but Tolbert started both halves with anxious moments.

The game opened with Tolbert guarding Breuer, who, at 7-2, stands five inches taller than Tolbert. In the first four minutes of the game, Minnesota jammed the ball inside to Breuer once for a turn-around jump shot that he hit and another time for a left-handed hook shot that swished.

"I said to myself right then, 'It's gonna be a long day,'" Tolbert admitted.

"But the other guys' sagging really helped me out and we did a little better job the rest of the way."

When IU came out the second half to try to generate a fast take-off to get out of a 26-18 hole, Tolbert had the ball stolen from him on the Hoosiers' first possession, Breuer scored from inside on Minnesota's first possession, and on IU's second possession, Tolbert wheeled around Breuer for an apparent basket and possible three-point play but lost everything when he was called for charging. "I thought I was by him," Tolbert said. "That one hurt, but we had to just keep going at them."

For all Tolbert's anxieties about having to take on Breuer, it was the opposite match-up that kept Minnesota playing zone defenses most of the way, Dutcher said.

"We had pretty good success with our man-to-man when we went to it late in the game," he said, "but the problem we had with it was Randy can't cover Tolbert. So to get some defense there, we had to hurt ourselves on offense.

"We also had some crucial turnovers late. And for us to win, Trent Tucker and Darryl Mitchell have to make a jump shot. I'm not sure either one of them ever did (each hit one, Tucker adding a rebound basket that made the two 3-for-13).

"I don't know what it is. We play well till we get 10 or 12 points ahead, and then they stick a pin in us."

Dutcher refused to let the overtime loss panic him about the Gophers' Big Ten championship chances. But he had to dabble in the league's version of new math to maintain any cheer.

"We're not really in bad shape yet," said Dutcher, whose team went off into the night with a 3-4 league record, two games behind tri-leaders Indiana, Iowa and Ohio State, and now has two of its next three games on the road.

"If we beat Northwestern (Saturday night at home and again the next Saturday at Evanston) and win at Purdue (next Thursday), we're right back in it," he said.

"But certainly we've got to some time be able to win a damned home game."

The loss to Indiana was the third the Gophers have taken in their four league games played at Williams Arena so far this year. They lost a fourth game there to Marquette in December. It takes better research than Gopher records permit to establish the last time the home folks went home so deflated so often in one season, but it surely transcends the era in which Minnesota has been packing its old basketball hall — an era of hyped basketball interest that dates to the arrival in 1971 of coach Bill Musselman, a man more commonly remembered in Gopherland in infamy than as a program-builder.

"This was a big boost for us," Wittman said, "but now we've got to go on from here and have a two-win week. We haven't had one of those since the first week of the Big Ten season. The only way we're going to win this thing is to have some of those.

"We've got to stop our rollercoaster. We can't have a good win on the road and then come back home and let it get away."

Both Wittman and the Hoosiers made a sharp reversal of form in the second half to get the current week off winningly.

"Randy forced them out a little," Tolbert said. "I was screening for him out there, and then when they covered him, the other guys were able to punch it in to me.

"We wanted to take it right to their big men."

"It means a lot to us to win this one," Wittman said, "because the close games we've lost we didn't lose on bad breaks or on a great play somebody made at the end. We had to make some plays to win those games and that just didn't happen.

"We talked about that out there tonight. I think it helps us a lot to win an overtime here."

"The difference in our offense the second half?" guard Isiah Thomas said, repeating a question. "I'd say Randy's shooting — that was the *only* difference.

"The reason why it was so special," he said, "is because of how awful it feels to lose."

Indiana 69, Purdue 61

Not with a roar but a symphony of whistles, Indiana moved into the Big Ten basketball lead by outscoring Purdue, 69-61, at Assembly Hall.

It was a mutually unsatisfying sort of sortie between two of the college game's sharpest rivals. It began with three technical fouls in the first two minutes and had its flow interrupted by 53 more whistles for personal fouls.

Somewhere in among it all, there were some bursts of basketball — enough of which had Isiah Thomas in the middle to give Indiana control, or the closest thing to it that the wild afternoon contained.

The bursts that made the difference were two 10-point Indiana runs in the first seven minutes of the game to enable the Hoosiers, down 6-0 at the start, to go ahead, 20-8.

There wasn't much orderliness to it, but the game did go on from there with a separation established. Purdue never got the margin under five, and the one point when that occurred in the second half produced the game's key play.

The play became vital because a Ted Kitchel tip-in that would have opened a 64-55 Hoosier lead was ruled a climbing foul on Kitchel instead: his disqualifying fifth foul, his basket wiped out, and freshman Greg Eifert of Purdue sent to the free-throw line for a one-and-one conversion that cut the Hoosier lead to 62-57 with 4:13 left.

Indiana broke the Purdue press by getting the ball to Thomas, who weaved through the backcourt challenge to charge in on the last defender, Purdue's Drake Morris.

Charge is a pejorative word in the Thomas vocabulary. He picked up two charging fouls trying to force fast breaks through to a fruitful end in the first half.

This time, he drove at Morris, pulled up short about six feet in front of the goal and arched a high, soft shot into the basket.

With the shot in the air, Thomas said and officials ruled, Morris "moved up a little to try to draw a charge," the two players bumping together. Instead of the charge, Morris drew his own fifth foul, and since the bump between the two came after the shot, Thomas got a one-and-one free-throw opportunity that he converted into a rare four-point play.

As quickly as the Boilermaker highwater mark had come, with an apparent nine-point lead chopped to five, the margin was back at nine with 4:04 left. Nothing so telling, nor even particularly worth telling, came afterward — Indiana blowing a chance to run up a fat victory margin by missing five straight one-and-ones and Purdue just as profligate with the chance all those misses afforded.

Purdue's first-year coach, Gene Keady, found something cheerful in the nine straight shots the Boilermakers missed during the two teams' wobbling finish.

"We had a chance to beat Indiana," Keady said. "Probably we should have beaten them. I think now we can win another Big Ten game. Before today, I wasn't so sure."

He got a ribald introduction to the rivalry. He hadn't quite survived two minutes of it before he was one technical foul away from leaving the premises.

IU's Bob Knight drew one only 94 seconds into the game. "I thought there were a couple of missed walking violations," said Knight.

His references to the perceived oversights followed a two-shot foul called on IU's Tony Brown against Purdue's standout freshman, Russell Cross. The combination let Cross stand at the line and pitch in four straight free throws to open a quick 6-0

Purdue lead and kept the ball in Purdue hands with a chance to go up 8-0.

But the Boilermakers lost the ball out of bounds, and simultaneously, Keady lost his temper. Keady saw Knight clamp a hand on the belt of official Dick Bestor and move him out of his way. "All I was trying to do was see what was going on," Knight said. "I can't see the game with a guy's butt in my face. That's probably the 50th game I've grabbed that third official. They make a hell of a mistake in their mechanics putting that guy there."

Keady said, "Bobby *grabbed* him. I have the highest respect for Bobby, but I'm not going to let anybody intimidate me."

Charging onto the floor to deliver that message to the officials cost Keady two technical fouls. So IU's Ted Kitchel, he of the 18-for-18 free-throwing afternoon earlier this year, got his own chance to play pitch-till-you-win. Kitchel matched the four in a row by Cross to get IU on the scoreboard, and when Thomas broke free for a layup on the Hoosier possession after the free throws, the whole 6-0 Purdue lead was gone and still the game was only a minute and 56 seconds along.

Thomas came back with a jump shot and a fast-break layup after a steal to round out the Hoosiers' first 10-point streak.

Mike Scearce broke it for Purdue with a jump shot, but Thomas's quick hands and feet to match had IU's running game in gear by then. He contributed six more points to another 10-point run that opened a 20-8 lead with 13:22 left in the half.

Steve Risley tries for save as Greg Eifert defends

The Hoosiers' first-half lead topped out at 29-16 with 7:44 left, after five straight points by Randy Wittman. Purdue closed within 33-28 late in the half before Indiana beat the Boilers back with a basket by Kitchel and two free throws by Thomas, ahead of a buzzer-beating jump shot by Tony Brown that opened a 39-30 halftime margin.

Purdue missed its first seven shots of the second half, and Thomas and Kitchel did most of the Hoosier scoring as IU edged out to a 47-34 lead, then a game-high 15-point margin at 56-41 with 9:58 left.

"That was probably the most important part of the game for us, when we got 15 up," Knight said. "It's pretty tough to knock that down. They had a nice little spurt, but we still had a pretty good lead."

Purdue never really did get its shooting problems cured, finished 9-for-36 in the second half (.250) and just .304 for the game. Free throws fueled the comeback attempt, Purdue squeezing 17 points out of the nine one-and-one chances it had during the game, one point below maximum, and Indiana — the Big Ten leader in free-throw shooting — getting just 11 points out of 13 one-and-ones, 15 points below the maximum.

Thomas finished with 26 points, on 10-for-12 shooting from the field and 6-for-7 at the free throw line. Kitchel was the only Hoosier to join him in double figures, totaling 19 — including 9-for-11 at the free throw line.

Cross had 19 points, 14 in the first half, to lead Purdue (4-4 in the Big Ten and 11-6 overall), and Morris added 12. Purdue also had a crushing 40-28 lead in rebounds and a slim edge in turnovers (18 to IU's 20) to make Indiana's vastly more proficient shooting (.571 for the game) the difference.

Cross impresses Tolbert, Hoosiers

IU senior Ray Tolbert went away from his first meeting with Cross a loser on points, Cross outscoring Tolbert, 19-4, and limiting Tolbert's day to 21 minutes because of foul trouble.

But Tolbert also took away the comfort of a 69-61 team victory that kept his club atop the Big Ten standings. He was impressed by Cross. "He's big (6-10), he's quick, and he's got good moves inside," Tolbert said. "And I think he plays hard."

"But I could have been in better position. It seemed like I was a second behind all day. I thought we had pretty good positioning against him, but the trouble we had was mostly my fault for not being where I should have been."

No stopping Isiah Thomas for Brian Walker (20)

PURDUE 61

	M	FG	FT	R	A	BS	St	PF	TP
Edmonson, f	25	1-10	0- 0	4	1	0	1	2	2
Scearce, f	16	1- 6	2- 2	4	0	0	0	3	4
Cross, c	38	5- 9	9-13	7	0	0	2	4	19
Walker, g	32	0- 6	2- 2	0	6	0	1	3	2
Morris, g	27	4-11	4- 4	5	0	0	2	5	12
Barnes	16	2- 3	0- 0	4	0	0	0	4	4
J.Kitchel	6	0- 1	0- 0	0	1	0	0	1	0
Benson	15	1- 1	4- 4	3	0	0	0	0	6
Stallings	10	2- 8	0- 1	1	0	0	0	4	4
Eifert	14	1- 1	6- 6	5	0	0	0	1	8
Hall	1	0- 0	0- 0	0	0	0	0	0	0
Team				7					
Totals		17-56	27-32	40	8	0	6	27	61

INDIANA 69

	M	FG	FT	R	A	BS	St	PF	TP
T.Kitchel, f	31	5- 8	9-11	7	2	0	1	5	19
Wittman, f	40	4- 8	1- 2	0	2	0	1	2	9
Tolbert, c	21	2- 7	0- 0	3	0	1	1	5	4
I.Thomas, g	39	10-12	6- 7	4	3	0	3	3	26
Brown, g	20	2- 4	2- 6	2	2	0	1	2	6
Turner	5	0- 1	0- 0	1	0	0	0	5	0
Risley	14	0- 1	0- 0	2	0	0	0	1	0
Bouchie	8	0- 0	0- 0	1	0	0	0	1	0
J.Thomas	22	1- 2	3- 4	6	5	0	0	2	5
Team				2					
Totals		24-42	21-30	28	14	1	7	26	69

SCORE BY HALVES

Purdue		30	31— 61
Indiana		39	30— 69

Turnovers—Purdue 18, Indiana 20.
Technical fouls—Indiana bench, T.Kitchel (grabbing the rim), Purdue bench 2.

SHOOTING

	FG	Pct.	FT	Pct.
Purdue	17-56	.304	27-32	.849
Indiana	24-42	.571	21-30	.700

Officials—Phil Robinson, Phil Bova, Dick Bestor.
Attendance—17,269 (sellout).

Cross also fouled out Tolbert's back-up man, Landon Turner, in just five minutes on-court for Turner. "Steve Risley came in and helped us around the boards," Knight said.

Kitchel called Cross "a hell of a player. By the time he's a senior, he ought to be one of the best in the country."

Kitchel, who grew up in Galveston much closer to Purdue than IU and shared the court Saturday with a cousin, Jon, who opted to do his playing as a Boilermaker, came up with more rebounds (seven) than the three Hoosier centers combined to forestall any Hoosier disaster under the boards.

As it was, Purdue — outrebounded in 10 of its first 16 games and five of its first seven Big Ten games — amassed a 40-28 rebounding edge over IU, although most of the day's missing was at the Purdue end, where the defensive team, IU, should have all the advantages in positioning.

Kitchel got five of his seven rebounds in the second half. "Ray was out a lot and I knew they were outrebounding us," Kitchel said. "I just tried to go to the boards as hard as I could."

What could have been his eighth rebound and an important tip-in for IU was wiped out because officials ruled he went to the boards a bit too hard with a Boilermaker in front of him. So, Kitchel stopped going to the boards and went to the bench, with five fouls.

"I thought Kitchel was very helpful to us," Knight said. "The second half in particular, he got some buckets and made some free throws at a point when they were really big."

Kitchel was impressed with the play of both youngsters who came out of Chicago's lavish high school coverage the last two years with impossible billing to live up to and really haven't done badly at trying: Cross (Class of '80) and Thomas (Class of '79).

"We tried to put some pressure on Cross," Kitchel said, "but he kept his cool pretty well. He's a hell of a player. By the time he's a senior, he ought to be one of the best in the country."

Thomas led both teams with 26 points, though his renown is for playmaking, not pointmaking.

"I thought Isiah took it to the basket pretty well all day," said Kitchel, who combined with Thomas for one of the game's eventful plays.

Tolbert already had gone to the bench with four fouls early in the second half when, for one of the rare times during the afternoon, Kitchel found himself deep in the Purdue backcourt when a shot went up.

IU's Jim Thomas rebounded it and hurried a pass up-court to Isiah Thomas. "I saw there was just one man back with Isiah," Kitchel said. "So I took off for the basket.

"If you're open, Isiah usually gets you the ball. He got it to me."

When the defender closed on Thomas to try to thwart the break in its infancy, Thomas lofted a quick, early pass that Kitchel fielded and converted into a two-handed dunk. It's recorded for history. In the process of dunking, Kitchel also grabbed the rim and drew a technical foul. "I don't get a lot of those (dunks)," Kitchel said.

The basket opened a 47-34 lead for IU (the technical free throw was missed) and started Kitchel on an 11-point burst in the middle six minutes of the second half.

Randy Wittman meets opposition from Keith Edmonson

Brian Walker deflects ball away from Isiah Thomas

With a person like Coach, who's so out in the open, everything is blown out of proportion. But he runs a camp for kids 9 to 14 every summer and he gets thousands of kids whose parents want them to go there. That's got to say something.

Al McGuire

Indiana 89, Wisconsin 64

Sophomore guard Tony Brown led Indiana on a shooting rampage, and when the smoke lifted, there were gaping holes in a couple theories. Namely that:

• The Hoosiers might get caught peeking ahead a bit to their emotional rematch with Purdue two days away;

• Assembly Hall, somehow and some way, is a virtual second home for Wisconsin.

Whatever the allure of a Purdue rematch, whatever past magic Wisconsin had managed in IU's arena, the Hoosiers went to work with concentration and thoroughness and put the Badgers away early in an 89-64 victory.

Thus, Indiana reached the halfway point of the Big Ten race 7-2, a game ahead of Illinois, Iowa and Michigan and two games up on Purdue.

Brown was 9-for-12, mostly from 16 to 20 feet, in scoring a career-high 18 points as the Hoosiers riddled Wisconsin with the best shooting night an IU team ever has had in Big Ten play. Indiana closed at .667, topping the .650 the 1978 Hoosiers shot in beating Purdue — the previous IU best in league play and the former Assembly Hall record.

The Hoosiers got there although coach Bob Knight went to the bench early. That didn't make any difference. The starters wound up 26-for-39; the eight reserves, each of whom scored, 12-for-18 — .667 for both groups.

Badger coach Bill Cofield was generous enough in his appraisal of the Hoosier performance ("tonight, they were the best we've played"), but he implied listless play by his own team had something to do with IU's glossiness.

"They handled us early," Cofield said. "I'm not too certain no matter who we were playing would have handled us tonight.

"We just did not play very well."

The Badgers stayed even through 6-6, but Isiah Thomas ignited the Hoosier zoom-away with a couple inventive plays.

Thomas broke the tie by slashing through the Wisconsin zone at an angle, laying off a pass to Brown for a lay-up.

Before Wisconsin could get a possible tying shot launched, Thomas stole the ball from guard Greg Dandridge and dashed to a layup that made it 10-6.

"It should have been 10-2," Knight said. "We gave up a couple baskets we shouldn't have.

"But the next five minutes I thought we played pretty well."

Brown's outside sniping was the problem that Wisconsin couldn't solve during the pullaway stretch. He hit three in a row to open a 16-10 lead. It became 21-12 when Brown, only 6-foot-2, pulled off a rebound at the Wisconsin end and led Thomas with a pass that blossomed into a layup.

A dunk by Ray Tolbert and a short jump shot by Randy Wittman widened the lead to 27-15 with 10 minutes left in the half. It became 33-19 on a Thomas basket, but when Thomas was charged with a foul for an illegal screen, he went to the bench with three personals, and Mike Kreklow converted the free throws awarded him to move Wisconsin within 33-23 with 4½ Thomas-less minutes left for the Hoosiers before halftime.

Those were Isiah Thomas-less minutes. He was replaced by Jim Thomas, who didn't try to be Isiah ("he's one of a kind") but didn't hurt the surname any. Wittman broke whatever momentum Wisconsin might have been building by working free for a jump shot, and the Hoosiers pulled away.

It was 43-27 at halftime and 44-29 only 95 seconds into the half when Knight called a time out — concerned that things were starting a little too much like the second half of IU's late, lamented Iowa game (a 56-53 home-court loss that turned around with a 10-1 Iowa burst opening the second half).

After the time out, IU outscored the Badgers, 8-3, to open its first 20-point lead of the night (53-32 with 14:37 left) and start Knight thinking about what starters to get out and what reserves to get in.

It was 55-35 with 13:06 left when Jim Thomas replaced Wittman; 61-37 with 11:18 to go when Chuck Franz replaced Isiah Thomas; 65-38 with 9:36 left when Glen Grunwald sent Brown to the sidelines to be greeted by smiles and handslaps there and a standing ovation from the 16,223 spectators.

Wisconsin's bulky inside pair, Claude Gregory and Larry Petty, led the Badger offense. Gregory, Wisconsin's career scoring recordholder, totaled 23 points to lead both teams while Petty had 17 and John Bailey 15.

Behind Brown's 18 points, IU had Tolbert with 14, Wittman 12 and Isiah Thomas 10, and Tolbert's five rebounds led Indiana to a 28-25 board edge.

WISCONSIN 64

	M	FG	FT	R	A	BS	St	PF	TP
Gregory, f	38	7-18	9-11	6	0	0	1	3	23
Kreklow, f	24	0- 0	2- 2	0	0	0	0	3	2
Petty, c	38	7-16	3- 5	5	2	0	0	5	17
Bailey, g	30	6-10	3- 4	3	2	0	0	4	15
Dandridge, g	31	0- 0	0- 0	3	5	0	1	0	0
Hastings	27	3- 4	0- 0	0	2	0	1	1	6
Renfroe	4	0- 0	0- 0	0	0	0	0	0	0
Lake	2	0- 0	0- 0	1	0	0	0	0	0
Mitchell	4	0- 1	0- 0	1	0	0	0	1	0
Zinkgraf	2	0- 1	1- 2	2	0	0	0	0	1
Team				4					
Totals		23-50	18-24	25	11	0	2	18	64

INDIANA 89

	M	FG	FT	R	A	BS	St	PF	TP
Kitchel, f	9	2- 3	1- 2	0	0	0	1	4	5
Wittman, f	27	5- 9	2- 2	1	3	0	1	1	12
Tolbert, c	28	5- 8	4- 5	5	0	0	0	3	14
I.Thomas, g	25	5- 7	0- 0	3	5	0	2	3	10
Brown, g	30	9-12	0- 0	4	4	0	2	3	18
Risley	18	1- 2	2- 3	4	1	0	0	3	4
J.Thomas	10	2- 2	0- 0	3	2	0	1	0	4
Bouchie	15	1- 4	0- 0	1	0	0	0	2	2
Franz	11	2- 2	1- 2	0	3	0	0	0	5
Turner	10	3- 3	0- 1	1	0	0	0	4	6
Grunwald	6	2- 3	0- 0	1	2	0	1	1	4
Isenbarger	7	1- 1	1- 1	0	2	1	0	0	3
LaFave	4	0- 1	2- 2	2	0	0	0	0	2
Team				3					
Totals		38-57	13-18	28	22	2	9	24	89

SCORE BY HALVES

Wisconsin		27	37— 64
Indiana		43	46— 89

Turnovers—Wisconsin 16, Indiana 12.

SHOOTING

	FG	Pct.	FT	Pct.
Wisconsin	23-50	.460	18-24	.750
Indiana	38-57	.667	13-18	.722

Officials—Rich Weller, Fred Jaspers, Malcolm Hemphill.
Attendance—16,223 (capacity).

Brown's jump shot survived slump

Last seen by the outside world, Brown was having a terrible time hitting the basket from 15 feet away, unguarded — on free throws. Four times in a row, the goal successfully avoided his pitch when IU whipped Purdue. He didn't stir anyone to rank him with the all-time great shooters.

But Brown wasn't really crushed even after the Purdue problems. "I have a little adjustment to make with my free throw," he said, "but I'm not going to change my jump shot any."

He is convinced the free-throw problem is behind him ("I wasn't using my knees".) The outside world is convinced he was right about not tampering with the jump shot. In leading Indiana's takeoff to an 89-64 victory over Wisconsin, Brown took eight jump shots and hit seven, which inspired a touch of tolerance even in his unequivocating coach, Bob Knight.

"We talked all week about a necessity to stick the ball in the basket from the guard spots if they were open," Knight said. "I was really pleased with the way he shot.

"I thought he took one really questionable shot, but by then he had hit four or five in a row so I guess we could give him that one.

"I think it was (assistant coach) Jimmy Crews who pointed out at the half he had done some other things besides shooting the basketball — he had some rebounds and a couple steals and assists. I just think without question it was his best all-round game."

Brown has started five games and the Hoosiers are 5-0 in them. Cause and effect are for Knight to decide, but the last four have come in Big Ten play (his first was the Ball State opener, when Isiah Thomas was hurt), and there aren't odds long enough to cover the possibility that Brown won't get a chance to try for 6-0 next time out against Purdue.

Brown is a Chicagoan who was, to a degree, the discovery of the fellow who operates beside him in the IU backcourt these days, Isiah Thomas. Brown was the pesky defender who took Thomas on in the game that ended Isiah's high school career, a tournament battle that went to Brown and De La Salle over Thomas and Westchester St. Joseph's. Thomas wasn't so sore a loser he didn't have warm words to pass along to IU recruiters about Brown, and he's happy to be operating in tandem — happy even while being aware that Brown isn't always going to hit nine of 12 shots.

"Tony gives me a lot of help," Thomas said. "When he's playing, I don't have to bring the ball up and I don't have to get things set up outside, so I can concentrate more on doing what we want to do inside.

"And on defense, he really helps out because he's so quick."

The shots Brown hit probably were there to be had before, he admitted. "Coach told the guards to get ready to step up and shoot," Brown said. "He wanted us to catch the ball ready to shoot every time. That was the key. That's what we haven't been doing before."

Cofield said he "knew Brown was a tremendous player, but he has some nights when he hits the basket and some when he

Dan Hastings looks for something to develop as Isiah Thomas coils

Larry Petty's innocent look didn't elude foul as Landon Turner sprawls

doesn't. He is potentially a very fine player, and he will be one by the time he leaves here."

Cofield credited more than the scorching Brown-IU shooting for the Hoosier edge in the teams' first meeting.

"Very early we let them physically take us out of the ball game," he said. "They just ran right through our arms and took our pass. They just overpowered us, and that hurt us mentally.

"Indiana is a good team. They have excellent depth and excellent strength and quickness. They've got the ingredients to win this thing. I said that before the season started and I'm not changing."

The Hoosiers had nine steals and converted six of them into immediate baskets.

Included was a first-half play when a Badger pass went into the backcourt, an automatic turnover as soon as a Wisconsin player touched the ball again.

However, when the Badgers were slow in going back to retrieve the lost basketball, Brown's quickness got him to it first and he shot a pass to Isiah Thomas for a fast cash-in.

Jim Thomas still had the pressure on the Badgers in the second half. He punched the ball away from a Wisconsin guard, beat everyone to it on the sidelines and then outran his chasers to ram home his first collegiate dunk.

"I was going for it as soon as I got the ball and looked up court," the 6-3 Floridian said. It was, predictably, a crowd pleaser, for an already well-pleased crowd.

Purdue 68, Indiana 66

Reserve Kevin Stallings hit two free throws with five seconds left for the appropriate difference as Purdue jerked Indiana back with the Big Ten pack, 68-66, at Mackey Arena.

The free-throw line was poison to the Hoosiers, who seemed to have Purdue put away twice but let the Boilermakers revive on missed Hoosier free-throw chances and their own 18-for-22 free-throw accuracy.

Indiana shot 25 free throws, with a chance to get 29 points out of the opportunities. The Hoosiers managed only 12. It was a breakdown that the Hoosiers survived in a 69-61 victory at Assembly Hall, but this time it was fatal.

The defeat dropped the Hoosiers to 7-3 in Big Ten play, even with Iowa and Michigan and a game ahead of Purdue.

Indiana hit 10 shots in a row early in the game to jump out to 16-6, 21-9, and 28-14 leads.

The margin was 14 points several more times in the first half, the last 36-22 with 5 minutes left. It was 41-29 with two minutes left — although Indiana managed only one point out of three one-and-one chances in an 85-second stretch just ahead of that. Purdue used the last two minutes to jam in eight quick points, the last two on a rebound basket by Mike Scearce just ahead of the buzzer, to close within 42-37 at the half.

"I think that was the turning point," Purdue freshman Russell Cross said. "We came out of the first half with our heads up."

The Boilermakers pulled around IU, 47-46, on a breakaway lay-up by Brian Walker with 15:40 left. But Indiana exploded from a 49-48 deficit with a 10-1 burst that gave IU command again, 58-50, Tolbert contributing three of the five baskets in the spurt.

Purdue coach Gene Keady took a time out with 11:39 left, after Ted Kitchel's shot had opened a 58-50 margin.

"I told our players if they would be patient and pass the ball around about 10 times every time we got it, they would win the basketball game," Keady said. "They were about to quit fighting."

Purdue worked the ball 29 seconds before Drake Morris hit a jump shot, which Isiah Thomas nullified with a baseline jump shot that gave IU a 60-52 lead — and put Keady off his feet and on the edge of the playing floor, challenging the full house of 14,123 to whip up some noise.

The noise came, but it built lots faster and louder from what was happening on the playing floor. Purdue ran in eight points in a row to catch up, 60-60, on freshman Greg Eifert's rebound basket with 6:41 left.

Thomas broke the tie with another baseline shot, but Cross scored five points in a row for Purdue to put the Boilermakers up 65-62, with 3:42 left.

The Boilermakers got the ball back on a double-dribble call against Thomas, and Purdue appeared to be going to a four-corner game when Brian Walker saw an opening, went to the basket and had his shot smothered by Tolbert.

Just that quickly, momentum swung back to IU. Roosevelt Barnes of Purdue was charged with his fifth foul, and when he lay flat on the floor in a gesture of shock, surprise and disagreement, he drew a technical foul, too.

Kitchel hit both halves of the one-and-one granted him to edge IU within 65-64 with 3:07 to go, but he missed a chance to tie with the technical free throw. IU kept possession, however, and Randy Wittman was fouled with 2:52 to go. He tied the game with his first shot on a one-and-one chance, and IU reclaimed possession again after his second shot missed but was fumbled out of bounds by Purdue.

Sideline patrol — Purdue's Gene Keady, IU's Bob Knight

Ray Tolbert, coach Bob Knight seek answers

The Hoosiers had three more chances to break that tie. Tolbert missed from close in, but after Purdue rebounded, Wittman intercepted a pass. Thomas was called for traveling but reclaimed the ball with a steal, then missed a one-and-one with 1:45 left.

Cross hit one of two free throws with 1:11 to go — on Tolbert's fifth foul — to give Purdue a 66-65 lead, but Thomas hit one of two at 0:59 to tie it again.

The Boilermakers ran the clock down, and with 11 seconds to go, Keady bounded off the bench signaling for a time out.

Stallings was dribbling the ball above the foul circle at the time. "I saw him," Stallings said, "but I didn't want to take the ball in my hands myself and signal for a time out. I was waiting for someone else to call it."

Nobody did, and as he dribbled, IU's Steve Risley slapped the ball loose. Risley, Stallings and IU's Jim Thomas went for the ball, and Thomas was called for diving into Stallings.

Even after Stallings hit both free throws, there was lots of action. IU took two time outs, then sent Thomas on a football-like pattern up court, Risley dropping a pass in his hands on the fly near center court. Thomas cut through some traffic and bounced a pass to Kitchel open on the baseline, but an official ruled Thomas double-dribbled before he made the pass.

"I've watched Isiah Thomas play for three years and I've never seen him double-dribble," IU coach Bob Knight said. "And it was called on him twice today, by people 30 to 50 feet behind the play."

And still the game wasn't over. Purdue had the ball out with two seconds left, but Walker ran into Cross and lost the ball out of bounds, turning it back to IU with a second left.

Thomas used the second to get free for a pass and launch a 30-foot shot that bounced off the backboard and rimmed out.

"Stallings is a very cool young man," Keady said. "I felt very sure he was going to make his free throws. But I also was sure Isiah was going to make his. You can't tell in this game."

Cross had 20 points (and a game-high 10 rebounds) for Purdue. Isiah Thomas had 20 points (and a team-leading 8 rebounds), Kitchel 16, Tolbert 14 and Wittman 13 for the Hoosiers, who outshot Purdue from the field .529 to .410, but couldn't make up for the free throws that got away.

Knight statement defends Thomas

Before a shot was fired, a shot was fired.

Indiana and Purdue basketball teams hadn't taken the floor at Mackey Arena yet when Knight, steaming over printed references to a "sucker punch" thrown by Thomas against Barnes in the previous IU-Purdue game at Assembly Hall, dictated a press statement that defended Thomas and left 'em steaming in Purdue's athletic hierarchy.

"It is a sorry commentary when a singular incident in a game such as what took place between Isiah Thomas and Roosevelt Barnes is taken totally out of context and used to bring a pseudo-emotional state to a college basketball game. An extremely unfair and undeserved reflection has been cast on the character of Isiah Thomas by insinuations coming from Purdue and then written by the press. Isiah Thomas did slap Barnes in the face as retaliation for being slapped on the chin by Barnes just seconds before. This occurred after several such instances directed not only toward Isiah but at other members of our team. I had warned the officials repeatedly about what was happening from early in the game.

"The Purdue film of the Thomas-Barnes incident apparently does not show the aforementioned, but our game film does.

This will be shown at an open press conference at Assembly Hall in Bloomington Monday at 11 a.m. Any of you interested in what actually happened instead of reporting from hearsay evidence are cordially invited to see exactly what happened and why on my television show Sunday.

"I make this statement because of the totally unwarranted and unjustified verbal attack on one of the finest young men I have ever known, Isiah Thomas."

The effect of the exceptionally rough first game between the two schools, the three early technical fouls slapped on the two coaches in that game, the IU victory followed by a quick return visit to Purdue, and the late-week revelations of the Thomas punch created a tense atmosphere in Mackey Arena. The Knight statement wasn't involved; it wasn't released until halftime and never was given general knowledge within the arena.

But Barnes had the feeling someone had read a story in the *Lafayette Journal and Courier* that told of his charges, his denial that he was out for revenge ("There's no bad blood or anything . . . he's a good guy, but sometimes you just get frustrated out there"), and Barnes's intentions to "muscle him."

Barnes wasn't sent into the game until IU led 23-13, with 11:19 left in the half. He arrived to a thunderous ovation, and eight seconds later, he had a personal foul, charged with bumping Thomas as the Hoosier sophomore attempted to drive.

"I think they (officials) kinda protected Isiah a little," Barnes said. "I couldn't touch him. It looked like they read the paper and decided to be extra-careful." Barnes eventually played 13 minutes and fouled out, departing with a technical foul assessed, too, for his fall on the floor in reaction to the foul call.

"I was shocked," he said of the technical. "I don't think what I did was a hot dog move. I'm an emotional player. That was my reaction."

Meanwhile, Thomas was getting some special attention from officials, too. The guard widely recognized as the Big Ten's best ball handler was charged with three violations in the last four minutes — plus a charging foul assessed when he drove the baseline with Purdue ahead, 63-62, squirmed inside the defense and went up among the biggest of the Boilermakers to try a lay-up. He drew the contact he wanted in pursuit of a three-point play, but the call was that his leap outward from the baseline drive caused the contact.

His last unfriendly whistle came in his desperate burst downcourt in the last 10 seconds, seeking a tying basket. Thomas was called for double-dribble as he cut through defenders Walker and Morris to get a pass away.

"I didn't double-dribble — no way," Thomas said in the subdued IU dressing room.

He didn't pin the blame for the defeat on that call or any that preceded it. "The reason we lost was we missed so many free throws and we had too many bad plays," he said. "If we had hit our free throws, we would have won . . . and it was me more than anyone else."

The No. 3 free-throw shooter in the Big Ten going into the game (34-for-38 for .895), Thomas missed four in a row, three of them one-and-ones. IU as a team missed 13 of its 25 chances, and it was in that one phase of the game that the advantage built with solid play in most of its other components flitted away from the Hoosiers.

"From our standpoint, the biggest part of the ball game was the last five minutes of the first half," Knight said. "We had a chance to take the game over completely and we just didn't. We could have gone in 12 or 15 points ahead, but we made a couple turnovers and missed some shots and free throws." The Boilermakers closed within 42-37. "It was a lot to their credit, too," Knight said. "You just don't do that by yourself."

Keady said the Boilermakers fell behind (frequently by as

Ray Tolbert dunks between Purdue defense

much as 14 points) in the first half because "we shot the ball too quickly — we weren't patient enough.

"Rosie got us going again. And you have to give a lot of credit to Brian Walker. He was playing hurt, but he's really a courageous player and a super leader.

"Russell played great again, and Eifert earned a starting berth. He played a great game the second half against Kitchel."

Cross had 19 points in the first IU game, but he felt the 20 came harder. "Tolbert really played aggressive defense today," he said. "He was much more intense than in the last game. This time, I think he was kinda ready.

"But it wasn't as physical a game as it was at Indiana. There was some talking out there today, but mostly positive talk. At Indiana, it was mostly negative."

Cross said the Boilermakers "had been looking forward to this game all week." That's not the recommended way to survive in the Big Ten, but Purdue handled Minnesota by 15 points to survive the one in-between hurdle.

With the year's series squared, Keady seemed eager to patch over the Thomas-Barnes issue.

"I think it's been blown out of proportion," he said. "Nobody from our program has made any comment. I wish they'd cool it. Isiah's a great player, and Roosevelt is a very good player."

A tale of Knight and 'Jack' and 'Purdue mentality'

Indiana basketball coach Bob Knight's offensive against Purdue — in the wake of "sucker-punch" charges circulated against Isiah Thomas and Knight's claim that the charge was part of a "Purdue mentality" he had observed before — reached a milestone with "Jack," a guest on Knight's television show.

Knight invited Purdue athletic director George King to be a guest on the Sunday show. After King declined, Knight brought out a mule wearing a Purdue cap.

"I had a guy call me when he read that King wouldn't come on our TV show and he told me he had a guest for us that, if we'd like to use him, would probably express the same kinds of views and be very, very symbolic of a lot of the thinking at Purdue," Knight said, "and we're very fortunate to have him as our guest today.

"His first name is Jack. I'll let you figure out the last name."

The reactions to the incident included the predictable outrage in West Lafayette, complete with a formal complaint to the Big Ten, and some equally predictable chortling among Knight-IU fans, complete with "Jack" T-shirts that became an instant hit. Among other reactions were the following remarks in a column written in the Lafayette Journal and Courier by Purdue alumna and sports writer Paula Waltz:

"Sorry if you missed it, because I haven't laughed that loud and long for free since the networks ran out of the old, old 'I Love Lucy' reruns. Coach Bob Knight, that underhanded, no-good IU basketball coach, got Purdue's goat — er, not exactly goat — again on his television show.

"As the cameramen went into hysterics, the camera panned to a mule — see, the guy doesn't even know his mules from his donkeys — a mule in a Purdue hat, bridled by a stoical guy in a plaid, flannel shirt and a straw hat.

"True to his internationally renowned diplomacy, Knight predictably extended his hand in fellowship to Purdue's Russell Cross (Knight named him the Big Ten freshman of the year) and coach Gene Keady (Knight said he and Michigan's Bill Frieder were his choices as the league's coaches of the year).

"So, there, that dastardly Knight can be a nice guy, if you can take the Black and Gold blinders off long enough to notice.

"What exactly does Knight get blamed for here? Violating the

conference code of conduct? Maybe, but since when does a Big Ten coach not have the right to speak his mind, be it on a 'Purdue mentality' or whatever, in a country that guarantees a right to free speech?

"Is he guilty of bruising Purdue's pride? Apparently, and Purdue has asked the conference to protect the university's honor.

"Why can't Purdue carry its own banner? Why does Knight seem to be having all the fun? What's to stop Purdue from trading humor for humor?

"Why doesn't Purdue put its comedy writers to work and get into the fun and games?"

You're talking about a kid in Isiah Thomas that's as good a kid as I've ever been around in my life. I've never seen a kid who's gotten knocked around, knocked down, banged up more in basketball games than he has in the two years he's been here. And he never complains, he just keeps right on playing. This is one of the really fine kids playing college basketball today. Nothing that's happened in the 10 years that I've been at Indiana infuriated me more than the left-handed, ridiculous slaps, undeserved and unwarranted, that have been taken at Isiah Thomas

Bob Knight

INDIANA 66

	M	FG	FT	R	A	BS	St	PF	TP
T.Kitchel, f	40	4-8	8-11	6	1	0	1	2	16
Wittman, f	40	6-9	1-2	3	3	0	3	3	13
Tolbert, c	36	7-12	0-3	7	2	0	0	5	14
I.Thomas, g	40	9-16	2-6	8	7	0	2	4	20
Brown, g	24	1-6	0-1	0	3	0	0	2	2
J.Thomas	16	0-0	0-0	3	0	0	0	3	0
Risley	4	0-0	1-2	1	0	0	0	1	1
Team				5					
Totals		27-51	12-25	33	16	0	6	20	66

PURDUE 68

	M	FG	FT	R	A	BS	St	PF	TP
Edmonson, f	30	3-5	3-4	3	1	0	0	5	9
Benson, f	8	0-2	0-0	1	0	0	0	3	0
Cross, c	39	7-19	6-8	10	2	3	1	1	20
Walker, g	34	3-6	4-4	2	2	0	1	2	10
Morris, g	33	5-13	2-2	8	3	0	0	3	12
Scearce	17	2-5	0-0	4	1	0	1	1	4
J.Kitchel	5	0-0	1-2	0	0	0	0	1	1
Barnes	13	2-4	0-0	3	1	0	1	5	4
Eifert	13	2-4	0-0	3	0	0	0	0	4
Stallings	7	1-3	2-2	0	0	0	0	1	4
Hall	1	0-0	0-0	0	0	0	0	0	0
Team				3					
Totals		25-61	18-22	37	10	3	4	22	68

SCORE BY HALVES

Indiana	42	24— 66
Purdue	37	31— 68

Turnovers—Indiana 16, Purdue 13.
Technical fouls—Purdue bench, Tolbert (grabbing the rim), Barnes.

SHOOTING

	FG	Pct.	FT	Pct.
Indiana	27-51	.529	12-25	.480
Purdue	25-61	.410	18-22	.818

Officials—Jim Bain, Verl Sell, Ralph Rosser.
Attendance—14,123 (capacity).

I came back. I was a professional. I didn't expect to be praised. I still don't feel like I was a hero, but who am I to tell that to 220 million people who are expressing their appreciation?

Cmdr. Donald Sharer
Iranian hostage, IU alumnus

Life's all thumbs-up now for Don Sharer

Indiana 86, Northwestern 52

Randy Wittman admits he thought his night's work was over when he went to the bench with 15½ minutes to play and Indiana routing Northwestern, 46-19. Ray Tolbert followed 47 seconds later and it seemed a starters' exodus was under way.

But odd things happened as the two watched. Northwestern's shackled offense escaped its bondage with unsuspected ferocity, chewed up Indiana for a 17-1 point difference in little more than five minutes, and with 10:24 to go, for one of the rare times in his 10 big seasons and many such merciful blowouts at IU, Hoosier coach Bob Knight had to reach back to his bench to return Wittman and Tolbert to a rout that had become a contest.

It reverted almost as fast. Tolbert hit from near the basket, Isiah Thomas ran in six straight Hoosier points, and the lead jumped from its low point of 48-36 to 56-38, on its way to another of the mystifyingly regular Hoosier romps over Northwestern, 86-52, at Assembly Hall.

The victory kept IU even with Iowa atop the Big Ten, each 8-3. Four more teams are 7-4 — Michigan, Purdue, Illinois and Ohio State.

Knight wasn't happy to see the fat lead melt, but he liked his team's reaction to the situation.

"We got a little sloppy," he said, "but Northwestern had a very good streak. It was more a case of something they did than something we didn't do.

"But as the game started to go away from us, instead of letting it get to a point where we had to be cautious, our kids just took it away again.

"That really doesn't happen very often."

Wittman's shooting was a major reason the Hoosiers were so far out front early.

He hit his first five shots over the Wildcat zone defense to help the Hoosiers get out fast, 20-8.

Another big reason for that lead was defense: solid at all spots for the Hoosiers, particularly crucial with Tony Brown taking on

Northwestern scoring leader Rod Roberson and Tolbert going against the Wildcats' hard-working forward, Jim Stack.

At halftime, Roberson was 1-for-7 from the field with four points; Stack, 1-for-6 with five. Indiana was sailing freely, 35-13, and Roberson and Stack were the Wildcats' hot men. The other players they had on the floor were 1-for-10 that half as Northwestern missed 16 shots in a row in one 14½-minute stretch without a basket and finished the half 3-for-23 (.130).

"I thought those were the key match-ups," Northwestern coach Rich Falk said of the Tolbert-on-Stack and Brown-on-Roberson battles.

"We had a lot of problems getting our two key people untracked."

Both got rolling in the second half to lead the one brief Wildcat charge. Stack hit his first four shots and finished with 16 points and a game-high 11 rebounds, while Roberson also ran in four shots in a row and led the 'Cats with 17 points.

Wittman hit 9 of the 11 he shot in getting his IU high, 18 points. Indiana also got 12 points each from Tolbert and Isiah Thomas. Tolbert's 10 rebounds gave the Hoosiers 43-41 command of the backboards.

It was the 20th straight victory for IU over Northwestern. No. 19 came three weeks earlier at Evanston, 93-56, when, unlike this game, the Wildcats turned their firepower loose early.

"We hit our first six shots," Falk recalled, "and they beat us badly.

"They just play extremely well against us. Last year, we played two games against Indiana and the scores were pretty close (81-72 and 83-69), but I really didn't thnk we were in either game."

Multiple injuries sideline Kitchel

Kitchel a 6-8 sophomore who has started 18 of the Hoosiers' 23 games and averaged 10.8 points a game, took a hard fall going for the basket on a fast break during the victory.

Kitchel was taken to Bloomington Hospital for x-rays that showed no fractures. All on one play, however, he landed heavily on his back, taking a deep bruise in the area where he had back surgery that kept him out most of his first season on campus two years ago; pulled a groin muscle, and banged his head on the floor.

Kitchel went into the game with a big wrapping on his leg, to protect a thigh bruise that kept him out of practice a day.

Meeting Sharer 'thrill' for Isiah

Isiah Thomas met and shook hands with the President of the United States last summer. He was more stirred — "it was definitely a bigger thrill' — when Navy Cmdr. Donald Sharer, one of 52 American hostages freshly returned from Iran, walked into the Indiana dressing room before the game, talked briefly to the Hoosiers and shook hands with each of them.

"I have a lot of respect for the guy and I don't even know him," Thomas said. "He walked in, and he just had a presence about him."

Thomas clearly recalled Sharer's remarks inside that dressing room — by a man who said earlier in the day that memories of

Randy Wittman pulls rebound away from Rod Roberson

Fast break collision with NU's Michael Jenkins brings leg, back, head injuries all at once for IU's Ted Kitchel

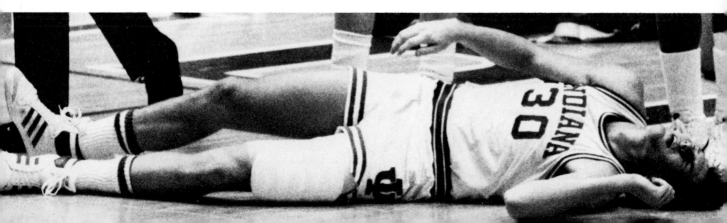

his student period at IU and such campus highlights as Hurryin' Hoosier basketball as played by fraternity brother Jimmy Rayl and others helped him while away the maddening hours during his 444 days in Iranian captivity.

"He just wished us luck," Thomas said, "and he told us it was the first time he had ever been invited back to a game since he left here.

"It's a shame he had to go through all that just to get back here."

The 15,229 inside Assembly Hall did their part to make the return memorable by giving Sharer a long and loud ovation after his pre-game introduction. Thomas and his Indiana teammates took it from there in the one-sided victory.

It was an emotional return of sorts, too, for Thomas, whose last game on the Assembly Hall court was the wild Purdue game that got him pounded around a few more times than usual and rebuked for a retaliatory punch he threw at Purdue's Roosevelt Barnes. In the intervening days, Thomas heard himself accused of a "sucker punch" at Purdue and defended ardently by Knight.

"To tell the truth, I didn't read all the stuff that came about it," Thomas said. "I read the statement he (Knight) released before the game at Purdue, and that's about all I read.

"I was aware he stuck up for me, and I *really* appreciated that."

Somehow, some way, the issue moved into the background neatly for the Hoosiers, who hardly figured to respond to the attention-diverting contretemps with the crisp basketball they played in ripping Northwestern.

It's supposed to be difficult to come up with a serious effort against a team once mastered as thoroughly as Northwestern was earlier this year by IU (93-56). Why, 'twasn't tough at all, the game's scoring leader, Wittman, said.

"The way we look at it, we just have to go into every game trying to play the best Indiana basketball we can," Wittman said.

It was an accurate rephrasing of the challenge Knight said he laid before the Hoosiers in the rematch. "We told our players they could either play Northwestern as if they had already beaten them pretty badly once before, or they could just go out and play their own game as well as they could," Knight said.

"They did that, and actually they have done that pretty well the last several games. The big thing you want to do is keep from losing games mentally. I would say since the Iowa game (four weeks and a 7-1 record ago), they have played pretty well, mentally. The one game we lost (68-66 at Purdue), if we put the ball in the basket at the free-throw line, we win. It wasn't mental."

Knight would settle for nothing more from Wittman the rest of the way than repeats of his play against Northwestern.

"The ball was going in," said Wittman, who hit nine of his 11 shots. "It was going up," Knight might have said. Knight never has questioned Wittman's shooting accuracy, but he has wondered at times if the man with the feathery touch was thinking shot as frequently as his skill would justify.

"It seemed like I had a lot of open shots," Wittman said. "And I felt good shooting it."

Thomas even got to the place in the game where he felt good shooting free throws again, after tumbling into a slump that made him 2-for-6 at Purdue.

"I hit my first one tonight," he recalled, "and then I missed my next two. All I heard was Coach screaming from the bench, 'Quit jumping around.'"

Thomas steadied, hit his last five free throws and went away feeling the stroke was back. "I hope so," he said.

Tolbert had a solid offensive night (12 points, on 6-for-7 shooting by the league's percentage leader, and 10 rebounds),

NORTHWESTERN 52									
	M	FG	FT	R	A	BS	St	PF	TP
Stack, f	37	5-13	6- 6	11	1	1	0	3	16
Rathel, f	11	1- 3	2- 2	1	0	0	0	0	4
Murray, c	32	1- 4	0- 1	3	0	2	0	2	2
Roberson, g	38	5-18	7- 8	3	1	0	0	3	17
Egan, g	21	2- 3	0- 0	1	1	0	0	3	3
Jenkins	16	0- 1	0- 1	1	0	0	0	2	0
Schultz	28	1- 5	1- 1	6	0	0	1	2	3
Aaron	13	3- 8	0- 1	1	0	0	2	2	6
Blackard	2	0- 0	0- 0	0	0	0	0	0	0
Schner	1	0- 0	0- 0	0	0	1	0	0	0
Schnepp	1	0- 0	0- 0	0	0	0	0	0	0
Team				4					
Totals		18-55	16-20	31	4	3	3	17	52

INDIANA 86									
	M	FG	FT	R	A	BS	St	PF	TP
Kitchel, f	14	2- 7	0- 0	4	2	0	0	1	4
Wittman, f	25	9-11	0- 1	5	2	0	0	1	18
Tolbert, c	27	6- 7	0- 0	10	0	0	2	2	12
I.Thomas, g	34	3- 8	6- 8	5	5	0	2	2	12
Brown, g	20	2- 7	1- 2	5	2	0	2	3	5
J.Thomas	26	2- 6	2- 2	6	4	0	3	2	6
Bouchie	20	4- 7	0- 0	2	0	0	0	2	8
Franz	9	0- 1	4- 4	0	2	0	1	3	4
Risley	4	0- 1	2- 4	1	0	0	0	0	2
Turner	9	4- 5	1- 1	1	2	0	0	1	9
Grunwald	3	1- 1	0- 1	0	0	0	0	2	2
Isenbarger	6	1- 2	0- 0	2	1	0	1	1	2
LaFave	3	1- 1	0- 0	0	0	0	0	0	2
Team				2					
Totals		35-64	16-23	43	20	0	11	20	86

SCORE BY HALVES

Northwestern		13	39— 52
Indiana		35	51— 86

Turnovers—Northwestern 23, Indiana 15.
Technical foul—Northwestern bench.

SHOOTING

	FG	Pct.	FT	Pct.
Northwestern	18-55	.327	16-20	.800
Indiana	35-64	.547	16-23	.696

Officials—George Solomon, Tom Rucker, Don Edwards.
Attendance—15,229 (sellout).

but his defensive work against Stack was Tolbert's primary contribution.

"I knew I had to start bearing down and playing better defense," Tolbert said. "I've had a tendency to let my man flash and get away from me. I had to know where Stack was and where the ball was, all the time.

"He's a good player — smart with the ball. He shoots jumping in, which gets him a lot of free throws."

Before even the player introductions, Knight went to the courtside microphone to deliver a compliment to the Assembly Hall audience that sharply contrasted with the criticism that has been directed at the home crowds of both Purdue and Notre Dame this week.

"One of the really great things about coaching and playing at Indiana is being able to play in front of you people," Knight said.

"I know that sometimes we haven't played as well as you would have liked, and sometimes I haven't coached as well as you would have liked, but we have always been extremely proud to play in front of what we think is the best basketball crowd in America.

"You have been tremendously supportive of our team and tremendously courteous to our opponents. Let's make sure we keep it that way. Just keep being the same kind of crowd that you've always been."

Indiana 59, Wisconsin 52

Randy Wittman's consistent outside sniping carried the day offensively for Indiana as the Hoosiers stayed tied with Iowa for the Big Ten basketball lead by edging Wisconsin, 59-52.

Only nine days earlier at Bloomington, Indiana embarrassed the Badgers, 89-64. That one didn't help the Hoosiers this time. "We knew for sure Indiana wasn't 25 points better than us," said Badger guard Greg Dandridge, a leader of the Wisconsin upset attempt.

In the Assembly Hall game, Dandridge never put up a shot and he was victimized frequently by Hoosier guards Isiah Thomas and Tony Brown — stripped of the basketball a couple times when he was trying to play offense and singed by long-range shots when he was in his out-front position in the Badger zone defense.

This time, Dandridge did some burning.

Wisconsin shut out the Hoosiers for the first four minutes, and the 6-0 lead the Badgers built during that time included a mid-court theft and layup by Dandridge.

Wittman finally got Indiana going with a banked jump shot with 15:47 left in the half, but the Hoosiers didn't get ahead until Landon Turner sank two free throws with 6:48 to go in the half for a 16-15 margin. In the last minute of the half, two free throws by Tony Brown and a steal and lay-up pulled off by Steve Risley and Jim Thomas sent Indiana to the dressing room with its biggest lead, 33-28.

Just when Badger spunk seemed to be easing, though, Dandridge's quick hands came through — twice.

IU was ahead 36-32 and Wittman appeared headed for a good shot or foul on a drive up the baseline when Dandridge stepped in front of him and picked the ball out of his hands as he went up to shoot. "I just rotated over there the way we're supposed to do when someone gets by his man," Dandridge said. "I was just fortunate to reach out and get the basketball."

He hurried the Badgers downcourt for a jump shot by Claude Gregory and the IU lead — seven points after Wittman's shot opening the second half — was down to 36-34.

Dandridge almost wiped it out entirely. When Isiah Thomas tried to dribble away from him and set up the Hoosier offense, Dandridge flicked out a hand again and punched the ball loose.

All the elements of a supreme moment were there for the aroused Badger crowd (a season-high 9,026) and for Dandridge. After his steal from the most noted guard in the league put the crowd on its feet, Dandridge left Thomas hanging with a behind-the-back dribble that raised the decibel level a little higher and opened a 2-on-1 invitation for a tying basket. Dandridge did everything perfectly, pulling the defender to him and dropping off a pass to teammate Dan Hastings for a wide-open lay-up.

Hastings missed.

"We missed some bunnies, there's no question about it," Badger coach Bill Cofield said.

Wisconsin got the ball back with one more chance to tie, and Cofield remembered that possession well, too. Larry Petty went for the tying basket with a short hook shot but missed. Gregory muscled his way to the rebound, but missed from in close. He kept muscling to get his own rebound and missed from closer. "We had four shots to tie it," Cofield said. "You just can't beat a team like Indiana missing shots like that."

Wittman beat back the Badger rally with a jump shot, and IU moved the lead on up to 41-34 before Wisconsin scrambled back again. Gregory's three-point play with 8:17 to go cut the IU lead to 45-44 and set up another Cofield memory. Risley went to the free-throw line for IU with a one-and-one and missed, but Wittman wrestled away the rebound to maintain Hoosier possession and drew a foul on the play. He hit both chances to restore a three-point lead. "That was the key play — we didn't get the rebound and we ended up letting them score," Cofield said.

Still, the Hoosiers had to do their best job all year of protecting a slim late-game lead with a possession game before they could go home as winners. The lead was only three when the Hoosiers picked Risley loose for a lay-up at 6:08, Wittman for one at 4:01 and Isiah Thomas for a short jump shot at 2:40. Each time, the Hoosiers ran off some time before getting the shot, and each time Wisconsin retaliated with a basket to keep the heat on.

It didn't diminish till Isiah Thomas broke the Wisconsin press for a close-in shot that lifted IU to a 57-52 lead with 38 seconds left. Jim Thomas gave the Hoosiers possession again by rebounding John Bailey's miss, and Ray Tolbert dropped in a rebound basket at the IU end with 20 seconds left for the final padding.

Knight noted the 18 points and 10 rebounds the Hoosiers got from Risley, Turner and Steve Bouchie, who filled in for injured Ted Kitchel.

"They really helped us," Knight said. "But the things that had been good for us didn't work out so well, with the exception of Wittman's play. I thought he did an excellent job."

Kitchel didn't make the trip, staying home for treatment of the groin pull and back bruise he sustained in a fall during the Northwestern game.

Wittman was IU's only double-figure scorer with 15 points. Gregory had 21 points and 11 rebounds for Wisconsin.

The day's play left IU and Iowa 9-3 and tied for first, with three weeks and six games left in the Big Ten race. Illinois took second place by itself (at 8-4) by winning at Ohio State, while Michigan and Purdue lost to drop to 7-5.

'I'll take it,' says unapologetic Knight

Knight never has been one to rejoice over an inelegant performance, even a winning one, but the Hoosier basketball coach took a Valentine's Day gift with neither hesitation nor remorse.

"We played poorly enough to lose, and we won," Knight said after the Hoosiers escaped.

"I'll take it. Damned right I'll take it.

"I keep going back to so many games we could have won if we just made the play, or made free throws. Games we *should* have won.

"I'm not going to apologize for this one."

It wasn't pretty. Neither was it fun, a mildly gloomy winner, IU guard Isiah Thomas, indicated.

"We were just so lethargic," Thomas said. "We were just out there.

"You can kinda feel it. I'm sure people can see it. Just . . . blah."

The natural suspicion was that the 25-point Hoosier victory over the Badgers dulled the IU edge for the return match.

"I don't think that had anything to do with it," Thomas said.

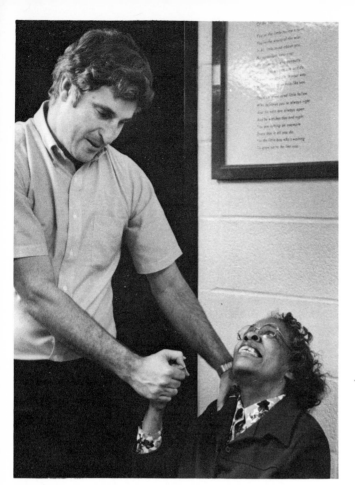

Bob Knight congratulated by Odessa Woodson

"Speaking only for myself, I thought I prepared myself to play.

"But I didn't play like it. It was like I was trying to think of everything I should do and by the time I got ready to do it, it was too late.

"Coach kept yelling at me about moving sharp and making quick cuts, but I'd just get out there and the pace of the game was slow and I just went with it.

"We won. We didn't play particularly well and we didn't deserve to win, but we won."

Thomas had a day when even his good plays became bad ones. IU led 49-44 with less than six minutes to play when Wisconsin's Greg Dandridge missed a shot from the side. Thomas went up to clear the rebound — for possession, *with* a five-point lead.

The possession didn't last long. "I tried to dribble away," Thomas said, the play vivid in memory, "and Petty hit the ball." Dandridge snatched it up and bolted to a lay-up that picked the Badgers up again.

It took more than five anxious minutes and three trade-offs of baskets by each team before IU again got the ball when five points ahead.

It could have been worse for the Hoosiers. Wisconsin was down 47-44 when Tolbert, playing behind the 6-9 Petty, slipped and fell just as Wisconsin tried to lob a pass leading Petty to the basket. Petty's feet got tangled with Tolbert's, and the Badger fell, too, the ball going out of bounds and over to IU.

Cofield wasn't sure the officials did him in on the play, but he was convinced Lady Luck did. "Larry was trying to be a nice guy and not step on Tolbert, and he hurt himself instead," Cofield said. "He strained a calf muscle. He didn't seem to have the explosion under the boards after that."

Petty said, "I think they should have called a foul. He (Tolbert) didn't mean to, but he tripped me. It just shocked me that they got the ball."

A couple minutes later, IU's lead was 49-46 when Wisconsin got the ball back on a Hoosier turnover. Cofield took a time out, urged patience from his ballhandlers and got it, then watched in anguish as Petty set up his wide body in position to take a pass just to the left of the basket, spun for a five-foot shot and missed.

"Tolbert got a hand on that one and tipped it just a little," Petty said. "That's why it missed." Tolbert also came through with a big rebound to complete the fruitless assault for the Badgers.

"We missed a lot of chippies — 8, 10, 12-foot shots," Cofield said.

Cofield made the Hoosiers his pick to wind up on top.

"I think Indiana's the best team, and I think Iowa's the second-best," he said when asked to assess the title race.

"And maybe Ohio State's beginning to come on."

The Buckeyes let him down before his lines hit ink. Illinois dumped the Bucks at Columbus to shove OSU two full games behind Iowa and IU.

"I have to rate Indiana up there because I think they have a beautiful blend of quickness and intelligence," Cofield said. "And they have depth. We got their big men in foul trouble and it didn't make any difference to them. They just kept coming in with players who did a good job.

"We tried to do some things differently this time against them. They switch very well on downscreens and cross-screens. They gambled on leaving some of our guys open in the first game, and we didn't really try to take advantage of it. This time, everyone had the green light to shoot if there was an opening.

"I thought we did a pretty good job of that, and we were patient enough. We just have to play a flawless basketball game to win, and we didn't do that."

INDIANA 59

	M	FG	FT	R	A	BS	St	PF	TP
Risley, f	26	4- 8	0- 1	7	1	0	0	4	8
Wittman, f	40	6-10	3- 5	4	1	0	0	1	15
Tolbert, c	35	3-10	2- 3	7	1	1	0	3	8
I.Thomas, g	34	4- 6	1- 2	2	2	0	0	2	9
Brown, g	24	1- 3	4- 4	3	0	0	1	1	6
J.Thomas	22	1- 4	1- 1	2	2	0	0	0	3
Turner	17	3- 5	2- 3	3	1	0	1	5	8
Bouchie	2	1- 2	0- 0	0	0	0	0	1	2
Team				5					
Totals		23-48	13-19	33	8	1	2	17	59

WISCONSIN 52

	M	FG	FT	R	A	BS	St	PF	TP
Gregory, f	39	7-19	7- 8	11	0	0	0	5	21
Kreklow, f	26	0- 2	2- 2	3	3	0	1	5	2
Petty, c	40	3- 8	3- 4	4	1	2	0	3	9
Bailey, g	26	7-11	0- 0	0	1	1	2	4	14
Dandridge, g	40	3- 6	0- 0	4	1	0	1	1	6
Hildebrand	6	0- 1	0- 2	1	0	0	0	1	0
Hastings	16	0- 3	0- 0	2	2	0	0	1	0
Mitchell	7	0- 0	0- 0	0	0	0	0	0	0
Team				3					
Totals		20-50	12-16	28	8	3	4	20	52

SCORE BY HALVES

Indiana		33	26— 59
Wisconsin		28	24— 52

Turnovers—Indiana 15, Wisconsin 13.
Technical foul—Bailey (grabbing the rim).

SHOOTING

	FG	Pct.	FT	Pct.
Indiana	23-48	.479	13-19	.684
Wisconsin	20-50	.400	12-16	.750

Officials—Rich Weiler, Darwin Brown, Eric Harmon.
Attendance—9,026.

Iowa 78, Indiana 65

Iowa has the Big Ten basketball lead all to itself, but the pressure hasn't eased much for either the Hawkeyes or their primary pursuers, Indiana and Illinois.

Iowa broke a tie with Indiana by turning back the Hoosiers at rollicking Iowa Fieldhouse, 78-65. That made Iowa 10-3 in league play, a game up on Indiana and Illinois.

The Hawkeyes' victory margin belies the struggle that went on before they sent Indiana home beaten.

The Hoosiers led at halftime, 37-35, and still were tied at 49-49 after Landon Turner's basket with 10:29 to play.

Iowa took charge in one dizzying half-minute flurry.

Sophomore Bob Hansen broke the tie for the Hawks by hitting two free throws with 10:13 to go. IU drove through the Iowa press, but Ray Tolbert missed an off-balance lay-up. The Hawks, working their running game for one of the rare times in the game, broke guard Kenny Arnold loose for a driving lay-up that opened a 53-49 lead.

A midcourt turnover sent Arnold on the way again, and his lay-up opened a 55-49 lead with 9:30 to go.

That was the margin that Iowa successfully worked with the rest of the way. Indiana cut it to four points a few times but never got the ball back with the lead that slim.

The closest the Hoosiers came was after Isiah Thomas hit a jump shot that cut the Iowa lead to 65-59, then drew a foul from Vince Brookins when the Hawkeye forward tried to break past him to get an inbounds pass against an IU press. When Thomas hit both halves of the one-and-one awarded him, it was 65-61 with 1:14 left.

The Hoosiers' two Thomases, Isiah and Jim, double-teamed Iowa's Kevin Boyle in the backcourt, and Isiah punched the ball free. But he made contact doing it, officials ruled, so Boyle went to the free-throw line with 1:07 to go.

For Iowa down the stretch, trips to the free-throw line meant an automatic two points. The Hawkeyes responded to game and season pressure by hitting 13 straight free throws in the last two minutes, helping them to finish with a 30-9 free-throw margin that nullified Indiana's 28-24 field-goal edge.

After Boyle sank his free throws, Isiah Thomas struck back with a drive than penetrated the Iowa defense and produced a close-in basket and a 67-63 score with 1:03 left.

Iowa got the ball up-court after that basket, and with 49 seconds left, Hansen drew Randy Wittman's fifth foul.

It was Hansen who hit four free throws in the last 10 seconds to clinch Iowa's 56-53 victory over IU at Assembly Hall Jan. 22. "Bobby's got so much confidence now he doesn't think he's ever gonna miss," Iowa coach Lute Olson said.

Hansen hit both after the Wittman foul to restore the six-point edge and start a wild finish.

It blew open when Isiah Thomas tried to get open inside the Iowa defense while Tony Brown was rushing the ball up-court for IU. Krafcisin cut off Thomas with an extended arm, Thomas flailed back with his own right arm as he broke through, and his back-handed swing popped Krafcisin in the mouth.

Official Gary Muncy stepped forward in a hurry, calling it a flagrant foul (two shots, plus ball out of bounds) and ejecting Thomas. Krafcisin hit the two free throws, and one playing second later, Hansen was back at the free-throw line to shoot a one-and-one plus a two-shot technical foul assessed against Knight. Iowa wound up scoring seven points without Indiana's ever getting possession, and the margin ballooned.

"I thought it was an excellent basketball game, very well-played by both teams right up to the end, when some circumstances made the score look more one-sided than it really was," Olson said.

Indiana had an odd night offensively. The Hoosiers solved the Iowa defense for good shots virtually throughout the game, but two of the best shooters on the IU roster, Kitchel (who played 18 minutes after being out a week with a groin pull) and Wittman, combined to go 2-for-14.

Turner made up for some of that by coming off the bench to lead IU with 18 points. Tolbert had 17 and Isiah Thomas 16, and those three hit 22 of 35 shots.

They did most of the scoring as Indiana stood off Iowa's attempt to break free in the first half. The Hawkeyes scored 11 points in a row to take a 17-10 lead, but IU stuck back with an 11-1 flurry of its own to go up, 21-18.

Twice in the first half, Iowa came up with four-point plays. Each time the Hawkeyes hit a shot that was in the air when officials called a Hoosier for an under-the-basket foul, and each time the Hawks capitalized fully by adding one-and-one free-throw conversions to the basket.

The second of those gave the lead back to Iowa, 22-21, but with 1:40 left in the half, Isiah Thomas scored to give Indiana a 35-30 lead. Hansen's three-point play and his corner shot three

INDIANA 65

	M	FG	FT	R	A	BS	St	PF	TP
Risley, f	25	1- 2	0- 1	9	1	0	2	2	2
Wittman, f	27	1- 6	0- 0	1	4	0	0	5	2
Tolbert, c	34	8-13	1- 2	7	1	2	1	3	17
I.Thomas, g	39	7-13	2- 2	1	4	0	1	4	16
J.Thomas, g	13	0- 0	0- 0	0	3	0	0	1	0
Turner	27	7- 9	4- 4	5	3	0	0	5	18
Kitchel	18	1- 8	0- 0	2	2	0	0	3	2
Grunwald	4	0- 0	2- 2	1	0	0	0	2	2
Brown	9	3- 4	0- 1	0	1	0	0	1	6
Bouchie	3	0- 0	0- 0	1	0	0	0	1	0
Franz	1	0- 0	0- 0	0	0	0	0	2	0
Team				1					
Totals		28-55	9-12	28	19	2	4	29	65

IOWA 78

	M	FG	FT	R	A	BS	St	PF	TP
Brookins, f	34	8-11	3- 6	4	2	0	1	3	19
Waite, f	23	1- 2	3- 6	4	1	0	1	3	5
Krafcisin, c	32	6-13	6- 7	6	0	1	2	3	18
Boyle, g	37	1- 5	5- 6	5	3	0	0	1	7
Arnold, g	31	6-10	1- 2	2	5	0	0	5	13
Hansen	25	2- 4	10-11	3	3	0	1	2	14
Carfino	9	0- 0	2- 2	0	0	0	0	1	2
Henry	3	0- 0	0- 0	0	0	0	0	0	0
Anderson	6	0- 0	0- 0	1	1	0	0	0	0
Team				6					
Totals		24-45	30-40	30	15	1	5	18	78

SCORE BY HALVES

Indiana	37	28—	65
Iowa	35	43—	78

Turnovers—Indiana 14, Iowa 14.

Technical fouls—Tolbert (grabbing the rim), I.Thomas, Indiana bench.

SHOOTING

	FG	Pct.	FT	Pct.
Indiana	28-55	.509	9-12	.750
Iowa	24-45	.533	30-40	.750

Officials—Gary Muncy, Bob Showalter, Bill Herzog.
Attendance—13,365.

seconds ahead of the halftime gun pulled Iowa within 37-35 at the break.

The Hawks jumped out, 43-39, on three Krafcisin baskets and one by Arnold early in the second half, but Indiana took a shortlived lead, 47-45, on Tolbert's basket at 13:20, and the Hoosiers followed two straight Vince Brookins baskets with the shot by Turner that created the 49-49 tie and set up the decisive flurry.

"We had some very, very clutch shooting by Vince Brookins and by Bobby Hansen at the free-throw line," Olson said.

"We felt going in Indiana has too many good shooters for us to beat 'em with a few fast-break baskets and we'd need one or two spurts. And that was basically what happened.

"We went in thinking we could win. If you can win in Bloomington, you can win anywhere."

Brookins had 19 points, Krafcisin 18, Hansen 14 and Arnold 13 for Iowa. The Hawks became the first Big Ten team to outshoot Indiana, hitting 53.3 percent of their shots to 50.9 for IU (16-9).

Thomas leaves Iowa ejected, embarrassed

If there were such a thing as a red carpet at black-and-gold-loving Iowa, Isiah Thomas would have received it when he was a warmly welcomed recruiting prospect a couple years ago.

After being thrown out of a basketball game for the first time in his life, he left Iowa City chagrined.

Thomas was feverishly trying to rally Indiana from behind in the last minute of the Hoosiers' battle with Iowa for the Big Ten lead when he ran afoul of an official (Muncy).

Thomas had scored six straight Hoosier points, but IU still trailed, 69-63, when Thomas tried to burst open inside the Iowa zone defense.

He got open, but Muncy ruled he did it with an intentional rap in the mouth to Krafcisin.

Olson applauded the call at the time and said later, "I didn't see how there could be too much question. Isiah swung and hit Krafcisin in the mouth. I was disappointed in Isiah. I think it was totally out of place. I have more respect for him than that."

Olson's aggrieved player, Krafcisin, seemed considerably less outraged.

Krafcisin replayed the incident in post-game press questioning.

"I think the last three times before that when we were in a zone, Isiah got the ball inside on us," Krafcisin said.

"We talked about that at a time out. Then, out of the corner of my eye, I saw him coming from down low to get open, and I reached out an arm to try to delay him. I didn't want to grab him — I'm not a dirty player. I just wanted to reach out and hold him back a little.

"What he did was a reflex action. He tried to hit my arm away

Isiah Thomas — Hungry?

and hit me in the mouth. I think he was a little frustrated. I thought he hit me with an elbow, but the guys on the bench said it looked like the back of his hand.

"He apologized afterward. He said he didn't mean it. It was the kind of thing that happens all the time. I got hit in the mouth here last year, too.

"I think he (Thomas) is a heck of a player. He had a good night tonight — what was he, 7-for-13?

"I don't think he's a crybaby or anything like that. He's done a whole lot for Indiana basketball, and for the country, really, with the Pan-American Games and everything."

Thomas called his own play "just dumb. It was stupid on my part.

"It was the first time I've ever been ejected from a game, but I can't blame the official for throwing me out."

He was the lowest of the Hoosiers on the trip home from Iowa, and he wasn't in a particularly analytical frame of mind. But he did have a concise explanation of how things got away from the Hoosiers in the second half. "We missed a lot of opportunities, and we made a lot of mistakes," he said.

Olson fully enjoyed the victory. "The thing that really pleases me is that we met an outstanding basketball team that played outstanding basketball," he said, "yet we stayed with what we were doing and we were able to win.

"I'm very pleased with the outcome. But at the same time, I want to emphasize that this is just one game. The big concern to us is that this isn't overplayed. I still feel both of us (Indiana and Iowa) have a tough row to hoe from here on. It would be a minor miracle if either one were to go undefeated the rest of the way."

> *I remember when wrestling was the big thing here, and basketball took a back seat. Now we've come into our own. Last year people around the state were wondering if we'd be going to the NCAA tournament or the NIT. Now there's no doubt where we'll be going. We have a great shot at winning the title, but we could get knocked off, too. We've seen other teams lose, and it could happen to us.*
>
> **Bob Hansen**
> Iowa

Where it all began — Ray Tolbert gets opening tip from 7-2 Randy Breuer at the start of 10-game championship drive

Indiana 74, Minnesota 63

Tenth-year pro George McGinnis sat on the Indiana bench in Assembly Hall for the first time and watched a play unfold that was routine for him in his one IU year.

Indiana — which at game's end was to look like a breezing winner in the history books, 74-63 — was struggling when the play came. The Hoosiers had blown a big early lead but fought back to cleave open a 47-42 edge over Minnesota when 6-10 Hoosier Landon Turner cleared a rebound off at the Gophers' end, wheeled, started up court and found nobody in front of him.

Isiah Thomas was running alongside him, like a terrier beside a Great Dane. "Isiah was saying, 'Gimme the ball — *Landon*, gimme the *ball*,'" Turner said later.

Landon wasn't giving the ball to anybody. "All I saw was dunk," he said. Never allowing memories of a dunk that he missed at Iowa to haunt him or cow him, Turner bolted right on up the middle to slam home a dunk that put the Hoosiers up, 49-42, and touched off a vocal explosion in Assembly Hall.

"I just wanted him to give me the ball, let me take it to the foul line and give it back to him," Thomas said. "I just *didn't* want a turnover."

From the sidelines, IU coach Bob Knight let the results speak for themselves. "Thomas was so close to him," Knight said, "I'm not sure if he gave it up if they were going to be able to take it all the way.

"He did what he should have."

In reviewing terms, the play was the production's dramatic highlight but not its *denouement*. Minnesota scrambled back by scoring the next two baskets and the battle was on again.

It was 54-52 when the Gophers got the ball back on an IU turnover. John Wiley tried to tie it with a jump shot but missed. The Gophers' 7-foot-2 center, Randy Breuer, got the rebound but missed the shot. Minnesota recovered one more time but Mark Hall, one of the best percentage shooters in the league the last three years, missed. "We had three straight medium-range jump shots to tie it, and we missed all three," Gopher coach Jim Dutcher said. "That really hurt us."

The margin was still two when Thomas slipped the ball to Turner for a press-beating lay-up that made the IU lead 58-54. The gigantic Breuer tried to cut into it by pulling off an offensive rebound, but he brought the ball down to terrier range, Thomas ripped it away, took off on a sortie of his own and beat Wiley for a lay-up that gave the Hoosiers 60-54 command with 6:45 to play.

It shrank to 60-57, but Indiana had worked Minnesota into one-and-one foul problems by then and the Hoosiers were playing things cautiously. Also, well.

Ray Tolbert eased the tension of the moment by hitting both halves of a one-and-one, then capped a minute of Hoosier passing and weaving by spotting a hole in the Gopher defense and driving through it for a lay-up that amounted to a back-breaker.

"Breuer was on me and he had four fouls," Tolbert said. "Isiah told me just before that if he came out to guard me on the high post I could get around him. I saw an opening, just took off and fortunately I got the basket."

Indiana's ball-control game worked equally well the rest of the way. Once, Randy Wittman popped free for a lay-up after a screen and a pass from Thomas. Four other times, Hoosiers went to the free throw line with one-and-one chances and came away with both points: Wittman twice, Thomas and Steve Risley once each.

With nine seconds left, Knight had his first chance in a while to pull his starters for an appreciative round of applause at the end of a tight and winning game.

Minnesota arrived on a high. The Gophers came in from a victory at Ohio State that had eased them back into the NCAA tournament picture, if not the Big Ten championship fight. "I think we were playing well," Dutcher said. "I didn't think we had a great one today.

"But we did have some pretty good spurts."

The Gophers appeared out of the game when Indiana — with five early baskets by Tolbert — broke away to a 20-8 lead. Thomas hit three shots in a row to make it 30-16 with 4:35 to go in the half, and even after Knight pulled Tolbert and Thomas to avoid a third foul for either before the half, the Hoosiers used five points by Risley and a couple Turner baskets to move ahead 39-24 with a minute left in the half.

It was a long, long minute for the Hoosiers. Minnesota's press tore holes in the revised Hoosier lineup, and the Gophers ran in eight points in a row to get to halftime down only 39-32.

MINNESOTA 63

	M	FG	FT	R	A	BS	St	PF	TP
Holmes, f	15	1- 5	0- 0	6	1	0	0	0	2
Wiley, f	27	2- 6	0- 0	5	5	1	1	4	4
Breuer, c	25	1- 7	7-12	4	2	0	1	4	9
Tucker, g	35	5-11	2- 2	1	4	0	2	5	12
Hall, g	34	7-11	0- 0	5	1	0	1	3	14
Mitchell	18	7-12	0- 1	2	3	0	4	2	14
Coleman	19	2- 7	0- 0	3	0	0	0	0	4
Howell	19	2- 6	0- 0	3	0	0	1	3	4
Petersen	5	0- 0	0- 0	1	1	0	0	1	0
Thompson	3	0- 2	0- 0	2	0	0	0	0	0
Team				1					
Totals		27-67	9-15	33	17	1	10	22	63

INDIANA 74

	M	FG	FT	R	A	BS	St	PF	TP
Kitchel, f	35	3- 6	0- 0	2	4	0	1	4	6
Turner, f	37	8-11	0- 0	9	2	1	0	2	16
Tolbert, c	35	7-10	5- 6	5	1	5	0	3	19
I.Thomas, g	37	4- 8	5- 6	3	8	0	4	4	13
Wittman, g	39	3- 5	7- 8	1	2	0	1	2	13
Risley	7	1- 1	5- 6	1	0	0	0	0	7
Brown	1	0- 0	0- 0	0	1	0	0	0	0
Bouchie	3	0- 0	0- 0	0	0	0	0	0	0
Grunwald	1	0- 0	0- 0	0	0	0	0	1	0
J.Thomas	2	0- 0	0- 0	0	0	0	0	0	0
Franz	1	0- 0	0- 0	0	0	0	0	0	0
Isenbarger	1	0- 0	0- 0	0	0	0	0	0	0
LaFave	1	0- 0	0- 0	0	0	0	0	0	0
Team				8					
Totals		26-41	22-26	29	18	6	6	16	74

SCORE BY HALVES

Minnesota		32	31— 63
Indiana		39	35— 74

Turnovers—Minnesota 15, Indiana 19.

SHOOTING

	FG	Pct.	FT	Pct.
Minnesota	27-67	.403	9-15	.600
Indiana	26-41	.634	22-26	.846

Officials—Richie Wieler, Darwin Brown, Malcolm Hemphill.

Attendance—16,915 (sellout).

A straight-down view of Ray Tolbert going straight up for rebound

It was a comeback that the Gophers continued in the opening minutes of the second half. Two free thows by Breuer with 17:02 left pulled Minnesota within 40-38.

Wittman, whose outside shooting was a key factor in IU's earlier overtime victory at Minneapolis, turned the Gophers back with a jump shot off a screen. But Gary Holmes made it a two-point game again with a baseline shot, and Tolbert avoided a catch-up chance for the Gophers by hitting a 15-foot jump shot for a 44-40 lead.

The Turner breakaway and the Hoosiers' game-closing efficiency followed, "I was as pleased with the way we played the last five minutes as I was perturbed about the last two minutes of the first half," Knight said.

Tolbert led the Hoosiers with 19 points, his season high, and he also had five rebounds and five blocked shots. "Tolbert's playing about as well as I've ever seen him play," Dutcher said.

"Tolbert played very hard and very well," Knight said.

The Hoosiers also got 16 points and a team-high nine rebounds from Turner in his first Big Ten start this year, and Thomas and Wittman scored 13 each. Minnesota had 14 points each from Hall and Darryl Mitchell and 12 from Trent Tucker.

IU shot .634, the Hoosiers' fourth time over .600 this year and third in Big Ten play. Minnesota managed only .403, about par against the Hoosiers in league competition this year — except for Iowa's .533 at Iowa City.

The "Three-I League" at the top of the Big Ten stayed in step. Iowa climbed to 11-3 with a 67-62 victory at Purdue, and Illinois joined Indiana at 10-4 by beating Michigan State, 82-62.

Hoosiers tired, Knight admits

Against Illinois, Indiana led by 19 points late in the first half, staggered into the last few minutes and got to the intermission with a lead down to nine. At Purdue, the Hoosiers led by 14, but last-minute problems dropped that to five by halftime and the Boilermakers went on to win. Against Minnesota, a Hoosier lead that was 15 with a minute to go in the half was seven when halftime came.

"We don't try to make 'em close — believe me, we don't," Tolbert said.

"Everything collapsed in on us," said Wittman. "We're lucky it didn't cost us."

"Instead of them going to the lockerroom thinking they're beaten, they were thinking they were the ones that had momentum."

Isiah Thomas, who was on the sidelines to protect against foul trouble when the last-minute chaos came, felt he over-reacted to the problem.

"When I went into the lockerroom, I just wanted to get back out there and get things re-established," he said.

"The first time we had the ball, we made one pass and I took a jump shot from the top of the key. It wasn't a bad shot, but at the time we could have got a better shot. I wasn't thinking enough about the situation."

The Hoosiers on this day were a little more harsh in criticism of themselves than their tough grader, Knight, was.

"We were tired," Knight said.

"I made a mistake Friday. We worked about 45 minutes and it should have been 10. That was my fault.

"We played hard at Iowa. We went right down to the last minute and we lost. When you play a game like that and win, it sorta carries itself through, but when you lose, it's tough. Our kids were really drained.

"We had to prepare for some things Minnesota was doing differently than the first time we played them. They're pressing now and they didn't press us at all in the first game. Breuer has improved. We had some things to go over, but perhaps we could have done it talking, not working."

So the Hoosiers, who were about as precise at both ends of the court as they have been all year in opening a 37-22 lead, jerked momentum away from the Gophers when the lead had shrunk to two and pulled smoothly away from them again at the end.

Breuer had scored 55 points in his last two games. "Obviously, we've got to try to take that away from them," Knight said. "If he gets 27 against us, we're not going to win."

Tolbert got the primary assignment, "but it wasn't me guarding Breuer, it was our team defense," Tolbert said. "Every time he got the ball below the foul line, our guys sagged in on him."

"We just had to take some things away from him. The first game (Breuer scored 21), we let him come across the lane at will. We changed that a little today."

Breuer scored only one field goal all day, and he was charged with five turnovers. "Randy just was struggling," Dutcher said. "He missed some shots he normally would hit. He's our best free-throw shooter and he missed his first four free throws. That was an indication right away that he wasn't at the top of his game."

Minnesota tried to counter the Hoosier sag by using Breuer as a feeder. He passed off for a couple of driving lay-ups early in the second half, but more frequently than that players put up shots that Dutcher didn't really want.

"They didn't guard our forwards," Dutcher said. "They gave either Wiley or (Zebedee) Howell or (Andy) Thompson the shot and they didn't have enough patience not to take it.

"It's hard to tell a guy not to take an open shot, but that's what you have to do."

Image unwelcome, Isiah Thomas says

Isiah Thomas has known more notoriety in the last few weeks than at any previous time in his basketball life. His inglorious exit in the last minute of the Hoosiers' loss at Iowa, when he was thrown out for what an official saw as a flagrant foul, plainly disturbed him.

"I don't want people thinking of me and saying, 'That's him who punched so-and-so,' " Thomas said softly, under press questioning.

"I'd rather they'd say, 'That's him who helped so-and-so.' "

But Iowa memories, or earlier ones involving Purdue, weren't distractions when it came time to get ready for Minnesota, Thomas said.

Bob Knight, Jim Dutcher exchange pre-game views

"The only thing that distracts me is when we lose," Thomas said, "especially when I'm pretty sure I helped the cause."

Thomas admitted that, as Knight said of the entire squad, he felt tired as the game moved along.

"But every game, you have to be ready to play," he said. "We can't lose any more. We have to survive. If we played another game tonight, or a game Sunday, we'd have to be ready to play."

Turner and Tolbert started together for the first time in Big Ten play, and they had one of the most solid games they've ever had as a tandem.

"We look for each other," Tolbert said. "What you have to do is talk and anticipate.

"Really, I think I looked for him too much. I ended up throwing the ball away a couple of times. I've got to know when to take my shot."

Turner had 12 points in helping to lead IU to its big first-half lead, and Tolbert said nothing about Turner's play surprised him. "It's up to him to be ready," Tolbert said, "and he was."

Turner said he "wasn't really disappointed" when he spent most of the first five weeks of the league season on the bench.

"I knew what the problem was," he said.

"I knew I just had to play my hardest without making mistakes, because coach Knight won't play guys who make mistakes."

Turner was charged with two turnovers in 37 minutes in this one.

A player who preceded him in going from the Indianapolis playgrounds to IU, McGinnis, had an enjoyable afternoon as a spectator in his first game sitting on the Hoosier bench.

McGinnis and fellow Indiana Pacer Tom Abernethy were introduced before the game, and McGinnis took back memories of a warm reception: loud and long applause that brought a wave from the muscular 6-8 giant.

McGinnis talked to the Hoosier squad in the dressing room after the game, and he indicated he won't be so long in making a return.

"That was all right — that was fun," he said.

"And I had the best seat in the house."

Indiana 74, Ohio State 58

Indiana made it through another checkpoint with a late-game pullaway that whipped Ohio State, 74-58, and left the Hoosiers:

• Still one game back of Iowa, which escaped from Michigan at Iowa City, 69-66;

• Alone in second place, thanks to Minnesota's 76-59 home-court victory over Illinois.

Defense saved the Hoosiers in a victory that forever will look much easier in the record books than it came.

With 16:34 to go, IU's Isiah Thomas drew a two-shot foul and hit both free throws for a 41-37 lead.

There, the Hoosier offense dried up. Thomas took the ball to the basket against the giant Buckeyes three straight times and couldn't get a shot to drop, losing one opportunity when teammate Ted Kitchel was called for offensive goaltending for touching a Thomas shot while it still was bouncing on the rim.

The misses were followed by a couple traveling calls — five straight Hoosier possessions without getting a point in a tight, crucial game.

Ohio State had it even worse. Through that whole stretch, the Buckeyes didn't even get a shot.

"We made seven turnovers in a row," Buckeye coach Eldon Miller said, pained at the memory of a grand chance blown.

"If we had handled the ball better, it would have been a different game. You have to give a lot of credit to the Indiana defense. They're the best defensive team in the league."

It was the pursuit of some offensive punch during that dreary stretch that prompted IU coach Bob Knight to make a move that became one of the game's keys.

Knight tried Kitchel, then Steve Risley at a forward spot in the second half. Each is 6-8 and equipped to give and take with the bulky front-court players who are Ohio State's hub.

After watching the five straight pointless possessions, Knight went a third direction at the forward spot: 6-3 Jim Thomas, who was a surprise starter and an exceptional contributor in IU's 67-60 early-season victory at Ohio State. He delivered nine points in just 11 minutes in his latest Buckeye surprise.

"He made us a quicker team, which was what we really needed right then," Knight said.

The quickness didn't manifest itself immediately, though the Hoosier drought ended. Thomas had been on the floor only 10 seconds when Ray Tolbert popped free for a jump shot that missed, but Randy Wittman rebounded it and laid it back in — the first points by either team in just under four minutes.

"Once we got the hell off 41-37, we played pretty well," Knight quipped.

Once Ohio State started getting shots launched, the Bucks did better, too. When Carter Scott freed himself for a jump shot that he hit with 11:52 to go, it was the first shot the Buckeyes had managed in just over five minutes.

The Bucks followed with another basket by Mitch Haas to trim the lead to 43-41 with 10:55 left.

About then, the Jim Thomas quickness became prominent.

Thomas beat his defender with a cut to the basket, took a perfect pass, spun and laid the ball up gently from the left side of the basket — and missed the easy shot.

"I thought, 'Here we go again,'" Thomas said. "But fortunately I was able to get the rebound basket — for which I was very thankful."

His errant lay-up rolled obligingly around the rim to come back to him, and he laid it in accurately on the second chance.

The Hoosier pullaway followed, the Thomas basket starting a nine-point run.

Twice in a row, Indiana scored by beating the Bucks downcourt. Tolbert got one, after Jim Smith's miss and Wittman's rebound, to make it 47-41 and get the crowd of 17,089 into the game — roaring while play continued, the hint that a kill is sensed.

Tolbert delivered again, deflecting a Buckeye pass that Isiah Thomas came up with, and he shot the ball downcourt to Jim Thomas for a three-point play and a 50-41 Hoosier lead.

The margin was never smaller than that the rest of the way. The Hoosiers had only two turnovers and one missed shot in almost nine minutes of running a spread offense — "our regular offense, just spread out a little more," Knight said.

It wasn't exactly a delay game. The Hoosiers scored 22 points in the stretch when they employed the spread.

Neither team could get a grip on the game in the first half, which was tied 30-30 until Landon Turner hit his sixth straight shot, a baseline jumper with 40 seconds left in the half, and Tolbert looped in his longest shot as a Hoosier — a 22-foot rainbow launched just because time was running out in the half but centered perfectly in the basket.

Indiana widened the lead to 39-32 opening the second half

OHIO STATE 58

	M	FG	FT	R	A	BS	St	PF	TP
Kellogg, f	36	4- 6	3- 4	3	2	1	1	4	11
Haas, f	9	2- 2	0- 0	0	1	0	0	0	4
Williams, c	39	4- 9	3- 4	5	0	4	0	1	11
Scott, g	31	7-11	2- 2	2	3	0	0	2	16
Huggins, g	28	1- 2	0- 0	0	1	0	2	2	2
Smith	24	1- 2	1- 1	5	1	0	0	4	3
Kirchner	7	0- 1	1- 2	1	0	0	0	1	1
Penn	26	4- 6	2- 2	2	3	0	1	1	10
Team				4					
Totals		23-39	12-15	22	11	5	4	15	58

INDIANA 74

	M	FG	FT	R	A	BS	St	PF	TP
Turner, f	39	9-15	2- 2	5	2	1	0	2	20
Risley, f	8	0- 1	0- 0	1	1	0	0	1	0
Tolbert, c	39	8-12	0- 0	7	3	1	3	3	16
I.Thomas, g	39	4-13	6- 7	5	8	0	5	3	14
Wittman, g	39	5- 7	2- 2	2	2	0	2	1	12
Kitchel	19	1- 6	1- 1	1	3	0	0	2	3
J.Thomas	11	3- 4	3- 3	2	1	0	1	0	9
Franz	1	0- 0	0- 0	0	0	0	0	0	0
Isenbarger	1	0- 0	0- 0	0	0	0	0	1	0
Grunwald	1	0- 0	0- 0	0	0	0	0	0	0
LaFave	1	0- 0	0- 0	0	0	0	0	0	0
Bouchie	1	0- 0	0- 0	0	0	0	0	0	0
Brown	1	0- 1	0- 0	1	0	0	0	0	0
Team				2					
Totals		30-59	14-15	26	20	2	11	13	74

SCORE BY HALVES

Ohio State		30	28— 58
Indiana		34	40— 74

Turnovers—Ohio State 25, Indiana 15.

SHOOTING

	FG	Pct.	FT	Pct.
Ohio State	23-39	.590	12-15	.800
Indiana	30-59	.508	14-15	.933

Officials—Jim Bain, Verl Sell, Ralph Rosser.
Attendance—17,089 (capacity).

Landon Turner eases shot over Herb Williams (32)

Last time together for Tolbert, fans

When Tolbert was recruited at Indiana four springs ago, his coach at Madison Heights, ex-Hoosier Phil Buck, promised only one thing:

"The fans down there will love him. That's the kind of player he is."

The love affair that Buck predicted became as ardent as he could have imagined. It reaches a milestone with the next game: Tolbert's last game as a Hoosier at Assembly Hall.

He steps on the floor as the No. 8 scorer in IU's long basketball history. He passed Tom Bolyard's 1,299-point total with his first basket against Ohio State.

He's also the No. 5 rebounder in Hoosier history with 815, ranking him behind Steve Downing (889), Archie Dees (914), Kent Benson (1,031) and recordholder Walt Bellamy (1,088).

And he's the Hoosiers' modern king of the dunk, the exuberant and ebullient master of bringing 'em out of their seats in the balconies and the main arena at Assembly Hall.

All the excitement doesn't come in the spectating areas, Knight indicated after the victory over Ohio State.

Turner turned in his fifth straight strong performance, Knight said. But when a writer suggested that Turner's play tends to rev up the rest of the Hoosiers, Knight said, "It's Tolbert who does that. And I thought he had another very good game."

For a man of zest and flair, Tolbert does a journeyman's unglamorous labor uncommonly well.

There is no record-book entry for defense, but Tolbert got the No. 1 assignment again: Ohio State's Herb Williams. Williams, about to become Ohio State's all-time leading scorer, hit the game's first shot and a few more to total 11 points by halftime.

He finished with 11 points. The entire second half, he got one shot, and two rebounds. "I guess our guards were doing a good job of pressuring their guards out front so they couldn't make a pass," Tolbert said.

Miller blamed Herbie's cohorts. "I feel we're making life very difficult for our big center," he said. A one-shot half for a Williams "is a farce," Miller said.

Williams was cognizant of Tolbert's presence. "I thought he played great," Williams said. "We're good friends. We roomed together at a camp this year. And we were together at the Pan-American Games trials here (in summer, 1979)."

Tolbert insists Williams doesn't light any special psychological fires for him. "I just play," Tolbert said.

But the truth is that Williams was considerably better known and higher ranked nationally when the two came into college basketball, and the first meeting of the two set the tone for their series: Tolbert the eager challenger who introduced himself with a 24-point game at Williams's expense.

After four years and nine head-on meetings, the two are dead-even in points (133 each). Another was a semifinal step toward IU's 1979 championship of New York's National Invitation Tournament, where Tolbert and teammate Butch Carter shared the tourney's MVP award.

Tolbert is trying for his third NCAA tournament trip. Mark it down, trivia buffs, if he makes it. Only one other Hoosier ever has started on three teams that made the NCAA field: Quinn Buckner.

All those are extraneous matters at the moment to Tolbert.

"Right now, the only thing in my mind is the next game," he said. "It's a game we've got to win, and Michigan is really good."

before the Bucks cut it back to 41-37, setting up the stretch with the Indiana-dominated dual: a suddenly ineffective Hoosier offense offset by a never more effective Hoosier defense. It would take considerable research to find the last time even a Knight team stubbornly protected a skinny lead through seven straight possessions without letting a shot go up.

Game figures indicated the Hoosiers were fortunate they didn't allow the Bucks free-firing. Ohio State shot .590 to IU's .508, but all those turnovers — 25 for the game, another statistic that Miller noted and winced over — left the Bucks with only 39 shots in the 40-minute game. Indiana had 59, because the Hoosiers threw the ball away 15 times and outrebounded the Buckeyes — Big Ten rebounding leaders going in — 26-22. Tolbert led both teams with seven rebounds, and the league's runaway rebound leader, 6-7 sophomore Clark Kellogg, managed only three.

Turner had 12 first-half points and a season-high 20 for the game to lead both teams. Tolbert added 16 points, Isiah Thomas 14 and Wittman 12. Scott, the Bucks' scoring leader in the first IU game when he was attempting to win back a starting spot, repeated with 16 points, while Kellogg and Williams had 11 each and sub Todd Penn 10.

Quickness helped, says I. of J. Thomas

The speed of Jim Thomas was an unquestioned key in the Hoosiers' late-game breakaway, but the Hoosiers' other sophomore Thomas, Isiah, didn't feel the nine points Jim racked up in 11 minutes represented his chief contribution.

"I think his quickness helped us more on defense than on offense," Isiah said. "We were able to apply a lot more pressure inside and outside with him.

"But he did help our offense, too. He made us much quicker getting down the floor.

"James coming in was the biggest turning point of the game. We had hit a dead spot until then."

Thomas arrived with the Hoosier lead 41-37, where it had stayed for about four minutes. The margin dipped to two points once, but during Thomas's time on the court, IU outscored the Buckeyes, 33-20.

Much of that time, the Thomas quickness was being exploited with the Hoosiers in a spread offense. "That made it hard for Ohio State to cover us," Thomas said.

Miller agreed. "If we hadn't given Turner so many baseline shots, our zone would have been pretty effective in the first half," Miller said.

"We couldn't use it at all the last half, because we were behind. I believe it would have been effective, if we could have used it."

Williams had his own first half-second half differential — 11 points in the first 20 minutes, zero in the second.

"I thought the difference was they were shooting the basketball and we were turning it over," Williams said. "They were taking the ball to the bucket and getting fouled and we weren't."

The Hoosier defense made its own big contributions to the victory. Twice, Buckeye guards drove the baseline on one side of the floor and tried to fire a blind pass to the other side, only to have Hoosier Randy Wittman intercept.

"I just followed our defensive rules for weakside help," Wittman said. "But that was something they hurt us with in the first game. They got a couple passes to guys for lay-ups that way so we were kinda looking for them."

Wittman's two interceptions were part of 11 steals the Hoosiers pulled off — five by Isiah Thomas, three by Tolbert and one by Jim Thomas completing the list.

Carter Scott, Randy Wittman meet

83

Indiana 98, Michigan 83

It was Indiana's traditional day for seniors, but it wasn't one when they could act like senior citizens.

The pace was so fast the Assembly Hall scoring record almost fell — for one player, and for everybody — but Indiana finally closed its home season with a 98-83 victory over Michigan to stay in step with Iowa and Illinois atop the Big Ten.

Sophomore Isiah Thomas scored 39 points to fuel the Hoosier victory charge, but lots more was needed to stay ahead of the fast-firing Wolverines in a game that fell a point short of the Assembly Hall two-team record for a college game (182, when Indiana outscored Iowa, 101-81, late in the 1975-76 season).

Thomas also just missed a Hall record. Steve Downing's 41-point total against Illinois in 1973, threatened earlier this year when Ted Kitchel scored 40 against the Illini, barely made it through again on sophomore Thomas' highest-scoring day as a Hoosier.

It was a day that didn't appear gilt-edged for Indiana when Michigan opened a 30-23 lead with about five minutes left in the half. "I'm not sure we were particularly struggling," IU coach Bob Knight said. "They shot extremely well."

The Woverines had a chance to widen the lead to nine, but Thad Garner's bank shot dipped far into the basket and popped out. For the next 15 minutes, Indiana's offense hummed with Hall of Fame efficiency to win one that, for a change, got out of the Hoosier defense's control.

The beginning of the stretch of brilliance was appropriate. Glen Grunwald, one of the four Hoosier seniors honored at the final home performance, took a Thomas pass for a lay-up to start the Hoosier comeback and his own 10-point day, his highest in two seasons.

It took Michigan's highest scorer ever, senior Mike McGee, only seven seconds to get that basket back with a shot from the corner.

But another Hoosier senior, Ray Tolbert, rebounded Landon Turner's miss and jammed it in with a crowd-rousing dunk. Thomas stole the ball back for IU, and Tolbert's one-and-one conversion pulled the Hoosiers within 32-29.

Seconds later, it was Thomas at the free-throw line, a sight available 21 times during the record-challenging afternoon. He hit both free throws (and 17 for the day) to make it 32-31.

McGee hushed the Hall's 17,072 habitues again with two free throws and a basket, restoring a 36-31 lead with 2:40 to go in the half.

Indiana's comeback formula was the same as before: Grunwald working loose in the offense for a basket, followed by a Tolbert rebound basket that became a game-tying three-point play.

The Hoosiers rushed on past Michigan to lead 44-38 until McGee's three-point play beat the halftime buzzer by three seconds.

Thomas opened a 27-point second-half scoring show by hitting jump shots on IU's first two possessions of the second half. Still, it was 52-49 and Turner — who had 15 points in the game's first 22 minutes — had gone to the bench with four fouls when IU took off again.

Thomas had six of the points and Kitchel a three-point play in an 11-point Indiana streak that put Michigan down, 63-49, with 13:30 to go. Thomas added eight more in a burst that opened the lead to 75-57 with 9:58 left.

IU got there from the 30-23 hole by scoring 52 points in just 33 possessions.

Congratulatory hug for Isiah Thomas from Bob Knight

By then, Michigan had abandoned any thoughts of patience or patterns and gone to a fire-when-able style that long-range gunners McGee and Johnny Johnson made work.

Suddenly, the score was 82-75 with 3:58 still left on a clock that seemed to be moving like a calendar.

Long before that crisis point, six minutes before, Thomas was tired, he admitted later. He lost what would have been his 40th point when he prepared to shoot a free throw with 9:58 left, took a deep breath, re-cocked and — just before he launched a shot that went in — was called for exceeding the 10 seconds the rules give him to get a free throw in the air.

"I was aware of the 10-second rule," he said, "but I've never seen it called. I was tired — I just wanted to get some more rest."

The one wiped out was the first of two free throws, and he hit the second. He wasn't any fresher when he went back to the line six minutes later with the eight-point lead down to seven, but he hit both free throws.

McGee offset those in five seconds with a hurry-up basket.

Indiana beat the Michigan press and ran off 23 seconds before Tolbert got a one-and-one chance. He hit both.

And in 11 seconds, Johnson nullified those to make it 86-79 with 3:04 still to go.

A fond Assembly Hall farewell for four-year favorite Ray Tolbert

IU worked with patience again before springing Ted Kitchel for a lay-up and an 88-79 lead with 2:20 left. McGee finally missed, but sophomore Ike Person of Michigan was fouled on the rebound, and his two free throws cut the lead back to seven with 2:07 remaining.

Finally, Indiana put the game away with a burst that included a close-in Thomas jump shot, McGee's fifth foul (for charging into Tolbert), two free throws by Kitchel, a Tolbert rebound of Johnson's miss, and a lay-up by Kitchel. The score was 94-81 and Knight at last was free to give the crowd its chance for a last salute to senior Tolbert, who left the floor with a wave at 0:53.

Thomas was 11-for-15 from the field in his 39-point game, which also included six rebounds, five assists and three steals. "He played extremely well," Knight said. "It was by far his best all-round game."

Turner, though playing only 20 minutes on his foul-shortened day, scored 15, Kitchel and Turner 13 each and Grunwald 10 as IU outshot Michigan (.599 to .458) and outrebounded the Wolverines (38-34 for the game, 24-10 the last half.).

McGee had 29 points, Johnson 14 and Paul Heuerman 10 for Michigan, which lost to IU for the ninth straight time at Assembly Hall.

Before sizzling, Isiah had to cool it

Tolbert has been learning the finer points of basketball since the day he arrived on campus in August, 1977. In his 120th Indiana game and his 116th start, he learned something new.

Suddenly, the man whose athletic skills have IU track coach Sam Bell downright enchanted learned a Terry Bradshaw he is not.

Tolbert's teacher, Knight, took a time out with 4:26 left Saturday because he was worried. An 18-point Hoosier lead was down to 82-71 and a Michigan press was threatening to stop nibbling and start gulping away at the lead.

Knight passed on his concerns and his suggestions for easing same, then sent the Hoosiers back to the court to face the press anew. The ball went to Tolbert, deep in the Michigan backcourt, and he elected to beat the pressers all at once with a long pass.

What he threw, quarterbacks call a "duck." When he threw it, Tolbert wanted to duck.

"I didn't put enough zip on the ball," Tolbert said. "I don't know why. I knew Isiah could catch anything I could throw.

"But it floated so high on me, and I saw two of their guys going for it. There was nothing I could do about it but hope Isiah would catch it."

He didn't, but he caught Garner's fifth foul and Tolbert caught one more Knightian lecture. Another day, another lesson.

This was a day that Tolbert and Assembly Hall's legions who love him have both awaited and dreaded. It was farewell day for IU's Seniors of '81: Glen Grunwald, Steve Risley, Phil Isenbarger, Eric Kirchner and Tolbert.

Ironically, Tolbert made it into the game feeling rather normal. It was the young cast around him, particularly the most experienced sophomore in college basketball, Isiah Thomas, who found the emotion of the day discombobulating.

"It was the same feeling I had last summer in Indianapolis," Thomas said. That was the night he came back to his new "home state" with USA on his jersey, playing for the U.S. Olympic team, and pre-game introductions came to a roaring stop when his name was announced. The Hoosier crowd saluted him with passion at its loudest, and Thomas was so pleased and so stirred he promptly went out and did everything he didn't want to do, when the game began.

This time, he said, "I felt anxious early in the game — I think everybody did. Everybody wanted to do so well for those seniors."

After 7½ minutes of shaky play, with the score 14-14, Knight sat Thomas down. He stayed on the bench 82 seconds and went back with Michigan leading, 20-17.

"I just tried to relax and remove myself from all the other factors that were involved," Thomas said. "Michigan is a good ball club, but I never felt we were going to lose the game."

Such is the nature of youth that quite likely there were 10 players on the court for the first 25 minutes or so who shared the feeling of imminent victory. Thomas backed his feelings with 35 points after his short cool-down on the bench. Victory tends to favor optimists like that.

Knight was properly impressed with Thomas' play, and he has frequently commented on Tolbert's zeal and his contributions through his four seasons as a Hoosier starter.

"The guy who really did the job for us today was Glen Grunwald," Knight said. "He came off the bench and played very, very well."

Grunwald scored 10 points and admitted it "felt nice — I scored some points and did something else when I was out there besides just standing around and running around."

"I couldn't be more pleased to have Glen go out at home this way," Knight said.

Four seniors say goodbye

In Knight's second season at Indiana, he began the tradition of bringing his seniors out after their last home game and letting them and the Assembly Hall crowd have a few moments for mutual thanks.

It's the kind of festive occasion that defeat would complicate. The Hoosier seniors have been blessed with fortune and forethought. None yet has lost on that last time out.

And 1981's seniors didn't either, winning solidly and then going before the mob.

Grunwald had his own unique opening. "I've had a great five years here," said the Chicagoan who sat out what would have been his sophomore year (1977-78) because of recurring knee problems.

"What's made these years so great is the people I've been around — my teammates, my friends. And I also want to thank all of you people that I didn't really get to know, you fans."

Isenbarger, whose grandfather was an I-man and whose brother, John, is enshrined forever in Hoosier legendry as a sophomore star on the 1967 Hoosier Rose Bowl team, said his parents and older brothers "have had me coming down here to athletic events for 22 consecutive years. And I wouldn't like anything more than to stretch this last one out as long as possible."

"I'd like to thank the coaches and one person who usually goes unrecognized, the best trainer in the country, Bob Young. And, of course, my teammates — the ones that aren't here and the ones that are. They've all given me more than I can ever give back."

Risley made a minor slip — he described how upset he occasionally felt after practice with a common but earthy description

— but carried on unfazed. "These four years have gone so quickly," he said. "They're the greatest four years of my life, and my teammates and you people have made them so, and I thank you all.

"I think of guys like Wayne Radford and Mike Woodson and Butch Carter and Isiah Thomas — they're what IU's all about. It's an honor to have played for a coach like Bob Knight."

The applause reached a peak for the anchorman, four-year starter Ray Tolbert. It rolled for 40 seconds before he had a chance to break in and speak.

"First of all," Tolbert said, "I'd like to thank God for giving me the privilege to perform for you all. You fans are the greatest in the world.

"I hope I can leave a trail here for people to come up and fill my shoes. I especially want to thank Coach Knight for putting up with me for four years."

The audience that fell for Tolbert's exuberant style in his first Hoosier season and regularly responded to the dunks that became his trademark begged for one more in the post-game ceremony. Tolbert declined at first.

But as the cry went on, Knight — the man who once said of Tolbert, "When he came here, after a summer of all-star games, he thought the whole game centered around the dunk shot" — was the first to accede. He sent manager Steve Skoronski after a basketball, and one materialized.

And Tolbert, wearing a warmup jacket, left the center-court microphones for one last, majestic dunk.

MICHIGAN 83

	M	FG	FT	R	A	BS	St	PF	TP
McGee, f	35	11-22	7- 7	4	2	0	2	5	29
Garner, f	35	4-10	0- 1	3	6	0	0	5	8
Heuerman, c	30	4- 7	2- 3	9	2	1	0	5	10
Mt.Bodnar, g	34	3- 6	2- 2	7	4	0	0	4	8
Johnson, g	29	7-12	0- 0	0	5	0	0	4	14
McCormick	16	3- 6	2- 2	2	0	0	0	3	8
Person	7	0- 2	2- 2	1	0	0	0	1	2
Burton	8	1- 3	2- 2	3	0	1	0	2	4
Mk.Bodnar	2	0- 1	0- 0	0	0	0	0	1	0
Hopson	2	0- 3	0- 0	1	0	0	0	1	0
Pelekoudas	1	0- 0	0- 0	0	0	0	0	1	0
Brown	1	0- 0	0- 0	0	0	0	0	0	0
Antonides	1	0- 0	0- 0	0	0	0	0	0	0
Team				4					
Totals		33-72	17-19	34	19	2	2	32	83

INDIANA 98

	M	FG	FT	R	A	BS	St	PF	TP
Kitchel, f	29	5-12	3- 3	6	3	0	0	4	13
Turner, f	20	7-11	1- 1	1	0	1	0	4	15
Tolbert, c	39	4-10	5- 5	9	5	0	0	3	13
I.Thomas, g	37	11-15	17-21	6	5	0	3	3	39
Wittman, g	40	0- 3	4- 4	3	2	0	0	2	4
J.Thomas	11	0- 1	0- 1	2	2	0	0	0	0
Grunwald	16	4- 4	2- 2	4	1	0	0	3	10
Risley	4	1- 2	0- 0	2	1	0	0	1	2
Isenbarger	1	0- 0	0- 1	1	0	0	0	0	0
Bouchie	1	1- 1	0- 0	1	0	0	0	1	2
Franz	1	0- 0	0- 0	0	0	0	0	0	0
Brown	1	0- 0	0- 0	0	0	0	0	0	0
Team				3					
Totals		33-59	32-38	38	19	1	3	21	98

SCORE BY HALVES

Michigan		41	42— 83
Indiana		44	54— 98

Turnovers—Michigan 11, Indiana 11.
Technical foul—Indiana bench.

SHOOTING

	FG	Pct.	FT	Pct.
Michigan	33-72	.458	17-19	.895
Indiana	33-59	.559	32-38	.842

Officials—Gary Muncy, Bob Showalter, Bill Herzog.
Attendance—17,072 (capacity).

Indiana 69, Illinois 66

Steve Risley led Indiana on a second-half brush with perfection and it produced a 69-66 victory over Illinois and a boost into co-leadership in the Big Ten for IU.

The Hoosiers pulled even with Iowa, a 71-70 overtime loser at Michigan State.

Risley, a 6-8 senior from Lawrence Central, came off the bench with four minutes gone in the second half and IU down, 37-36.

He had been in the game just 31 seconds when he drove to the middle of the Illinois defense and put up a soft shot that gave Indiana a 38-37 lead.

The Hoosiers fell back, 49-45, before Risley and another reserve, Jim Thomas, found the same hole in the Illini 3-2 zone, on the left baseline, for baskets that tied the game, 49-49 with 9:40 to play.

Second-half hero Steve Risley works free among Illini

"Their wingman (6-8 Mark Smith) had to move up to cover Randy (Wittman), because he's one of our best shooters," Risley said. Smith agreed. "The center (6-10 James Griffin) has to come out," Smith said. "If he's not quick enough, you're in trouble."

The two baskets, which followed an earlier Risley shot from the same area, convinced Illini coach Lou Henson to make a countermove. He substituted 6-11 Derek Holcomb for Griffin and went to a man-to-man defense.

The game turned golden for a few minutes. The two NCAA tournament-bound teams scored on seven straight possessions, snatching the lead back and forth.

Illinois was ahead, 56-55, when IU coach Bob Knight took a time out with 6:13 to go.

"As long as they were in a man-to-man, we wanted to go with our spread offense," Knight said. The Hoosiers played it the rest of the way, and it paid dividends — both immediate and long-range.

Ray Tolbert set a screen that freed Wittman for a cut to the basket, and Risley's pass from the top of the foul circle gave Wittman the lay-up that popped Indiana on top for the final time, 57-56, with 5:50 left.

At 4:08, the same play worked: Tolbert picking off Illini freshman Derek Harper and freeing Wittman for a pass from Isiah Thomas and a lay-up that made it 59-56.

Indiana didn't score another field goal, and didn't have to. The Hoosiers packed away one of their biggest victories of the year by hitting 10 straight free throws in the last 3½ minutes.

Each time, some heat was on. Tolbert started the string by hitting both halves of a one-and-one with 3:20 left for a 61-58 lead. Risley rebounded Harper's close-in miss to give Indiana the ball for the first time with a 3-point margin, and Jim Thomas was fouled. He also hit both shots on a one-and-one for a 63-58 lead at 3:01.

Guard Perry Range scored a rebound basket for Illinois with 2:19 left, but Isiah Thomas hit both halves of a two-shot foul at 1:54 to restore the margin at 65-60.

Craig Tucker sliced into that with a jump shot at 0:37, but the Hoosiers avoided a foul by the desperate Illini until the clock was down to 0:18, and when fouled, Isiah Thomas hit two more free throws to lift IU out front, 67-62.

Griffin scored a rebound basket for Illinois and called time out with nine seconds left. Only two seconds ran off before Tolbert was fouled, and he clinched the Hoosier victory with a one-and-one conversion that gave IU the luxury of letting Johnson score for Illinois as time ran out.

"You just can't see a lot better game than that," Knight said. "I thought it was really well-played, just an awfully good college basketball game.

"We really only missed about three plays in the last eight minutes — we missed one lay-up and they got a couple put-back baskets on us. And that was it."

The Hoosiers shot .800 (12-for-15) from the field and .944 (17-for-18) from the free-throw line the last half. Risley scored 10 points, hitting all four shots he tried and both free throws awarded him.

Illinois, which would have pulled into a second-place tie with IU and kept its championship hopes alive going to the final day if it had won, may have muffed its victory chance in the first half.

With 5:32 to go in the half, Tucker drew foul No. 3 on Isiah

Jim Thomas pulls away from Eddie Johnson, Mark Smith

Festive Champaign day spoiled by IU

A folk singer from a Champaign radio station strummed a guitar and led an overflow Assembly Hall crowd in singing a lively tune at halftime. The refrain, the one that brought in the crowd for some music-in-the-round, ran:

"The '80s belong to Illini..."

The night's game, however, was played in the 60s. And that meant *it* belonged to Indiana.

"They controlled the tempo," Johnson said. "They cut off our running game, and we thought we had to run against them to win.

"The fast break is our game. The first half, we got them going for just a little while, but then they controlled the tempo again.

"Even in the second half when we were up by four (49-45 with 10½ minutes left), they just kept working with the ball. They didn't take a bad shot."

Perhaps that was the game's pivotal period — the stretch in which the Hoosiers refused to drop back and, once even, traded crucial shots with the revved-up Illini.

Or maybe it was the last six minutes, when Indiana's sharp passing and quick cuts from a spread offense picked apart Illinois' man-to-man defense. That was the phase that had second-guessers questioning Henson's decision to go with the man-to-man, rather than a zone.

Ironically, it was fear of the Hoosiers' long-range accuracy that led to the choice in Illini defenses, and Henson didn't second-guess himself for it.

"Indiana might be the best outside-shooting team in the country," he said. "We felt we had to alternate defenses.

"When they got ahead at the end, they had the opportunity to spread it out and make us come after them. If we had been up three points and had the ball in that stretch, we would have done the same thing."

Smith called the spread "a good move on Coach Knight's part. When they went to the wide-open offense, we couldn't put any pressure on."

Smith spoke readily of Indiana's tournament chances, though lots of teams have better records than the Hoosiers' 20-9.

"First of all, you have to figure who they lost to," Smith said. "They lost to some really good teams early in the year and in the conference, they lost to the best teams (Iowa twice, Purdue and Michigan once each).

"I think they'll do really well. They'll be tough to beat.

"They play so intently, and they help so much on defense. I've never seen a team so unselfish. There just are no selfish players on the team.

"And you rarely will see teams getting lay-ups on them, the way they help out on defense."

It was a surprise ending to a festive day in Champaign-Urbana. Champaign *News Gazette* sports writer Loren Tate called it the biggest March game at Illinois since the early '60s. Radio stations played the folk singer's tune throughout the day, interspersed with ribald doggerel called in by listeners forecasting a dire evening for Knight and his Hoosiers. The mood threatened to get ugly, but the atmosphere at the game never did. Knight had an obscenity or two shouted at him and some pejorative signs and T-shirts flashed his way, but the crowd in general was lively and enthusiastic, challenging its team to show its new Big Ten standing by felling the league's giant of the '70s, Indiana.

The '80s, whatever the tunesmith says, remain up for grabs. And Indiana is still alive and well and in there grabbing.

"The first half, we got kind of caught up in the crowd," Wittman said.

Thomas, sending the Hoosier guard to the sidelines for the rest of the half. Tucker's free throws gave Illinois a 24-20 lead.

But with a 28-26 lead and 2:36 left in the half, Henson took time out and put the Illini in their own spread offense. The Hoosiers backed off. Illinois ran off more than a minute before resuming the attack. It took a 25-foot shot by Smith a second ahead of the buzzer to give Illinois as big a halftime lead as it had when Thomas left (32-28).

Thomas didn't return shy. Barely more than a half-minute into the second half, he slapped the ball away from Holcomb for a steal and lay-up that tied the game, 32-32, the midpoint of an eight-point Hoosier run.

But three straight IU turnovers let Illinois score five points in a row, reclaim the lead, and bring Risley on.

"I went in mainly to help our defense," Risley said, "to drop off Holcomb and help jam up Johnson and Smith. They're two great offensive players. No one can cover them one-on-one.

"I just got open at the other end and hit some shots.

"This has to be the biggest game I've ever helped win here. It was a great team win."

Tolbert and Isiah Thomas had 14 points each and Wittman 13 for Indiana — 20-9 now for Knight's eighth 20-victory season in his 10 seasons as IU's coach.

The Hoosiers' big second half lifted their shooting to .531 for the game, only the fifth time an Illini opponent has topped .500 this year. Indiana did it in both games, shooting .587 in a January 78-61 victory over the Illini at IU's Assembly Hall. IU's .944 free-throw mark was the Hoosiers' best this year and the best by any team in a Big Ten game.

"We were coming down, making one pass and putting a shot up.

"The second half, we were much more patient. We worked the ball around three or four or five times and got good shots."

Henson saw things from a slightly different view.

"The first half, I felt we played pretty good defense," he said. "And I thought we did in the second half, too, until we had to go out and get the basketball there at the end. Then we let them get behind us. We did a very poor job. Our defense broke down.

"I thought it was a very good game. It was a game where whoever gets a break wins it, and we didn't get the break."

Knight called it "just an awfully good college basketball game" and noted:

"There weren't a hell of a lot of turnovers either way (IU officially was charged with nine, Illinois eight), and the kids on both teams made free throws. Illinois hit some in the middle of the second half (7-of-8 during a stretch when the lead was going back and forth) and almost put us out of the game, and our kids hit them at the end (10 in a row, 17-for-18 for the game).

"It was poetic justice that we would win a game there. We lost one at Purdue at the foul line.

"We never really had a chance to run away with this game. Illinois did maybe twice in the first half. There was a good sequence of plays for us at the end of the half, and we were a little lucky."

Tolbert's sore back concern to gametime

Tolbert rode home in the IU airplane with ice on his back. "Ooooo, it's cold," Tolbert said, "but there's no pain."

Probably, the Hoosier victory at Champaign couldn't have come without Tolbert, a leading candidate for all-Big Ten consideration though he hasn't had a 20-point game yet this year.

This time, he had 14 points and eight rebounds in a 40-minute contribution to victory. There was considerable question early in the week if he'd be able to contribute at all.

Tolbert's problems started at the Hoosiers' Monday practice, a light one during the Big Ten season for players who have played to any great extent in games the previous Thursday and Saturday.

"I was just shooting around and trying to get loose," Tolbert said. "I must have come down wrong in a jump. All of a sudden I felt a sharp pain.

"I tried to stretch it out, but it kept getting worse and finally I had to sit it out."

He rested Tuesday, too. Wednesday, he worked out, wearing a special brace, and he played with the brace on against Illinois. "I probably couldn't jump as high as I'd like," Tolbert admitted, "but the brace really helped me. It kept my back straight.

"I'm just glad I could contribute when I had to.

"I was really happy for Risley. The Michigan game, Glen (Grunwald) came off the bench and hit some shots, and this time it was Steve. We're going to need that the rest of the way."

Risley scored 10 points and had four rebounds in 16 minutes. "He just did a great job," Knight said. "And as I said before with Glen, it's really good to have a senior come through like that in a game that's so meaningful."

The Hoosiers were showered and dressed and about to get on the bus for the ride to the airport after the game when word came of Michigan State's 71-70 overtime victory over Iowa — the coupling of events that, with the Hoosiers' success at Illinois, made IU and Iowa Big Ten co-leaders.

"Thank God, thank God for Jay Vincent," Isiah Thomas reacted.

Perry Range is fenced in by Ted Kitchel, Ray Tolbert

INDIANA 69

	M	FG	FT	R	A	BS	St	PF	TP
Turner, f	24	3- 6	2- 2	0	1	1	0	3	8
Kitchel, f	19	1- 5	2- 2	3	1	0	0	1	4
Tolbert, c	40	5- 8	4- 4	8	2	1	0	4	14
I.Thomas, g	34	5- 9	4- 4	3	5	0	1	3	14
Wittman, g	40	6-10	1- 2	3	4	0	0	1	13
Grunwald	6	0- 3	0- 0	1	0	0	0	0	0
J.Thomas	21	2- 4	2- 2	6	1	0	1	1	6
Risley	16	4- 4	2- 2	4	2	0	0	1	10
Team				1					
Totals		26-49	17-18	29	16	2	2	14	69

ILLINOIS 66

	M	FG	FT	R	A	BS	St	PF	TP
Johnson, f	37	5-12	2- 2	11	2	0	1	4	12
Smith, f	35	6-12	4- 6	5	3	0	2	4	16
Holcomb, c	23	2- 4	0- 2	2	3	2	3	0	4
Harper, g	36	3-13	0- 0	2	4	2	1	0	6
Range, g	33	3-11	2- 2	6	2	0	0	2	8
Leonard	4	0- 0	0- 0	0	0	0	0	0	0
Griffin	10	3- 3	0- 0	3	0	1	0	0	6
Tucker	22	3- 5	8- 8	0	1	0	0	3	14
Team				2					
Totals		25-60	16-20	31	15	5	7	13	66

SCORE BY HALVES

Indiana	28	41—	69
Illinois	32	34—	66

Turnovers—Indiana 9, Illinois 8.

SHOOTING

	FG	Pct.	FT	Pct.
Indiana	26-49	.531	17-18	.944
Illinois	25-60	.417	16-20	.800

Officials—Jim Bain, Verl Sell, Ralph Rosser.
Attendance—16,663 (sellout).

Indiana 69, Michigan State 48

Indiana had the Big Ten championship door opened to it by Ohio State and went barging through it in championship style with a 69-48 victory over Michigan State.

The victory capped a tumultuous weekend that saw the Hoosiers move from a game out with two games to go to win their second straight clear-cut title.

Assists came from Ohio State, which dumped Iowa, 78-70, and from the Michigan State team that Indiana overpowered. The Spartans brought Iowa back to IU two nights earlier with a 71-70 home-court victory over the Hawkeyes.

A year ago, Indiana won its last six league games to win the championship outright.

"The difference between last year and this year is that last year we controlled out own destiny," said Hoosiers coach Bob Knight — whose IU teams now have won five championships and one co-championship in his 10 seasons.

"Last year, if we won our last six, nobody could beat us out of the championship.

"This year, we didn't have that after we lost at Iowa.

"I think that's a great tribute to these kids that they kept whacking away at it when they didn't have full control.

"This has to be a tremendous thrill for them, and it is for me, too."

Michigan State had a full house pulling for a second straight Spartan upset, and the 10,004 rocked old Jenison Fieldhouse's rafters when senior Jay Vincent — completing a second year as the Big Ten's scoring champion — sparked MSU to a 19-17 early lead.

By then, Vincent was 5-for-6, mostly from territory foreign to the burly inside specialist: deep on the left side, near the corner.

Indiana appeared doubly vulnerable when guard Isiah Thomas picked up two fouls in the first six minutes.

But Thomas didn't get another until the second half, and the Hoosiers moved ahead with a five-point run that came after Vincent's shot delivered the 19-17 lead with 8:05 left in the half.

Ray Tolbert, the Hoosier who started with Vincent as his assignment and was beleaguered by the sudden outside success, tied the game with two free throws at 7:28.

Another senior, Steve Risley, came off the bench for a second straight strong performance, including the points that put IU ahead for good. Risley broke the 19-19 tie with a free throw at 6:56 and broke free for a lay-up 36 seconds later to give the Hoosiers some room.

Consecutive baskets by Thomas, Landon Turner and Randy Wittman zoomed the Hoosiers to a 30-23 lead, and Wittman's 18-foot shot just ahead of the buzzer sent the Hoosiers in at the half with a 34-26 lead.

Indiana, which led the league in shooting, hit only four of its first 13 shots but ran in nine of 10 during the late-half stretch that gave them the lead.

"I think our offense just picked up a little bit," Knight said. "That basket Wittman hit gave us a damned good lead."

The second half, Turner took over on Vincent, who knew at halftime he needed only one more basket to top the point total of runnerup Mike McGee, whose last league season at Michigan had ended a few hours earlier.

It took Vincent a long while to get that title-winning basket. It finally came from the top of the foul circle with 8:50 to play, and it touched off an explosive reaction in the fieldhouse — Spartan fans following a burst of applause with a chant, "Jay! Jay! Jay!"

At that point, however, two champions were pretty well crowned. Indiana had a 50-38 lead and had the Spartans out of the zone defense they prefer, chasing the Hoosiers man-to-man.

"We tried to stay in our zone as long as we could," said Jud Heathcote, whose zone was a staple on his national championship team at MSU in 1979.

"There comes a time when you just have to go after them."

It came barely five minutes into the second half, with IU leading, 40-30.

"They went man-to-man just at a time when we were going to bring them out (of the zone)," Knight said.

State still was within 10 at 54-44 with 5:30 to play, but two free throws by Tolbert, one by Risley, then baskets by Thomas and Tolbert after a Spartan score put Indiana up, 62-46, with 2:50 to go and assured the meaningful victory.

Before Knight could get the clock stopped to remove his starters in the last minute and a half, the Hoosiers had celebrated the championship with crashing dunks by Turner and Tolbert.

They led the Hoosier scoring, Tolbert with 17 points and Turner 16 (plus a game-high nine rebounds). Thomas, despite an uncharacteristic 4-for-9 night at the free-throw line, had 14 points.

Vincent finished with 20 points, but the man expected to co-lead the upset effort, guard Kevin Smith, managed only five.

Freshmen forward Ben Tower took up some of the slack with unexpected 7-for-9 shooting and 14 points, equalling his season high.

Indiana shot .632 for the game — 24-for-38, which means the Hoosiers hit 20-of-25 shots after their chilly start. That charts out to the same .800 mark that carried the Hoosiers to victory in the last half at Illinois.

Heathcote's pick Oregon State

Heathcote is one of six active collegiate coaches who have taken a team to the NCAA basketball championship, and he frankly is picking Oregon State to win this year.

"We barely beat them in Portland two years ago (with Magic Johnson, Gregory Kelser and the rest of the '79 champions)," Heathcote recalled. "And their guys are still there — three of them, anyway." He spoke of center Steve Johnson and guards Mark Radford and Ray Blume. And just when Heathcote was working up some firm belief in his Beaver pick, someone told him Oregon State was no longer undefeated, dumped by 20 points at home by Arizona State that afternoon.

"Cancel everything," Heathcote said. "There's always some wise guy to spoil your fun."

Heathcote attempted to put Indiana in a national perspective as time comes for the giants to hit.

"Indiana is as good as any team in the country . . . if the game is even or they're ahead — if they can play their game," Heathcote said.

"I wouldn't be a bit surprised to see Indiana in the Final Four.

"But don't sell Illinois short. They're explosive.

"And I like Iowa, too. I like all our teams."

The tournament didn't really take on any significance at all for Indiana, however, until the most surprising weekend of the Big

Ten season had flip-flopped the Hoosiers and Iowa atop the league.

Knight admitted he had considered "the whole spectrum" of possibilities entering the final weekend, including the possibility that Iowa would clinch the title outright by winning its last two games (at Michigan State and Ohio State) and Indiana would lose its last two (at Illinois and MSU) and slide to third.

"There were all kinds of other possibilities, too, of course," Knight said.

"And down at the bottom of the spectrum in my thinking was Iowa losing two and us winning two."

Finishes like that have happened before. The 1973 Hoosiers got last-week help from Iowa and Northwestern in snatching away a clear-cut championship that Minnesota seemed to have clinched. That IU team, Knight's first of six championship clubs at IU, capitalized on its opening to move right on to the NCAA Final Four — the start, as things worked out, to a whole new tradition of basketball excellence at a school with roots deep in national success.

Knight refused to consider the Hoosiers' advance to the NCAA field a break over the teams from virtually all other conferences that had to go through post-season intra-league tourneys before moving on.

"We played two damned tough games this week," Knight said. "Nobody played any tougher games than we did. We haven't just been sitting around.

"Now we have to collect ourselves for the tournament. Last year, we had such a tough stretch coming down to the end, and (Mike) Woodson was so tired (after returning from back surgery) that I don't think we ever really did play well in the tournament.

"Now, I think you just go out and try to play as well as you can. The only thing you don't want to do is look back."

Heathcote promised Thursday night, after the upset of Iowa, to "do our best to win Iowa the championship." That meant, obviously, following one upset with another.

But after losing to IU, Heathcote said, "We could have played one of our best games and not won tonight.

"We got a good lesson on defense, for the second time this year. They do a great job of shutting off Kevin Smith and Jay Vincent, and then it's hard work for us to score.

"Indiana is just an awfully good basketball team, and that's why they're first and we're eighth, I guess."

Knight agreed "our defense tonight was good," and he supported Heathcote's reasoning on just why it was good.

"It was a different defense than we normally play," Knight said, "in that the whole thrust of our defense was aimed at two people (Smith and Vincent); instead of trying to play all five pretty straight.

"Vincent is obviously a great player who is tough as hell to play against. We tried to pay as much attention to where Vincent was as we have against anybody in the league — probably more. He just has a great touch."

Knight made a point of greeting Vincent before his last match-up with the Spartan senior, and he also talked with the other two MSU seniors, Mike Brkovich and Rick Kaye.

He made one other pre-game jaunt, turning to the bleachers behind him and calling an elderly, greenclad gentleman to the bench.

The man was an MSU economics professor, Walter Adams, who once was the school's interim's president. His seat for years has been directly behind the opponent's bench, and he is one of the league's champion coach-baiters. "He's been giving me hell for 10 years," Knight laughed.

This time, Knight surprised him with a bright red Indiana cap and an IU T-shirt, which Adams donned — then clasped Knight in a warm embrace.

An unusual night was off to a proper start.

Vincent's first goal was to go out a winner. He came in at Michigan State as one from Lansing Eastern High, and he was a leader instantly on two straight Big Ten championship teams.

Then, he was alone as a kingpin, buddies Earvin Johnson and Gregory Kelser moved on to the pros. The last two years, victories have been less frequent but Vincent has led the nation's toughest defensive league in scoring, twice.

That was a secondary goal Saturday night. He knew going in he needed exactly 16 points to pass Michigan's Mike McGee, who had 12 points in a losing effort against Purdue. When play was over, and Vincent had 20 points and IU a Big Ten championship, Vincent was philosophical and honest.

"I think if I hadn't had three or four fast-break jump shots, it would have been hard for me to get 16 points," he said.

"They're the best defensive team in America. They're tough. We couldn't even get into our offense."

Vincent was half of the Hoosier defensive concentration. The other half was junior guard Kevin Smith, who threw down a challenge to IU's Isiah Thomas after the Spartan victory over Iowa. Smith said then he considered Kevin Smith to be the Big Ten's best guard.

"I didn't hear about that." said Thomas.

He played as if he had. At game's end, Smith had two field goals, in part because Thomas played him cautiously, not with

INDIANA 69	M	FG	FT	R	A	BS	St	PF	TP
Kitchel, f	11	0- 1	3- 3	2	1	0	0	0	3
Turner, f	39	7- 9	2- 2	9	0	0	0	4	16
Tolbert, c	37	5- 9	7- 7	3	1	1	1	3	17
I. Thomas, g	37	5- 8	4- 9	3	5	0	2	4	14
Wittman, g	39	4- 7	1- 2	2	1	1	0	0	9
Grunwald	2	0- 0	0- 0	0	1	0	0	1	0
J. Thomas	2	0- 0	0- 0	0	0	0	0	0	0
Risley	28	2- 3	4- 6	4	1	1	0	0	8
Franz	1	0- 0	0- 0	0	0	0	0	0	0
Bouchie	1	0- 0	0- 0	0	0	0	0	0	0
Isenbarger	1	0- 0	0- 0	0	0	0	0	0	0
Brown	1	1- 1	0- 0	0	0	0	0	0	2
LaFave	1	0- 0	0- 0	0	0	0	0	0	0
Team				0					
Totals		24-38	21-29	23	10	3	3	12	69

MICHIGAN STATE 48	M	FG	FT	R	A	BS	St	PF	TP
Kaye, f	36	0- 2	3- 4	2	0	0	0	3	3
Tower, f	35	7- 9	0- 0	3	2	0	0	4	14
Vincent, c	38	10-17	0- 2	4	2	0	0	3	20
Smith, g	35	2- 8	1- 2	5	3	1	1	4	5
Brkovich, g	16	0- 4	0- 0	2	0	0	0	1	0
Bostic	14	1- 1	0- 0	0	1	0	0	2	2
Morrison	12	1- 1	0- 0	0	0	0	0	3	2
Perry	7	0- 2	0- 0	1	1	0	0	1	0
Bates	2	0- 1	0- 0	1	0	0	0	0	0
Cawood	2	0- 1	0- 0	0	0	0	0	1	0
Gore	2	0- 0	0- 0	0	0	0	0	0	0
Fossum		0- 0	0- 0	0	0	0	0	0	0
Radelet	1	0- 0	2- 2	0	0	0	0	0	2
Team				2					
Totals		21-46	6-10	20	9	1	1	22	48

SCORE BY HALVES

Indiana	34	35—	69
Michigan State	26	22—	48

Turnovers—Indiana 9, Michigan State 12.
Technical foul—Tower (grabbing rim).

SHOOTING

	FG	Pct.	FT	Pct.
Indiana	24-38	.632	21-29	.724
Michigan State	21-46	.457	6-10	.600

Officials—Art White, Fred Jaspers, Malcolm Hemphill.
Attendance—10,004 (sellout).

> *It's always nice to have personal goals, but I would have given it (a second straight Big Ten scoring championship) up to have the team win this one. They have to be the best defensive team in college basketball. We just could never get into our offense.*
>
> Jay Vincent
> Michigan State

his daring, sometimes reckless style that produces some steals and some burns.

"I just tried to play him head-up and stop him from penetrating," Thomas said.

"I did have to kind of control my hands a little. He's very good with the ball. He leaves it out there for you to grab at it, and if you do, he's good enough to take it right by you. I had to really concentrate on controlling myself."

As for the Smith declaration: "If he thinks he's the best, that's his prerogative," Thomas said. "Everybody thinks they're great."

Saturday, the Hoosiers thought Ohio State's Buckeyes had a touch of greatness themselves. It was Ohio State's televised afternoon victory over Iowa that gave IU a shot at a clear-cut championship.

Thomas said he didn't shout or bang the TV set when the Buckeye victory was final. "I just said, 'Thank you, Ohio State,' " he said. He insisted he wasn't surprised. "I would have bet my house Ohio State would win today, being their seniors' last game and everything," he said.

Risley, whose second strong reserve role of the week helped lift Hoosiers to the championship, said that after the Ohio State-Iowa game, "We just tried not to lose sight of what we had to do.

"We had a meeting ourselves right away after that game and we decided then that we didn't want a tie."

Knight said Risley "played another very good basketball game. It was just a great game for these kids."

Knight refused to watch the TV game. He didn't hear the outcome until about a half-hour afterward, although the explosive reaction in the halls around him probably gave him a clue.

He insisted he never was concerned about the afternoon outcome taking the edge off his team. "Not one bit," Knight said. "Not one bit."

He was left to celebrate a clear-cut Big Ten championship for the fifth time as Indiana's coach — and for the eighth time in his life.

That includes three as a player at Ohio State, from 1960 to '62.

Indiana has won only eight in its long history of championship contention. Knight's 1974 Hoosiers were co-champions, and his six titles overall are part of the 14 that IU now claims.

Thomas first IU soph on consensus all-America

Isiah Thomas became Indiana's first sophomore to make the consensus all-America team when he was selected on the first team of all four teams that determine the consensus team: the National Assn. of Basketball Coaches, the U.S. Basketball Writers Assn. and the two wire services.

Unanimous along with Thomas were Mark Aguirre of DePaul, Ralph Sampson of Virginia and Danny Ainge of Brigham Young. The fifth spot was divided: Kelly Tripucka of Notre Dame chosen by AP, Kevin Magee of California-Irvine by UPI and Steve Johnson of Oregon State by the coaches.

Jim Thomas gives Landon Turner two helping hands

Hoosiers pass Purdue in all-time standings

Indiana's 14-4 Big Ten record and four-game margin over Purdue moved the Hoosiers around Purdue by 3/10,000ths of a percentage point in the all-time Big Ten standings. Illinois had led until a few years ago. Indiana was fourth when Bob Knight took over as Hoosier coach in 1971, and under him the first team the Hoosiers passed on the all-time list was his alma mater, Ohio State.

ALL-TIME BIG TEN STANDINGS

	W	L	Pct.	Ch.	CC
Indiana	535	408	.5673	8	6
Purdue	554	423	.5670	8	7
Illinois	555	439	.558	6	5
Ohio State	470	436	.519	9	4
Michigan	435	423	.5070	5	5
Minnesota	499	486	.5066	3	3
Iowa	447	454	.496	4	4
Wisconsin	478	514	.482	6	7
Michigan State	224	242	.481	2	3
Northwestern	350	594	.371	1	1
Chicago	168	296	.362	4	2

Ray Tolbert — Seventh Hoosier named Big Ten's most valuable player

Tolbert easy winner as Big Ten's MVP

Ray Tolbert's long list of achievements in four seasons as an Indiana starter never did include selection on an all-Big Ten team.

But Tolbert did close out his career as the most valuable player in the Big Ten.

Tolbert, Hoosier coach Bob Knight's public choice for the award before the season ended, was the one-sided winner in balloting for the league honor, conducted by the Chicago *Tribune*.

Tolbert got three-fourths of the first-place votes from a 24-man panel that included the 10 Big Ten coaches, 10 officials, Big Ten Commissioner Wayne Duke and George Langford, Roy Damer and Bill Jauss from the *Tribune*.

He became the second straight Hoosier to win the award. Mike Woodson was named in 1980 after coming off the injured list to lead IU to six straight victories at the end of the season and a come-from-behind Big Ten title.

Tolbert also gave Indiana its sixth Big Ten MVP award in the last nine years and ninth overall in the 36 years the award has been given. Seven Hoosiers have won it, including Archie Dees (1957-58) and Scott May (1975-76) twice each.

Others besides Tolbert and Woodson were Kent Benson (1977), Steve Downing (1973) and Don Schlundt (1953).

Eddie Johnson of Illinois, scoring champion Jay Vincent of Michigan State and Mike McGee of Michigan were bunched in a group below Tolbert, *Tribune* officials said.

Other nominees, as MVPs on their own teams, were Vince Brookins of Iowa, Mark Hall and Trent Tucker of Minnesota, Rod Roberson of Northwestern, Herb Williams of Ohio State, Brian Walker of Purdue and Claude Gregory of Wisconsin.

All but the co-selections from Minnesota are seniors. Hall and Tucker are juniors.

Tolbert came out of Madison Heights in Anderson, where he was selected as Indiana's high school "Mr. Basketball" in 1977.

At Indiana, he moved into the starting lineup immediately, replacing 1977 all-America and Big Ten MVP Kent Benson.

He has played on:
• An NCAA champion (1981);
• Two Big Ten champions (1980 and '81);
• A National Invitation Tournament champion (1979; he and Butch Carter were named co-MVPs of the tournament);
• A Pan-American gold-medal team (1979, San Juan);
• Three NCAA qualifiers (including the 1978 team that finished second in the Big Ten).

Knight also predicted in pre-season that Tolbert will be a first-round selection in the National Basketball Assn. draft.

Indiana 99, Maryland 64

Dayton Arena was still reverberating with shock waves from the St. Joseph's elimination of No. 1-ranked DePaul when Maryland threatened a new tremor. In two fast-paced minutes, the not at all turtle-like Terrapins bolted to an 8-0 lead over Indiana's Big Ten champions.

"I was kinda surprised," IU guard Isiah Thomas admitted.

Thomas and the Hoosiers dealt out the rest of the afternoon's surprises, taking the Terps apart with superb play at both ends of the court in a 99-64 rout.

"We just got our fannies beat," Maryland coach Lefty Driesell put it.

"They played great. They dominated us on the boards. They dominated us on defense. If they'd been playing the 76ers today, they'd have beaten the 76ers."

Among the surprises the Hoosiers dealt out to Maryland were some medium-range jump shots by Ray Tolbert and Landon Turner, the big-man combination that suddenly clicked in IU's stretch run to the Big Ten title. "From the films we saw and the scouting reports, their big men don't shoot out there," said Maryland's all-America forward, Albert King. "It was very surprising."

Frequently, the same two were shooting from above the rim, freed for most of their eight dunks by a running game that wasn't supposed to be there, either, according to Maryland's intelligence reports. "We thought they'd slow it down and run if they had a chance to," King said. "We didn't think they'd run *that* much."

Tolbert had his IU high with 26 points, including five of the dunks. Turner scored 20 points, and the two combined to hit 19 of 26 shots.

Thomas shot even better (9-for-11) and passed better yet. His

Ted Kitchel clamps onto rebound

14 assists tied the recognized IU record (Quinn Buckner, vs. Illinois, 1974, and Bobby Wilkerson, vs. Michigan, 1976). "He played a super game," said Driesell, who found agreement from the NBC-TV selectors who made Thomas their player of the game.

The Hoosiers' .651 shooting and the 99 points were Indiana records for NCAA tournament play.

Neither mark seemed likely when Maryland's screeching start contrasted with a cough and a sputter as IU tried to move out.

The Hoosiers opened the game with a turnover, then four different players missed shots before Turner ended thoughts of a shutout by laying in a rebound shot.

The Indiana offense hummed, once it got in gear. Until it did, Maryland learned that IU's defensive reputation isn't all talk.

Three times in the first six minutes, Maryland lost the ball on offensive fouls. "We probably just forced our offense a little," Driesell said. "They play great defense."

Two of the fouls went against 6-foot-8 center Buck Williams, the quick and strong hub of Terp happenings on both offense and defense.

Williams was matched against Tolbert at IU's end, and the fouls plus the scouting information led him to back off and watch as Tolbert — surprised and delighted — went up for a 15-foot jump shot that gave IU its first lead, 14-13.

Next time downcourt, Tolbert ran to the same region, recognized the same Williams passivity and shouted "Isiah! Isiah!" A pass came, Tolbert went up again, and IU led 16-13.

Maryland's Greg Manning tried to get the Terrapins going again with a long-range jump shot, but Thomas blocked it, then scooted downcourt to set up Tolbert for the first fast-break dunk and push Driesell to a time out.

He didn't find any answers in the huddle. Indiana was in another of the nirvana stretches that have been habitual of late.

For 16 minutes, the Hoosiers played without a turnover, shot .710 (22-for-30) and outscored Maryland, 46-26, in exploding away to a 50-34 halftime lead.

In IU coach Bob Knight's view, things got better later. Maryland started the second half almost as quickly as the first, cutting the lead to 54-42 and whipping up some new-found hope within the optimistic Driesell. "I thought when we got it back to 12, we were going to get back in it," he said.

But Ted Kitchel hit from the side, Thomas beat the Maryland defense downcourt with a quick-break jump shot, Kitchel worked loose for a three-point play, Thomas supplied Tolbert with another dunk and the Hoosiers were out of sight again, 63-42. The lead reached 69-42 before the 3½-minute Indiana point run ended at 15.

"That was maybe the most important period for us," Knight said. "We were able to reassert ourselves."

More than 14 minutes remained, but all doubt was gone. Randy Wittman was the first of the Hoosier starters to be pulled, with 6:14 to go. Thomas left to a standing ovation with 3:18 remaining, and the other starters followed seconds later.

All five reached double figures, Thomas totaling 19, Kitchel 13 and Wittman 10. King fired 28 times to get his 10 field goals and 22 points in leading Maryland (21-10), while Williams had 16 points and Ernest Graham 14.

Landon Turner, Jim Thomas, Ray Tolbert have a ball

Coaching wives Nancy Knight, Kim Crews relish victory

'Best team I've played,'
Terps' Driesell says

Favorites were falling all over the country as college basketball began its serious pruning of candidates for the sport's most prestigious amateur championship. Champion Louisville is gone. And 10-time winner UCLA. And No. 1-ranked DePaul. It was an awful day to be regal.

But Indiana got through — with such total domination of Maryland that Driesell was reduced to awe and Knight to aw-shucks.

"They were the best team I've played against since I got my program going," Driesell said. "Nobody's beat us like that. There's nothing I can say but congratulations. I hope they win the national championship."

Knight's been there. He knows such a journey isn't made with one step, no matter how grand the step. When it was suggested that the day's events in Dayton Arena raised Hoosier stock for Final Four consideration, Knight scoffed. "Our stock is just one game better than it was two hours ago," he said.

No, he said, he wasn't shocked by DePaul's loss to unranked St. Joseph's. "I've seen a lot of teams get beat in this tournament. I've stood right here after we got beat . . ."

It was his one concession to sentiment. Six years ago, Knight's Indiana team was unbeaten and No. 1-ranked, but it fell, 92-90, to Kentucky and he had to step through the same curtain and step to the same rostrum and discuss how it had happened. Hoarsely that day, he congratulated Kentucky and said, "I really feel in today's game the best team won, and that's sure as hell the way it ought to be." That day, Knight was near tears as he closed his remarks: "It's been an enjoyable year for us. We'll be back some day."

They were back in the NCAA tournament a year later and stormed through it. It wasn't until this day that an Indiana team made it back to Dayton, and the result was equally overpowering.

But it was, Knight kept emphasizing, just one game, one day. "A lot of things really broke for us today," Knight said. "If we play Maryland again 10 times, they might beat us five.

"It might not have been the best thing in the world for Maryland to get off to the start they did (an 8-0 lead)." There may have been a reminder in there that awful things can happen to teams softened by an unexpectedly easy start.

"We just had things going our way," Knight said. "Maryland threw some passes away. We actually hit a couple shots I wasn't altogether enthused about them taking. The ball bounced our way. We must have had three or four baskets where we missed the shot, got the rebound and put it back up."

There were indeed three times when the IU shooter grabbed his own rebound and scored, plus five other times when a teammate reclaimed a Hoosier and scored — not bad on a day when the Hoosiers missed only 22 shots.

It was not a performance that Knight couldn't fault. "I don't think there is such a thing as a perfect game," Knight said. "In this one, I told our kids at the half we had already given up eight points on goaltending calls. At least we want to make the other team put in the hole to score."

Knight rejected a suggestion that the Hoosiers might have been extra-eager to win and qualify to go to their own party: the Mideast Regional at Assembly Hall Friday and Sunday. "I don't think so," he said. "These kids have played tournament games all over the country, and I think they're just happy to play anywhere."

Indiana is not a hard team to prepare for. They're going to play man-to-man defense. They're not going to press you, they're going to pick you up half-court. They do not do a whole lot of things, but what they do, they do very well. We know what they want to do.

Lefty Driesell
Maryland coach

MARYLAND 64

	M	FG	FT	R	A	BS	St	PF	TP
King, f	30	10-28	2- 4	4	2	0	0	4	22
Graham, f	30	7-18	0- 0	10	3	0	1	4	14
Williams, c	39	7- 9	2- 2	10	1	0	0	4	16
Jackson, g	24	0- 2	0- 0	0	1	0	0	3	0
Manning, g	37	3- 8	0- 0	0	2	0	0	3	6
Pittman	23	3- 3	0- 0	6	0	0	0	0	6
Rivers	8	0- 0	0- 0	0	1	0	0	0	0
Morley	9	0- 1	0- 0	1	4	0	1	2	0
Team				2					
Totals		30-69	4- 6	33	14	0	2	20	64

INDIANA 99

	M	FG	FT	R	A	BS	St	PF	TP
Turner, f	38	9-13	2- 2	7	2	1	2	2	20
Kitchel, f	30	5-11	3- 3	6	2	0	0	3	13
Tolbert, c	38	10-13	6- 6	8	1	4	1	1	26
Wittman, g	34	4- 9	2- 2	2	4	0	2	0	10
I.Thomas, g	35	9-11	1- 2	4	14	1	0	2	19
J.Thomas	6	0- 0	0- 0	1	0	0	0	0	0
Risley	8	2- 3	1- 3	3	0	0	0	1	5
Brown	3	0- 0	2- 2	0	0	0	0	0	2
Isenbarger	2	2- 2	0- 0	1	0	0	0	0	4
Bouchie	2	0- 0	0- 0	1	0	0	0	0	0
Grunwald	1	0- 0	0- 0	0	1	0	0	0	0
Franz	2	0- 1	0- 0	0	0	0	0	0	0
LaFave	1	0- 0	0- 0	1	0	0	0	0	0
Team				0					
Totals		41-63	17-20	33	25	6	5	9	99

SCORE BY HALVES

Maryland	34	30— 64
Indiana	50	49— 99

Turnovers—Maryland 16, Indiana 9.
Technical foul—Tolbert (grabbing rim).

SHOOTING

	FG	Pct.	FT	Pct.
Maryland	30-69	.435	4- 6	.667
Indiana	41-63	.651	17-20	.850

Officials—Hank Nichols, George Solomon, Willis McJunkin.

Attendance—13,458 (sellout).

Driesell expressed a skepticism growing in the college game about the value of the home court in big games, especially tournament games when the crowd isn't all local. "Sometimes, that (the home court) works against you," Driesell said. "It didn't seem to help a lot of teams last year.

"They've lost some games at home, I understand. That isn't going to make any difference.

"But if they play like they did today, there ain't nobody gonna beat 'em, wherever they play."

Driesell was sufficiently stirred by the enormity of his disaster that he peeked into his own record book to find when anything like that had happened before. His worst defeat in 12 highly successful seasons at Maryland was by a matching 35-point margin, 105-70 — at North Carolina, in 1971, the second year Driesell was at Maryland and, as he suggested, before he got the Terp program rolling.

"I'm a competitor," Driesell said. "We'll be back. This will just make me recruit a little bit harder.

"We're still a good ball club. I hate to get beat like this, but they just played great."

Driesell's biggest current star, King, won't be back. The most noted high school player in the country four years ago and Driesell's greatest recruiting catch, King left philosophically.

"They played like Louisville played against us," King said. "They couldn't do no wrong."

He found one consolation.

"It's better to lose this way than the way DePaul did."

'A clock that just kept ticking' — Isiah

The day was, Isiah Thomas decided, in a word, fun.

"It's always fun when you play well and do things right," Indiana's all-America guard said after a 19-point, 14-assist contribution to a spectacular team performance.

When the Hoosiers got rolling, Thomas said, "We were like a clock. We just kept ticking. Our offense worked. Our defense worked.

"The key was our defense. They could never get into their transition game."

That's the phrase that used to be called the running game. Fast breaks. Quick scores. Maryland stung the Hoosiers with a few of those early and then waited almost to the final minute before getting another.

When the score reached 8-0 during Maryland's fast start, Knight made no move toward a time out, expecting his players to realize the problem and correct it.

"We didn't get back quick enough," Tolbert said. "We knew we had to show some composure and just keep going. When we started to score, it stopped them from getting out on us."

Tolbert's primary concern was working against the high-scoring Maryland front line of King, Graham and Williams.

"Williams is such a strong player — tremendously strong," Tolbert said. "We wanted to try to go right at him and get him in foul trouble if we could.

"And Albert King is an excellent ballplayer. Landon was on him at the start."

That assignment was the continuation of a series of such roles for Turner, who has guarded quick forwards Kevin Boyle of Iowa, Mike McGee of Michigan and now King since his return to the Hoosier lineup.

"I knew I was going to have to play harder on defense against him," Turner said, "I had to move my feet. I knew he was a good shooter." King scored 22 points, but he had to fire freely to get them. He took 28 shots.

At IU's end, Turner said the poor start reinforced a Knight maxim. "You have to keep patient and the shots will come,"

Isiah Thomas to Steve Risley on 14-assist day

Indiana 87, Alabama-Birmingham 72

Two tournament opponents have left lasting memories with Indiana basketball followers in the last few years: Alabama, the team IU coach Bob Knight has called "the best we've ever played" because, in the Mideast Regional, it came closest to derailing the unbeaten Hoosiers on their way to the 1976 national championship; and Alcorn State, which was unbeaten but hadn't really won big-time recognition when it chased Indiana to the finish before losing in the 1979 NIT-champion Hoosiers' quarterfinal test at Assembly Hall.

Add Alabama Birmingham to the list. The Blazers went down, 87-72, but left some scars before moving aside in the NCAA Mideast Regional at IU's Assembly Hall.

Randy Wittman's best offensive night as a Hoosier, 20 points on 7-for-11 shooting, helped Indiana get away from UAB's upset attempt.

Wittman didn't feel as if he was off to a landmark game when the man he was guarding, Oliver Robinson, stung him for all the Blazer points as he put his team ahead, 9-8. "I was just trying to control him, but he came out and hit his first four shots," Wittman said. "That doesn't help your confidence a lot."

Robinson's fourth basket and three in a row by left-hander Chris Giles helped UAB open a 25-19 lead with 9:24 left in the half.

Wittman fired over the Blazers' zone to cut into the lead, then sniped again next time downcourt, missed but grabbed his own rebound and put it back in for a 25-23 game.

Indiana used the points for a springboard to a 38-31 lead that still was 42-37 at halftime — Wittman already the author of 14 points.

Wittman also had, not really reluctantly, handed defensive assignments against Robinson over to sophomore Jim Thomas by then. "If Alabama Birmingham was better known, Robinson would be up there on the all-America list," Wittman said. "He is really a good player.

"But when James came in (just after the two Wittman baskets, with 8:03 left in the half and UAB ahead, 27-23), it gave us a lift."

Thomas went in because Landon Turner picked up three fouls and sat down in the game's first five minutes and Steve Risley, vital to the Hoosiers in their two season-closing victories at Illinois and Michigan State, didn't have the answers this time for the problems posed by the swift Blazers.

"We needed a little more quickness," Knight said, "and Jimmy Thomas just about leads our club in rebounds per minute."

Thomas did enough closing out the first half to win a starting spot in the lineup for the second half. When Craig Lane opened the half with a rebound basket that pulled UAB within 42-39, Thomas stepped into an opening in the Blazer zone and hit the first Hoosier shot. Minutes later, he hit from the same place, and IU's lead had jumped back to 50-41.

Alabama Birmingham never got it under seven again, but the Hoosiers had to wait a while before edging into a comfortable lead. It was 68-60 with eight minutes left and Indiana already had gone to a spread offense to look for lay-ups and burn some time when Isiah Thomas cut for the basket but missed a lay-up in traffic. UAB hustled the ball downcourt to Giles in a bid to pull within six.

His shot missed, and Jim Thomas rebounded. Seconds later, Isiah Thomas zipped a pass to Ray Tolbert for a reverse dunk that restored a 10-point margin for the Hoosiers.

When UAB's Donnie Speer missed, Jim Thomas again rebounded and floated a pass to Tolbert breaking downcourt for

Landon Turner hooks over Leon Morris

another dunk that became a three-point play for a 73-60 IU lead with 6½ minutes left.

UAB had the lead down to 77-70 with 2½ minutes left when Isiah Thomas went to the free-throw line three times in 59 seconds and hit both halves of a one-and-one each time to get Indiana out of catching range.

Isiah Thomas had a couple shots rammed back at him when he went for baskets off the Hoosier spread but he had another big offensive night: 27 points (including 13-for-15 on free throws) and eight assists. Besides Wittman's 20, Indiana got 17 points from Tolbert, who led both teams with nine rebounds.

Robinson finished with 17 points for UAB (23-9). Giles and quick Glenn Marcus, Robinson's back-court partner, had 13 points each.

"I feel as though we could have beaten an awful lot of teams tonight," UAB coach Gene Bartow said. "But this is another outstanding Bob Knight team.

"We're obviously disappointed. We played hard and we played well. We wish them well in the tournament."

The Hoosiers did a lot of sweating on a night when they out-shot UAB, .525 to .429; had a 41-33 rebounding edge, and committed only seven turnovers.

"That's an excellent basketball team," Knight said.

Bartow pulling for Valparaiso

On a night when far more of Assembly Hall's seats than usual were filled by visitors and still the place rocked as it hasn't all year, Bartow soaked up the atmosphere and dreamed ahead.

"The regional's at our place next year," Bartow said.

"Boy, I hope we're in it . . . and I hope there's an Indiana team in it . . . but I hope it's Valparaiso."

Bartow had reason to leave The Hall with head high and humor intact, even though the NCAA tournament trail ended for his team.

This was the year that established the Blazers as a major league threat. This was the year UAB took mighty Kentucky out of the tournament. That's one Bartow can build on and his players can beam about all summer.

The variance from the heights scaled against Kentucky and the defeat that came against IU was not in UAB's play, Bartow indicated.

"The difference between Indiana and Kentucky is that Indiana shoots the lights out when you go to a zone, and Kentucky struggles," Bartow said.

"To me, this was a typical Bob Knight team. They played perfect in many ways — I'm sure not in his eyes, but in my eyes they looked pretty good.

"They do so many things so well. We changed defenses on them and just in an instant they adjusted their alignment. Lots of teams have some hesitation and a breakdown or two, but not Bob's teams. I didn't see them early this year, but I've heard they were struggling a little then. They're not struggling now."

Bartow stuck with his zone as long as he could, even with Wittman leading the Hoosiers' outside attack. "Indiana's so hard to cover man-to-man for very long," Bartow said. He went to a man-to-man early, and the first time downcourt against it, the Hoosiers worked 6-1 Isiah Thomas inside in their offense, operating against the 5-10 Marcus. Thomas went over

Nice try, but no success for UAB's Gene Bartow

for a close-in jump shot, and Bartow signaled a return to the zone.

"We thought Isiah might take us under some, and he did," Bartow said. "I never had the privilege of seeing Isiah Thomas play. He's a great team leader and an outstanding player.

"But Indiana's great defense was the key. They're tough, physical and very smart. We didn't shoot well (.429), probably because of their great defense. We thought we would have to shoot at least 50 percent to win.

"And still we were in it till the last two minutes."

Marcus is the only starting senior on a Blazer roster that will be brightened next year by the addition of 6-5 guard Raymond Gause and 6-10 forward Lex Drum, two players on campus now but sitting out the year. "They may be the two best players we have," Bartow said.

"I thought from the start we'd have a good program. (Former Alabama coach) C.M. Newton played Indiana's championship team a great basketball game, and I believe every one of his kids came from Birmingham."

Knight clearly was relieved that the Blazers were behind his team.

"There was a point in the second half when I really thought they might slip away from us," Knight said.

"I thought both Jim Thomas and Steve Bouchie came off the bench and played very, very well.

Randy Wittman finds an opening over Oliver Robinson

ALABAMA BIRMINGHAM 72

	M	FG	FT	R	A	BS	St	PF	TP
Giles, f	39	6-11	1- 3	8	1	0	1	3	13
Lane, f	13	1- 5	0- 2	3	0	0	0	4	2
Speer, c	23	3- 8	2- 2	7	0	1	0	3	8
Robinson, g	38	6-15	5- 5	2	1	0	0	4	17
Marcus, g	28	6-10	1- 1	1	4	0	1	5	13
Anchrum	18	2- 5	3- 4	3	0	2	0	5	7
Nicholas	7	0- 0	1- 2	1	0	0	0	0	1
Morris	24	1- 4	4- 4	2	1	0	0	0	6
Foster	5	2- 3	1- 1	1	0	0	1	5	5
Almquist	1	0- 0	0- 0	1	0	0	0	0	0
Simcik	1	0- 1	0- 0	0	0	0	0	0	0
McCammon	1	0- 1	0- 0	0	0	0	0	0	0
Richards	1	0- 0	0- 0	0	0	0	0	0	0
Bartow	1	0- 0	0- 0	0	0	0	0	0	0
Team				4					
Totals		27-63	18-24	33	7	3	3	29	72

INDIANA 87

	M	FG	FT	R	A	BS	St	PF	TP
Kitchel, f	17	3- 8	3- 4	1	0	0	0	3	9
Turner, f	11	0- 3	0- 2	1	0	1	0	3	0
Tolbert, c	39	8-12	1- 1	9	2	1	0	3	17
I.Thomas, g	39	7-12	13-15	4	8	0	3	4	27
Wittman, g	40	7-11	6- 7	4	3	0	1	1	20
Risley	7	0- 1	0- 0	2	0	0	0	2	0
J.Thomas	27	3- 4	1- 2	6	3	0	0	2	7
Bouchie	16	2- 7	1- 2	3	2	0	1	2	5
Isenbarger	1	0- 0	0- 0	1	1	0	0	0	0
Franz	1	0- 0	0- 0	0	0	0	0	0	0
Brown	1	1- 1	0- 0	0	0	0	0	0	2
Grunwald	1	0- 0	0- 0	1	0	0	0	0	0
Team				9					
Totals		31-59	25-33	41	19	2	5	20	87

SCORE BY HALVES

Alabama Birmingham		37	35— 72
Indiana		42	45— 87

Turnovers—Alabama Birmingham 11, Indiana 7.

SHOOTING

	FG	Pct.	FT	Pct.
Alabama Birmingham	27-63	.429	18-24	.750
Indiana	31-59	.525	25-33	.758

Officials—Bobby Dibler (WAC), Dale Kelley (SEC), James Howell (Southern).

Attendance—17,091.

"We started out the game in our accelerated one-pass-and-shoot offense that our kids devised in a 2 o'clock meeting.

"We're not going to have a 2 o'clock meeting tomorrow."

'Lot of improvement to make' — Wittman

Wittman heard the town and campus talk that everyone else did; that the Mideast Regional looked like such a rugged challenge for Indiana at one time, before DePaul, Kentucky and Wake Forest disappeared and St. Joseph's, Alabama Birmingham and Boston College showed up.

Respecting the Birmingham team, however, was no problem for the Hoosiers, Wittman said.

"They had done one thing that we hadn't: they beat Kentucky," Wittman said. "And Kentucky beat us here."

The latter point covered the other possible justification for Hoosier smugness going into the tournament: the home-court edge. Obviously, the folks who run the Knight basketball program had the researchers at work to deal with that item.

"Only four teams have ever won a regional on their home court," Wittman said. "Those aren't very good odds."

So, Wittman was primed going in, his career-high 20-point offensive performance no real surprise.

"We knew they would be playing mostly zone," he said. "I had to look for my shot." Uncharacteristically, he found eight of them in the first half and scored 14 points, including six free throws.

"We came out and shot much too fast," Wittman said. "We acted like we were playing with a 30-second clock.

"I think we got caught up in the crowd a little. Once we settled down, we went to the foul line a lot, which was what we wanted to do.

"This wasn't one of our better games. We've got a lot of improvement to make. We've got to keep going up now."

Knight felt Wittman's biggest contribution came on defense. "He did an excellent job of sliding over and taking a couple charges on Marcus," Knight said. Marcus scored on two drives to the basket in the first half but paid for both field goals with a foul after running into Wittman. "That bought us some time, when he (Marcus) had to go out," Knight said.

Wittman had his hands full at the time trying to keep UAB's leading scorer, Robinson, in check. But he did keep Marcus in view, too, and when he saw Marcus roaring to the basket on the two drives, he left his man long enough to get in the way.

"Marcus is such a fine ballplayer — I'd say he hurt us more with his quickness than anyone we've played," Wittman said.

Marcus was Isiah Thomas's headache — and vice versa — for most of the game. And Thomas was impressed.

"They were a really good ball club," Thomas said. "They never quit."

Anti-Thomas plan foiled for UAB

The plan was to prevent Isiah Thomas from penetrating. That was the plan, anyway.

It looked so good on the blackboard. Marcus and Robinson would stand out front in UAB's 2-1-2 zone and block Thomas whenever he made a move to the lane.

But Isiah's hummingbird quickness has a way of fouling up the best of chalkboard strategy. Repeatedly, he knifed between the two-man blockade and worked on the interior of the Blazers' zone. When all was said and done, Thomas had done enough penetrating to score 27 points and flip off eight assists (one more than the entire UAB team).

Jim Thomas closes in on Oliver Robinson

"Isiah is a great guard," said Robinson. "We wanted to keep him from driving the middle where he could shoot or pass off. But he did a good job.

"I expect them to win the national championship. Their defense is about the same as Kentucky's, but offensively they hit more shots. Without that outside shooting they'd be dead, but as long as they keep shooting no one is going to stop them."

The Hoosiers shot .525 for the night, hitting 31 of 59 shots. That's below their average. They were at .533 for the season going in, .541 in Big Ten play.

Giles said the Blazers "concentrated on the team as a whole but the main thing was keeping Isiah from penetrating inside and then dishing off to Tolbert."

To a man, the Blazers spoke of IU's sixth man . . . the crowd. Several times in the second half, when the Hoosiers fended off UAB's relentless challenge with flurries of points, the Assembly Hall noise reached deafening proportions.

"You just try to block everything out," said Robinson. "You always have to do that when you play on the road, but the noise here was awesome. We couldn't even communicate.

"It may have affected things. We didn't get some breaks.

"We just wanted to play with them. We wanted to play as hard as we could and prove that we have a team to be reckoned with. I think we did that."

Indiana 78, St. Joseph's 46

They weren't subtle at St. Joseph's about the game plan. It fluttered from a sign in the cheering section: "Four-to-Score to the Final Four."

"Four-to-score" is Hawk coach Jim Lynam's spread offense — players aligned in the four corners of the offensive court, a la the clock-killing ploy associated with North Carolina coach Dean Smith, but instructed in Lynam's system to look for opportunities to drive and set up scoring opportunities. It's not a stall but an offense, albeit a slow and patient one.

It was the threat that hung in the air when the throw went up for the opening tip. Control went to Indiana, and the first offensive sequence took on game-ending importance. The Hoosiers maneuvered and distorted the 2-3 St. Joseph's zone defense with passes and short drives till suddenly Ted Kitchel was open in the wing area right of the free-throw circle. "I thought it was really important to get ahead," Kitchel said. He sank the shot, Indiana was up 2-0, and "probably the most important part of the game," in the judgment of IU guard Isiah Thomas, already was over, 25 seconds into the game.

St. Joseph's did go to its "four-to-score" spread. John Smith, 6-5, had 6-10 Landon Turner of IU draped on all sides of him as Smith tried to find an open teammate. Turner stayed close enough long enough to get a jump ball, controlled the tip, and a few more passes opened Randy Wittman in the left corner for a jump shot that, like Kitchel's, swished.

The score was 4-0, Lynam waved his team out of the spread offense into regular movement, and Indiana was on its way to Philadelphia and to a 78-46 romp in the NCAA Mideast Regional's championship game at Assembly Hall.

Lynam hadn't panicked. "We didn't intend to run the spread the whole game," he said. "We wanted to go in and out of it."

And in the spread, he said, "We weren't trying to hold the ball. We just wanted them to come out and guard us. They did, and they did it extremely well.

"If their defense is not the best in the country, it has got to be tied for it."

The offense wasn't bad, either. The opening bullseyes by Kitchel and Wittman — just a day before, Lynam had them in mind when he said, "Those two kids from Indiana look to me like shooters" — started the second-best shooting show in IU history and the best ever in NCAA tournament competition.

The Hoosiers closed at .686. They shot 51 times and missed 16. It was the seventh time the current club topped .600 in a game. Only the 1979 team's .711 performance at Texas Tech in its NIT opener beat the performance that took a .684 mark set by San Francisco against Brigham Young in 1979 off the NCAA books.

Indiana hit five of its first six shots in taking a 10-4 lead. Just that quickly the chance for St. Joseph's to do anything drastic with a slowdown died. At the very least, Lyman conceded, it did "give them (the Hoosiers) an air of confidence."

Turner and Wittman led the early Hoosier charge, with assistance — a most apt word — from Isiah Thomas, who wasn't particularly afflicted with the hot-hand problem most of his teammates had but fed the ones who were warm to roll up 12 assists.

Turner was 3-for-3 and Wittman, after hitting three in a row from long range, found a path through the St. Joseph's zone for a driving shot that gave him a fourth field goal and the Hoosiers an 18-10 lead.

The basket also gave Wittman a seat for the rest of the day. "I

Contact sport for Ted Kitchel, Tony Costner

Net profit for Ray Tolbert after regional final

caught a knee in my thigh when I made the drive," he said. The problem was diagnosed as a bruise, ice and rest were prescribed, and Wittman became the only cloud on a glorious Hoosier day, his availability for the Final Four games at least somewhat questionable.

Jim Thomas came on to replace Wittman with 6:50 to go in the half, and the sophomore from Fort Lauderdale delivered his second strong reserve performance of the weekend.

"He played extremely well," Hoosier coach Bob Knight said. "He just had a very, very good tournament. He did a good job defensively and he scored well."

Jim Thomas had one field goal as Indiana pulled out to a 32-16 halftime lead. When St. Joseph's abandoned its zone and tried to surprise the Hoosiers with man-to-man pressure opening the second half, Thomas worked free to score the first three field goals of the half and puncture any hopes of the Hawks had of generating a comeback.

The Thomas spree made the score 38-17, and St. Joseph's never got the margin under 19 again.

It didn't really balloon until after Knight had pulled his last two regulars, one at a time to let the crowd of 17,112 lavish its appreciation — Isiah Thomas, pulled with 3:51 left and the score 60-34; then, for the last time at The Hall, Ray Tolbert, with 3:05 to go and the score 65-38.

Lynam also cleared his bench, and the Indiana margin zoomed past 30 to a high of 34 before settling at the final 32.

Turner, NBC-TV's pick as player of the game, and Tolbert

I sat on the bench as they were pulling away with a kind of helpless feeling. They were taking us out of anything we tried to do. I've lost a lot of games as a coach, but very few like that. I never felt more hopeless.

Jim Lynam
St. Joseph's coach

ST. JOSEPH'S 46

	M	FG	FT	R	A	BS	St	PF	TP
Williams, f	34	2- 4	0- 0	4	0	0	0	3	4
Smith, f	32	1- 6	0- 0	2	3	0	1	3	2
Costner, c	34	3- 8	1- 2	4	0	0	1	5	7
Clark, g	31	3- 4	5- 6	4	0	0	0	4	11
Warrick, g	38	3-10	3- 3	0	3	0	1	1	9
McFarlan	20	1- 7	4- 6	2	2	0	0	0	6
Mitchell	3	0- 0	0- 1	0	0	0	0	0	0
Kearney	3	0- 0	2- 3	1	0	0	0	1	2
Springman	3	1- 3	3- 4	0	0	0	0	0	5
DiCaro	2	0- 0	0- 0	0	1	0	0	0	0
Team				4					
Totals		14-42	18-25	21	9	0	3	17	46

INDIANA 78

	M	FG	FT	R	A	BS	St	PF	TP
Kitchel, f	20	1- 4	1- 2	3	3	0	1	4	3
Turner, f	29	7- 8	0- 0	5	2	0	0	5	14
Tolbert, c	37	6- 8	2- 4	5	2	0	0	1	14
I.Thomas, g	36	3- 8	2- 3	1	12	0	3	2	8
Wittman, g	13	4- 4	0- 0	0	1	0	0	0	8
J.Thomas	24	6- 7	0- 0	3	1	0	0	0	12
Risley	17	1- 2	0- 1	2	2	0	1	0	2
Grunwald	8	1- 1	2- 2	1	1	0	0	1	4
Brown	4	0- 1	1- 2	1	2	0	0	2	1
Isenbarger	3	3- 4	0- 0	0	2	0	0	3	6
Bouchie	3	1- 2	0- 0	1	1	0	0	0	2
Franz	3	1- 1	0- 0	0	0	0	0	1	2
LaFave	3	1- 1	0- 0	5	0	0	0	0	2
Team				6					
Totals		35-51	8-14	33	29	0	5	19	78

SCORE BY HALVES

St. Joseph's		16	30— 46
Indiana		32	46— 78

Turnovers—St. Joseph's 11, Indiana 9.

SHOOTING

	FG	Pct.	FT	Pct.
St. Joseph's	14-42	.333	18-25	.720
Indiana	35-51	.686	8-14	.571

Officials—Dale Kelley (SEC), James Howell (Southern), Bobby Dibler (WAC).

Attendance—17,112 (sellout).

shared Hoosier scoring honors with 14 points. They also shared the game's rebounding lead with a surprise third partner: freshman Mike LaFave, who matched their five rebounds in playing just two minutes and 53 seconds.

Jim Thomas had 12 points, hitting six of seven shots, Turner was 7-for-8, Tolbert 6-for-8. Because most of the rebounds were occurring at the IU defensive end, the Hoosiers claimed a 33-21 board edge.

Guard Jeff Clark had 11 points for St. Joseph's, but the Hawks' other guard, Bryan Warrick, made the all-tournament team along with Alabama Birmingham's Glenn Marcus and three Hoosiers — Wittman, Tolbert and the regional's outstanding player, Isiah Thomas.

Hawks unembarrassed by one-sided loss

St. Joseph's senior John Smith was slumped in a chair, towel draped around his neck and trickles of perspiration rolling off his chin.

His eyes were red, moistened by the knowledge that he had just played his last game as a Hawk — a 32-point blowout.

"I don't think we were embarrassed at all today," Smith said. "They went after us right from the start. But I won't hang my head. Regardless of the score, we were in it . . . we were in it."

Clark was the key figure in St. Joseph's battle plan. In the Hawks' spread offense, Clark was to handle the ball as much as possible, hoping to get the gambling Isiah Thomas in early foul trouble.

"I had confidence in myself that in the four-corner, I could drive around him and draw some fouls," said Clark. "We wanted to be patient and use the clock.

"It was pretty much the same game plan we used against DePaul, but today the tempo got away from us. We made some turnovers and missed some easy chances to score.

"DePaul didn't play nearly so aggressive on defense. Indiana plays a very aggressive man-to-man. But they still don't force turnovers; it was just our lack of concentration."

Smith also was surprised to see the four-to-score self-destruct so quickly.

"They give you the outside lane but they wouldn't let you get to the middle," Smith said. "They did a really good job of denying the ball and not letting us get to the middle of the court. This is the first time this year that a team has taken us out of our four-to-score with defensive pressure."

Warrick, a member of the all-regional team, said, "I don't

Jeff Clark (12), Isiah Thomas duel

He knows how to communicate his philosophy to his players to a degree few coaches can duplicate. You know what they're going to do. There's nothing overly sophisticated. But the way they implement their plan is so constant, so consistent. It's hard to believe the way Knight gets his athletes to sustain it the way they do from start to finish.

Jim Lynam
St. Joseph's coach

And a few days later, both St. Joe's and Indiana were in Pa. — and Hoosiers were happiest

know why their defense was so effective. You'd have to ask Bobby Knight about that. Whatever they did bothered us a lot."

Lynam considered Thomas the part of the Hoosier offense he had to stop, or at least control, to win.

"To beat them, you've got to contain him," Lynam said, "but that's obviously much easier said than done.

"And they have such a tremendous defense. One of the things that makes it so good is that Thomas puts such relentless pressure on the ball.

"I was hoping we would be able to spread the defense and create some openings. But when we spread the floor, they had definite things in mind *they* wanted to do defensively."

The crowd was a much-discussed subject in the Hawks' locker room

"I would love to play them on a neutral site," Smith said. "I'm not saying we would beat them there but it would be a lot closer."

Warrick felt the crowd "really got 'em pepped up. You could see it when they were warming up. It got so loud we couldn't hear. When you can't hear the play and have to use hand signals to communicate, it's going to affect you."

But Smith, weakened by the flu throughout the tournament, admitted there were some players who also made a contribution.

"What the crowd does doesn't have any effect on what happens on the court," he said. "What happens between the lines is determined by the players. The crowd can't make a basket or block your shot. Only players can do that."

Tolbert, Thomas thrilled by Final Four

Tolbert remembers the last time the NCAA Final Four played in Philadelphia's Spectrum, in 1976. "I was at the state tournament at Market Square Arena," Tolbert said. "At halftime, we went to a lounge and watched — us and about 85 other people. Indiana was playing UCLA, and I remember thinking, 'Hey, that's great. It must be great to play in the national finals.'"

Isiah Thomas watched that tournament in Chicago, a high school freshman at the time. He has watched several NCAAs since, last year's not among them. "I was too depressed last year," he said. But those other Final Fours he has watched were responsible for the tears that came as he sat on the bench with Indiana's trip to Philadelphia for this year's Final Four assured. "I feel great," he said. "I've never felt this way about anything else. It's the chance of a lifetime. If it's anything like they make it seem, it's tremendous."

Thomas was the fourth Hoosier starter to leave the floor late in the game. He leaped up seconds later when Tolbert made his last exit from an Assembly Hall game.

The two, Thomas and Tolbert, grabbed each other. "I just

Isiah Thomas, Randy Wittman swap congratulations

looked at Zeke," Tolbert recalled. "And I said, 'We're *going.*'

"It seems unreal."

The two had eyes for each other at vital times during the game as well. Indiana attacked the St. Joseph's zone defense in the traditional way, with outside shooting, but the Hoosiers also cracked it repeatedly for shots inside the zone.

Three times, Tolbert materialized in the middle of the zone like a mushroom popping out of the wooden floor. Each time, the ball arrived simultaneously, and he stung the Hawks for a quick turn-around jump shot. All went in. Turner made the same sort of sudden appearance. He cashed in his Thomas passes with a variety of short hook shots.

"We try to come up from behind their guy, where he can't see us," Tolbert said. "There is a lot of eye contact with Isiah.

"Isiah can see the whole floor. If we're open in there, he'll get to us.

"If we're not moving enough, he'll tell us to move more. He thinks ahead of time."

Thomas has been seeing whole floors for some time now. The ability to bark when necessary came a little later.

106

"He is the kind of kid who has a great respect for people," Knight said. "He was reluctant to say, 'This is the way we're going to do it.'

"But he has just done an excellent job of taking over out there and doing the things we want done.

"And in doing that, he is also more careful about what he does. So he has become not only a better contributor to the team but also a better player himself."

It wasn't easy, Thomas admitted. "It's the seniors' year," he said. "They've worked twice as hard as I have. I've only been here two years; they've been here four."

He overcame the reluctance to be a commander. "I had no choice," he said.

"Tolbert and (Glen) Grunwald were the captains at the beginning of the year. They can handle things off the court, but on the court, they're both inside players. They can't see things as well as I can on the outside looking in."

No one looks in better, Lynam implied.

"Thomas is a great passer against a zone," Lynam said. "If a guy's open in the middle, he finds him. They probably shoot more shots close to the basket than any team I've seen, and I have to attribute that to Thomas."

Turner learned one more time never to presume things when Thomas has a basketball in his hands. Early in the game, Thomas was open for a 16-foot jump shot, he went into the air and — whoosh, he zipped a pass instead toward Turner, past Turner, into the hands of a St. Joseph's defender trapped behind Turner in a spot where he could have done nothing to avert a lay-up if Turner had caught the ball.

"I thought he was going to shoot and I was looking up at the rim getting ready for the rebound," Turner said. "Next thing I know the ball is sailing past my face."

Standout passers have been known to bloody a nose or two with unexpected but accurate throws to open but unsuspecting targets. "He's never hit me in the face yet," Turner said, "but that one was pretty close."

Thomas confessed to some feelings of *deja vu*, triggered by the name of the game opponent. "My high school was St. Joseph's (in suburban Chicago)," he said.

"And the other guard with me was Ray Clark, who wore No. 12. When coach was going through the lineup, the St. Joseph's guy I was assigned to guard was Clark, and he wore No. 12. It freaked me out."

It's the first Final Four trip for each of the 13 Hoosier players. Knight is going for the sixth time: three in a row as a player at Ohio State, now three as IU's coach. "I feel very proud of our kids," Knight said.

When the game ended, Knight grabbed the courtside microphone and told the crowd of 17,112: "On behalf of the whole basketball team, I want to thank you for hanging in there with us in December and rooting like hell for us in January and February."

Later, he said the Hoosiers' development was not a sudden switch from bad to good.

"We had a 7-5 start with a fairly inexperienced team," he said. "I'm not sure how bad we played in doing that. We lost some very close games to some pretty good basketball teams.

There's nothing casual about what Indiana does. Forget that you've got a nice lead. With Knight, that's beside the point, and that might be why they're the best in the country.

Jim Lynam
St. Joseph's coach

Isiah Thomas gets a sendoff on way to Philly

"But I was glad they (IU fans) hung with us. A lot of places don't care how you lose, they just get on you. I've had 'em get on me when we won."

Tolbert, the most public of the Hoosiers with his exuberance and joy, went private in his biggest moment of IU success yet. He took a back way out of Assembly Hall, to duck interviewers and autograph seekers. "I just wanted to get out when I could so I could spend some time with my parents," he said. "I did, and it was great.

"I almost couldn't sleep last night. I just wanted to get out there and play. We were so close to going to the Final Four. I just wanted to get the game started.

"And now I come back home, and it doesn't seem like we're in a Final Four. It seems like we just got through another tough Big Ten weekend and there's another one coming up.

"I'm very happy. Everything has worked out well for us. Being in the Final Four is such a great honor. We've worked hard all year, looking forward to this goal.

"It's a good feeling, but now we want to go out there and do as well as we can."

The Spectrum — Site of two NCAA finals, two Indiana championships in six years

Upsets and all, tourney has classy Final Four

The wailings of a week ago are as forgotten today as the dear departed teams whose demise caused them. The 41st NCAA basketball tournament has worked down to as classy a Final Four as public concepts of national college basketball excellence could seek. At Philadelphia next weekend will be:

• Indiana, the champion of the Big Ten;

• Louisiana State, the champion of the Southeastern Conference;

• Virginia, the regular-season champion of the Atlantic Coast Conference;

• North Carolina, the ACC's post-season tournament champion.

There isn't an upsetter nor a potentially embarrassing national champion in the group, although Indiana and North Carolina weren't really supposed to be the best in the regions that they wound up dominating. DePaul and Oregon State were the top seeds in those regionals, but Indiana and North Carolina have been as consistent at winning crucial games of late as these recent DePaul and Oregon State superteams have been at losing them in tournament play.

The situation recalls a haughty sign shown in a *Sports Illustrated* picture after it was hoisted in the DePaul cheering section last year when the Demons first reached No. 1:

Isiah, eat your heart out.

Pitiful indeed, Isiah's plight.

Indiana, the school that Isiah Thomas finally chose over DePaul in his recruiting days to acquire the grandstand Demonic enmity, is in this year's Final Four with nine defeats. That is two more than any of the NCAA's first 40 champions ever had and five more than DePaul has suffered in the last two years.

But Isiah also has two Big Ten championships and one NCAA regional title. Likely, the huge Thomas heart doesn't have the first toothmark yet.

Phrases don't essentially reflect truth. Whoever coined the line, "We're better than ever," for IU booster pins this year has a terribly short memory.

The salient point is that IU is back — in Philadelphia, in national prominence, in production of basketball masterpieces that tend to awe. The current Hoosiers didn't enjoy their nine defeats, but they seem not in the least shamefaced about their chance at history, nor should they be. They're in the national semifinals legitimately, their latest Big Ten title sufficient ratification of their worth — and the eight-game winning streak that has carried them into the Final Four as shiny a stretch as any college team has put together for a while.

All four of the survivors were seeded. The bye that the NCAA's selectors gave them for their regular-season achievements wasn't the kiss of death for them that so many of the sidelined seeds claimed it was.

So much for myths.

IU's .686 against St. Joe NCAA tournament record

Indiana's .686 shooting against St. Joseph's in the NCAA Mideast Regional finals at Assembly Hall set an NCAA tournament record — after the Hoosiers had just missed the 41-year-old tournament's all-time Top 10 shooting performances by shooting .651 in their opener against Maryland. The top marks:

NCAA SHOOTING

	FG	Pct.
1. Indiana, vs. St. Joseph's, 1981	35-51	.686
2. San Francisco, vs. Brigham Young, 1979	39-57	.684
3. Princeton, vs. Providence, 1965	41-60	.683
4. Arkansas, vs. Wake Forest, 1977	34-50	.680
5. Ohio State, vs. California, 1960*	31-46	.674
6. Penn, vs. Providence, 1972	33-49	.673
Villanova, vs. Houston, 1981	33-49	.673
8. Notre Dame, vs. North Carolina, 1977	30-45	.667
9. VMI, vs. Tennessee, 1976	33-50	.660
10. Providence, vs. Penn, 1973	40-61	.656
13. Indiana, vs. Maryland, 1981	41-63	.651

*Record for championship game

Indiana 67, Louisiana State 49

The last time Bob Knight brought an Indiana basketball team to The Spectrum, it trailed at halftime and then won by 18. Five years have passed, and Knight hasn't improved the script a bit.

Knight's overnight wonders routed Louisiana State, 67-49, to move into position to try for a repeat of the national championship IU won under Knight in 1976, the last time the tournament was played in Philadelphia.

The Hoosiers, who broke the all-time tournament shooting record last time out, threatened to break the glass backboards with the shots they threw up against LSU.

They missed their last 10 shots of the first half, lost their on-court leader, Isiah Thomas, to foul troubles, and went to the dressing room behind LSU's Southeastern Conference champions, 30-27.

Thomas hit six of the eight shots he tried in the first half but couldn't get the tension out of the shooters all around him. When he picked up his third foul and sat down with 3:14 left in the half, the Hoosiers got tighter still.

"The best thing that happened to us," Thomas said, "was the halftime."

Knight didn't use the half to revise any planning.

"I just told them, 'Stretch out and breathe deeply,' " Knight said.

"I told them, 'We don't need to do anything differently. Let's just settle down and relax.' "

Thomas agreed with Knight. "Everyone was too excited," he said. "I woke up at 6 this morning thinking it was 9. Everybody was just so anxious to play.

"And that showed in the way we played."

When the Hoosiers returned to the playing floor to get a few practice shots, Knight gathered them around him again in the middle of the floor and talked for a few seconds. "We usually do that," Knight said, "when we're in trouble."

Ray Tolbert was the primary target of Knight's halftime advice. "He's such a 'hyper' kid," Knight said. "That first half, he was in the ozone." The Big Ten's 1981 shooting champion took five shots and hit one in the first half.

He also had one rebound in the half. When he opened the second half by snatching Ted Kitchel's miss out of the air and slamming it through the hoop with a robust dunk, the Hoosier charge was signaled.

The other big man who has helped to key the late-season IU charge, 6-10 junior Landon Turner, scored the basket that put the Hoosiers ahead for good, 31-30.

Another Kitchel miss was fielded by Thomas, who zipped the ball to Turner for a three-point play and a sudden 34-30 Hoosier lead that drove LSU coach Dale Brown to a time out, barely 2½ minutes into the second half.

If the purpose of the time out was to break momentum, it failed. Sub Willie Sims put up a quick LSU shot under defensive pressure and missed, and Turner's rebound basket jumped the Indiana lead to 36-30.

The turning point that came then was a shocker to LSU. Isiah Thomas drew his fourth foul and sat down again — 16:33 left in the game and Bayou hopes blazing anew with the Hoosier all-American out.

Sophomore Jim Thomas came on as his replacement, and he wasn't on the floor five seconds till he had pulled off a rebound — the first scorebook entry he was to make in a victory contribution so spectacular that he wound up sharing NBC-TV's award as the game's outstanding player with teammate Turner.

Landon Turner plays a high game against LSU

109

Jim Thomas — An unknown to LSU, but all-Final Four

Turner did it with points — 20, high for both teams. Jim Thomas missed all four shots he took and scored just two points, but he also led IU with nine rebounds, passed off for a couple baskets, blocked two LSU shots, made a steal and generally, in Knight's view, "played great."

His first rebound blossomed into a quick-break jump shot by Turner for a 38-30 lead.

More than five minutes of the second half passed, 8:19 in all counting a dry stretch at the end of the first half, before LSU scored a point. The Tigers had the ball 11 times without scoring in that long period, ended by Howard Carter's shot from the corner with 14:55 to go in the game.

The shot made the score 38-32, but the Tigers got no closer.

It was 40-34 when Kitchel fired from a distance rarely tried even by guards in the Knight era. "It was a little farther out than I thought," Kitchel admitted later. "But I was open and I thought I could hit it."

He did for a 42-34 lead. Jim Thomas, only 6-3, leaped high amidst the collection of big men on the floor to save an offensive rebound for IU and set up Randy Wittman for another long shot over LSU's zone defense.

After Tolbert cleared Tiger freshman Leonard Mitchell's miss, Wittman hit again from well out on the court to put IU up, 46-34.

Turner closed the back-breaking eight-point streak with two free throws for a 48-34 lead. It was 54-39 with 6:47 to go when

Isiah Thomas returned — the lead almost doubled in the best stretch of clutch play the Hoosiers have had without their quarterback in his two seasons of collegiate play.

Indiana celebrated his return by running off six points in a row to boost its lead over 20 for the first time at 60-39 — a margin that represented a stunning 33-9 Hoosier edge in the first 17 minutes of second-half play.

Reserves finished out for IU.

It was a crushing rebuff for Brown in his first trip to the Final Four. Instead of the national championship he hoped to take back to Baton Rouge, he watched his usually high-scoring club set a 17-year LSU low with its 49 points.

"The shooting was horrendous for both teams," Brown said. Indiana won with its season low in shooting, .365, but LSU underachieved that with .322, including .241 in the last half.

Besides Turner's 20 points, IU got 14 from Isiah Thomas and 10 from Kitchel.

Carter's 10 led LSU, which didn't get the season average in point production from any of the "starting six" who carried the Tigers to their big season.

Slump-shaking dunk by Tolbert 'helped'

For Tolbert, 1981 has been what no other year in his Indiana University career has been: marked by amazing consistency.

Tolbert led the Big Ten in shooting with the performances he strung together in winning Knight's nomination as the league's most valuable player. Against LSU, in the biggest game of Tolbert's Hoosier career, the shooting touch that had been there night in and night out through the Hoosiers' drive to the Big Ten title suddenly was gone.

He tried five shots in the first half and missed four. Some of the misses were by embarrassing margins. One of those went up just before Knight pulled him with 1:50 left in the half. "I wasn't doing the things I was supposed to do," Tolbert said. "He sat me down and let me think about it."

The second half began with LSU star Durand Macklin, who had a frustrating day of his own trying to find shooting room around or over Turner, spinning his wheels trying to shake loose from Turner and drawing a traveling call.

Kitchel, who missed the last 10 minutes of the half himself with three fouls, worked free for the Hoosiers' first shot of the second half but missed it.

As things turned out, it may have been a well-timed miss.

Kitchel remembered the thought that passed through his mind when he was resting the last 10 minutes of the first half and watching Tolbert struggle to find his shooting touch. "I was thinking, 'Ray really needs a basket,' " Kitchel said.

When both were back on court opening the second half and Kitchel's soft push shot bounced out, Tolbert was there to grab the rebound, take it back to the basket and jam it home.

It was a stimulator, that Tolbert dunk.

"I think it helped the other guys on our team," Tolbert said. "They knew I was trying."

Wittman read special meaning into the play. "We all knew he was wanting to score so badly," Wittman said. "That one helped."

Knight doesn't put much stock in single plays or single games representing anything significant or symbolic. So neither did Tolbert after his basket. "One dunk doesn't relieve frustration," Tolbert said. "I knew I had to keep making some plays."

The one play did help him return to something closer to his late-season norm, and the Hoosiers took off as if someone had lifted an anchor.

It seemed to have dropped again when four fouls took floor

Ray Tolbert between coaches Jene Davis, Gerry Gimelstob

Sweet time for IU leaders Isiah Thomas, Ray Tolbert

leader Isiah Thomas out of the Hoosier picture with IU up only 36-30 and 16½ minutes left.

Jim Thomas replaced him, and LSU, which earned a tag of explosive for its scoring bursts that frequently were triggered by the quick Tigers' full-court press, went after the Hoosiers immediately.

Jim Thomas was a front-court player in high school, frequently playing center. Ball-handling has been the slowest phase of his game to come around at IU.

But in Wittman's view, it has come around.

"I don't think I panicked when Isiah went out and I don't think Coach Knight panicked," Wittman said.

"James has proven himself. Tonight was just another example."

In a 17-minute performance that included lots of pluses, there wasn't a single turnover charged against sub Thomas.

"When I came in, I just tried to keep the offense going," Thomas said.

"The first half was just a matter of us being very tight. Coach told us to loosen up and play our game, and we came out the second half with a more relaxed attitude."

Thomas received some all-regional votes last week after two strong relief performances. Somehow, though, those apparently weren't really noticed by LSU scouts.

Brown said he made one of the game's key decisions — to take out his back-court leader, Ethan Martin, at the same time Isiah Thomas went out with three fouls with 3:14 left in the half — in part because of James Thomas.

"Ethan had two fouls," Brown said. "I was afraid that, psychologically, he might let up on the new guy, whom we

hadn't heard about, and pick up his third foul."

The move saved Martin, but it could have cost the Tigers their last real chance — as game events worked out — to take control of the game.

LSU led 30-27 when both Thomas and Martin went out, with 3:14 left in the half. Indiana didn't score the rest of the half without Thomas, but LSU didn't even get a shot the rest of the way without Martin — his replacement, freshman Johnny Jones, committing one turnover and missing a one-and-one free-throw chance.

When the Hoosiers survived that stretch and got Tolbert going in the second half, LSU's chances for controlling anything were gone.

If James Thomas was a surprise to Brown, he wasn't to Knight.

"He came in and did an awful lot of good things for us," Knight said, "but he has done that all year.

"We're better against a zone defense with Isiah in there, but we were ahead when he came out so LSU had to play us man-to-man. We were all right (with the James Thomas-Wittman guard combination)."

Ironically, James Thomas prepared for the LSU game by standing in for Wittman throughout the week's practice. Wittman stayed out of live work to protect the thigh bruise he picked up in the Mideast Regional championship game.

In the first half against LSU, Wittman hit only one of six shots, probably a reflection of the lack of practice time. "All I know is I felt all right," Wittman said. "The thigh didn't bother me. I got a little tired a couple of times, but that was all."

LSU unimpressed by IU's defense

Two years ago, LSU advanced to the final 16 of the NCAA tournament before losing to eventual champion Michigan State. Last year, the Tigers went a step farther, to the final eight, before losing to eventual champion Louisville.

This year, LSU was in the Final Four for the first time since 1953, and the Tigers hoped to end their string of losing to the ultimate champion. When the loss to Indiana was on the books, Brown indicated he expected his streak to continue. "I would be very surprised if Indiana isn't the national champion," he said.

His team gave almost reluctant agreement. The Tigers looked at the game more as one they lost than one Indiana won.

"Things just went bad in the second half," senior center Greg Cook said.

"It didn't have anything to do with Indiana's defense. I didn't see any defense. I've seen tougher defenses than theirs in the SEC. We beat ourselves."

Martin, admitted he was "really up" for a head-on meeting with IU's Isiah Thomas.

"Yeah, I was," he said. "I thought it was a great challenge.

"And I thought I held my own.

"They're a good team. They play a real aggressive team defense. But we took some bad shots.

"It's more disappointing to lose like this than just to have lost. I can't explain it. The only thing I can say is that we came out too loose in the second half. We had a nice lead and we got too loose.

"We should have taken advantage of it when Isiah went out (with four fouls, Indiana leading 36-30 with 16½ minutes left). But we didn't. We came down, fumbled the ball, and had two traveling calls.

"We panicked. When they got 10-up, we tried to get back in the game too quick.

"They did a great job of sagging, and we got a little unpatient and started putting it up from the outside."

Carter agreed. "We lost our composure in the second half," he said.

"I don't think Indiana hurt us too much overall. I think we hurt ourselves. We got out of our offense and never got back. We forced a lot of outside shots."

Sims called Turner "the key — he started taking the ball to the hole.

"When Isiah went out, we wanted to pump it up and raise the score up, but we couldn't hit from the outside. We won by the jump shot and now we lost by the jump shot.

"We did want to work it inside, but it didn't seem to work. Indiana's a good team. They've got some big guys. The first half, it was a strong defensive game inside."

Mitchell said Turner "played strong inside." But he also followed the team theme that the Tigers lost more than Indiana won.

"Indiana's defense wasn't what did it," he said.

"Our game plan was exactly what we did: take it to them inside. We felt we were more aggressive inside."

Macklin, the Louisville senior who led the Tigers in scoring and rebounding and made some all-America lists, was only 2-for-12 in scoring four points against the defense of IU's Ray Tolbert.

"They did a lot of overplaying," Macklin said. "We didn't execute offensively as well as we should have.

"They boxed out well. And our shot selection was bad. We just weren't hitting. The shots were there; we just didn't put them down."

"You have a tendency to be overanxious, and we tried to get back in the game in one minute. We wanted to get back in it so badly. We should have relaxed."

Macklin, a left-handed shooter, cut the little finger on his right hand in the Midwest Regional title game. He played with a bandage over the finger.

"It was a factor in that every time I'd catch the ball, it would slip out of my hand and I had to recatch it," he said.

"My first jump shot slipped out of my hand and I reshot it. Luckily, it went in.

"It didn't hurt much. It just seemed that I lost the feeling in my finger."

Sims discounted the finger as a cause of LSU's defeat.

"He didn't score because he started to put it up from the outside," Sims said. "Our game is on the inside."

The Tigers lived for a year with disappointment over their poor play in their tournament loss to Louisville last year.

"This game isn't comparable to the Louisville game," Sims said. "We were ready to play today. We just couldn't get anything going from the outside."

One thing the Tigers weren't ready for, however, was James Thomas, the Hoosier sophomore who came on when Isiah Thomas went out with foul problems.

"James Thomas is a good ballplayer," Sims said. "I thought we'd have an advantage when he came in, but we didn't."

Martin was more blunt: "I had never heard of James Thomas."

INDIANA 67

	M	FG	FT	R	A	BS	St	PF	TP
Kitchel, f	23	3-8	4-4	6	0	0	0	3	10
Turner, f	38	7-19	6-7	8	0	0	0	1	20
Tolbert, c	37	3-7	1-2	6	5	0	1	3	7
I.Thomas, g	26	6-8	2-3	2	4	0	0	4	14
Wittman, g	37	3-10	2-2	2	2	0	0	0	8
Risley	11	0-2	1-2	2	1	0	0	0	1
J.Thomas	17	0-4	2-2	9	2	2	1	1	2
Bouchie	3	0-1	0-0	2	0	0	0	0	0
Grunwald	2	1-2	1-2	2	0	0	0	1	3
Brown	2	0-1	0-1	0	0	0	0	0	0
Isenbarger	2	0-1	0-0	0	0	0	0	0	0
Franz	1	0-0	2-2	0	0	0	0	1	2
LaFave	1	0-0	0-0	2	0	0	0	1	0
Team				2					
Totals		23-63	21-27	43	14	2	2	15	67

LOUISIANA STATE 49

	M	FG	FT	R	A	BS	St	PF	TP
Macklin, f	35	2-12	0-0	8	0	1	0	1	4
Mitchell, f	37	3-10	3-4	10	0	0	1	3	9
Cook, c	34	3-5	0-0	5	0	0	0	5	6
Martin, g	30	2-8	3-3	3	8	0	0	4	7
Carter, g	32	5-10	0-0	6	1	1	1	3	10
Sims	13	2-8	1-2	1	0	0	2	0	5
Jones	10	0-2	0-1	2	1	0	0	2	0
Tudor	4	1-3	4-4	2	0	0	0	3	6
Bergeron	3	0-0	0-0	0	0	0	0	1	0
Costello	1	0-0	0-0	0	0	0	0	0	0
Black	1	1-1	0-0	1	0	0	0	0	2
Team				3					
Totals		19-59	11-14	41	10	2	4	22	49

SCORE BY HALVES

Indiana	27	40—	67
Louisiana State	30	19—	49

Turnovers—Indiana 10, Louisiana State 19.
Technical foul—Louisiana State bench.

SHOOTING

	FG	Pct.	FT	Pct.
Indiana	23-63	.365	21-27	.778
Louisiana State	19-59	.322	11-14	.786

Officials—Booker Turner (Pac-10), Lou Moser (ACC), Ken Lauderdale (SEC).
Attendance—18,276.

Happy times for Bob Knight, longtime adviser Pete Newell

IU-North Carolina: 'a coaches' final'

The all-time viewing record for a basketball game, college or pro, was set the night Larry Bird and Indiana State met Magic Johnson and Michigan State for the 1979 NCAA championship.

That was a fans' final, the first match-up of two captivating stars who still have an allure as professionals.

Tonight is a coaches' final. The profession is sitting back to watch the two accepted masters of the college coaching art, 40-year-old Bob Knight of Indiana and 50-year-old Dean Smith of North Carolina, send polished, well-drilled teams against each other to determine the new national champion.

Coaches Jack Hartman of Kansas State and Ralph Miller of Oregon State, in town to receive their peers' award as college co-coaches of the year, were excited about the match-up.

Hartman said "my philosophy might be more in line with Bobby's." Miller said he's more inclined toward Smith's coaching style. Hartman declined to pick a winner. Miller said, "I'm leaning, and there's really no common sense to it, I just feel that maybe Indiana has the advantage."

Hartman called it a match-up of "two coaches who have been very successful . . . two who have been copied tremendously."

And he considers it not so much a collision of contrasting philosophies as a meeting of like minds.

"They're very much alike," he said, "in what they want in shot selection, in their emphasis on execution, their emphasis on fundamentals, their emphasis on strong defenses, their emphasis on board play.

"Both will go into a possession game, although Dean will go into it early in the game to try to dictate the flow and Bobby is more traditional."

Miller said "There's only one key to winning and that's defense. And both of these coaches know that. Bobby is a solid one-defense coach, and Dean will use several things.

"It's a great game to watch. Both coaches have been to the trough.

"If Dean's various types of defense begin to upset Indiana to the point where their players start to think — that's why you do those things — Bobby's team is going to have a hard time catching up.

"Somebody's going to get his name in the papers for scoring a lot of points, but whichever best executes its defense will win."

The two front courts excite Hartman and Miller.

"There are some great match-ups right there," Hartman said. "(IU's Ray) Tolbert and (North Carolina's Sam) Perkins, (IU's Landon) Turner and (Carolina's James) Worthy. . . .

"There isn't a good match-up at the other spot (Indiana's Ted Kitchel with Carolina's Al Wood). Wood has the mobility."

Miller wasn't eager to speculate on the match-ups. "You never know," he said, reaching back 26 years for an example.

"When San Francisco played LaSalle (1955), nobody in the country would have guessed San Francisco would put K.C. Jones (6-1) on Gola (6-6). I know I wouldn't have. But he did it and did a great job."

Hartman allows for a surprise in the Wood match-up. "You

This is a game between two coaches who have been very successful, two who have been copied tremendously. It looks to me like it's Indiana's ability to cope vs. North Carolina's changing defenses.

Jack Hartman
Kansas State coach

know each team has a very good sixth man, too — and they don't match up," he said, referring to 6-6 Carolina sixth-man Matt Doherty and 6-3 James Thomas of Indiana.

"I was *really* impressed with James Thomas's play," Hartman said. "Good night! That kid is quicker than a cat."

Brigham Young's Danny Ainge was in town, too, to be honored as the coaches' national player of the year and play in the NABC's all-star game.

He won't be around tonight when the new college champion is crowned, but he made a reluctant choice.

"It's hard, but I kinda like Indiana," he said. "They've been playing so good. They won big Saturday without Isiah (Thomas, who sat out 14 minutes with foul problems).

"I think either team is capable of winning, but I just like the way Indiana has played in the tournament."

Long way from chance
K.C. meeting for finalists

The new year was hours away as the two men stood in a corridor of the Kansas City Airport. They were off by themselves, involved in a quiet and not at all jovial conversation. Nearby, a man said, "There stand the two best basketball coaches in America."

"Yeah," another said. "And they both just got their butt beat."

Defeat hasn't happened often to Dean Smith of North Carolina and Bob Knight of Indiana. But the night before the chance meeting in mid-America, Smith's North Carolina team had been walloped by Minnesota in Los Angeles, 76-60, and Knight's Indiana team had lost a consolation-round game in Hawaii to Pan American, 66-60.

Smith laughed as he recalled the meeting the day before his team and Knight's will meet to pick the 1981 national collegiate basketball championship.

"Bobby was telling me, 'I just can't play (Ray) Tolbert and (Landon) Turner together,'" Smith said.

"And I was asking him: 'Does Minnesota always shoot that well? From that far out?'"

Only 11 days earlier at Smith's home base, Chapel Hill, North Carolina had broken a tie in the last five minutes and whipped Indiana, 65-56.

North Carolina won because:
• The Tar Heels' front line outrebounded Indiana's, 24-8;
• Carolina guard Jimmy Black had one of his best games of the season, at IU all-American Isiah Thomas's expense.

The December game offered little hint of the championship game it was previewing. Play was sloppy; Indiana committed 18 turnovers and North Carolina 20.

Now, 99 days later, the two have stormed through NCAA tournament opposition to get to the championship game with few real scares behind them.

Trainer Bob Young gets Randy Wittman ready for Philadelphia workout

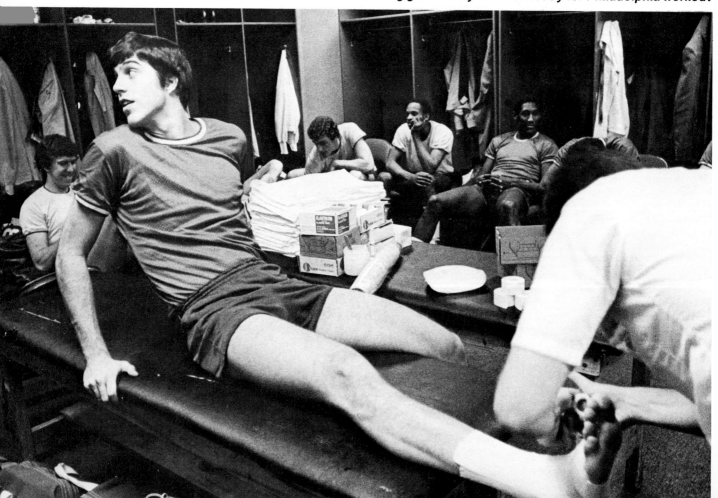

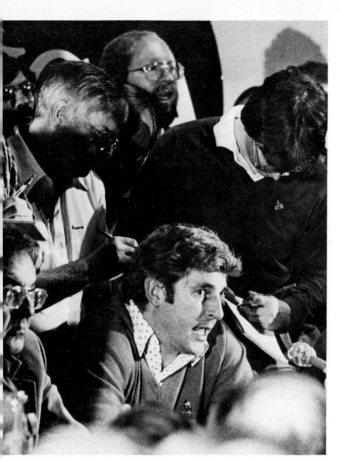

Bob Knight — A busy Philadelphia weekend

North Carolina had a five-point game with Utah on the Utes' homecourt in regional play, but otherwise the Heels have drubbed their tournament opponents.

Pittsburgh fell, 74-57; Kansas State, 82-68, and Virginia, the team that whipped Carolina twice during the season, 78-65.

After dumping Virginia in the semifinals, Smith quipped: "We will trade those other two for this one."

Knight knows the feeling. He's 0-2 against Smith at the moment, IU losing at Assembly Hall, 61-57, a year ago on the week that both Mike Woodson and Randy Wittman were ruled out, before this year's Chapel Hill game.

Smith has a team in the championship game for the third time, in the Final Four for the sixth time, in his brilliantly successful 20 years as Tar Heel coach.

His tenure doubles Knight's 10 seasons at IU. So do his Final Four trips. However, Knight is in the final game for the second time, and he's after his second national championship; Smith, his first.

Smith is 436-142 (.754) in his 20 Carolina seasons; Knight, 230-68 (.772) in his 10 at IU. For 15 years, Smith's teams have never finished lower than second in the Atlantic Coast Conference, and he has won nine regular-season ACC titles, eight

> It's a great game to watch. Both coaches have been to the trough. Whichever bests executes its defense will win. I'm leaning, and there's really no common sense to it, I just feel that maybe Indiana has the advantage.
>
> Ralph Miller
> Oregon State coach

more in the league's post-season tournament. The current season was his 11th straight 20-victory year, his eighth team to win at least 25 games.

Knight's IU teams have won six Big Ten championships in the last nine years. They are the dominant figures in the two dominant basketball leagues in the nation, and tonight they take their theories and their chess game into the main arena.

North Carolina did win an NCAA championship in 1957, when Frank McGuire coached the Tar Heels to a 32-0 season.

That one ended with a triple-overtime victory over Kansas and Wilt Chamberlain. The 1957 North Carolina team and IU's 1976 team share the record for the best won-lost mark for a champion, 32-0.

'I did the shoving, he did the insulting'

Knight tried to lock in on the national championship game after giving his version of his "Tiger Bait" encounter with a Louisiana State fan.

The incident occurred about four hours after Indiana's victory over LSU. Knight gave his version during a scheduled press conference, after reading a Philadelphia morning newspaper account that he called "unfactual."

Knight said he and some friends were headed for dinner at the Hoosiers' tournament hotel (the Cherry Hill, N.J., Inn). They were walking through the hotel restaurant's bar when an LSU fan — one of about 200 based at the same hotel — said, "Congratulations."

"All morning Saturday, when our players were walking back and forth in the hotel between our meeting room and the breakfast room, LSU fans kept hollering, 'Tiger bait, Tiger bait,' " Knight said.

"As I walked past this guy, I turned to him and said over my shoulder, 'Well, we really weren't Tiger bait after all, were we?' and I kept on walking with the people in my party."

Knight said the fan — Louis Bonnecaze, Jr., a public accountant from Baton Rouge — shouted an obscenity at him, then repeated it.

"I walked over — I did a little more than walk over, I walked *swiftly* over — and I said, 'Would you like to say again what you just said?'

"He said, 'I gave you a compliment and you were very sarcastic and rude to me.'

"I said, 'No, I wasn't sarcastic and rude to you. I just threw something back at you that our kids have been hearing all day long.'

"He said, 'Well, you're still an (obscenity).

"I grabbed him, shoved him up against the wall and turned and walked away."

One news account said Bonnecaze wound up in a garbage can. The story was headlined "Knight trades shoves, insults with LSU fan."

"We didn't trade shoves, I did all the shoving," Knight said.

"And we didn't trade insults, he did all the insulting."

Bonnecaze called the police, but a police spokesman said, "There were no arrests, no injuries, everybody parted friends and shook hands."

Knight said he has frequently been called names in arenas and "put up with it. I probably ignore 10,000 things for every one that I get upset about. But I'll be damned if I'll take that in a public place."

A writer asked: "After watching your team yesterday, I wonder: Did the fan go cleanly into the garbage can, or did he rim out?"

"I understand the bartender called it goal-tending and a charge," Knight said.

Indiana 63, North Carolina 50

The City of Hoosierly Love crowned another Indiana basketball team the national collegiate champion.

Five years and a day after the 1976 Hoosiers became the last unbeaten champion by beating Michigan at The Spectrum, IU returned to the building and claimed the 1981 championship with a 63-50 victory over North Carolina.

Indiana — a four-time winner now, behind only UCLA (10) and Kentucky (5) — did it with the same kind of second-half magic that whipped Michigan, 86-68, in the 1976 final game. The Hoosiers appeared in trouble for a half against the Tar Heels, then seized control at the start of the second half and won easily.

It was, said IU coach Bob Knight, remembering a 35-29 halftime hole in '76, "a little *deja vu*.

"We did play well in the second half."

The Hoosiers didn't lead for even a second in the first half, which ended with Wittman's shot in the air from a deep corner.

It went in to put Indiana ahead, 26-25, as the teams took a break. North Carolina had led early, 8-2, then 16-8. "It didn't look good then," Knight said. "We were on the verge of being blown out."

Wittman hit four shots from long range and Landon Turner powered to three baskets inside to deliver the halftime lead.

"They were playing zone and mostly giving us the outside shot," Wittman said. He had to ask for the last one. Isiah Thomas was scanning the court when Wittman thought he had lost track of time. "When it got down to :05, I yelled at him," Wittman said. "Al Wood was way off me, looking for something to the inside."

Wittman shouted, "Come *on!*" Thomas slipped him the ball and Wittman's shot was barely out of his hand before the buzzer sounded.

"That was the most important play of the game," Thomas said of Wittman's shot. "It gave us momentum."

Second and third on the "most important" list may have been a couple plays supplied by Thomas in stimulating the momentum early in the second half.

North Carolina controlled the tip at the start of the half and was working for the shot that could have put the Tar Heels on top again when Thomas snapped up a loose ball and drove to a lay-up.

"The ball was slippery," Thomas said. "It went right through (Carolina guard Jimmy) Black's hands. I was just in the right place at the right time."

The Thomas basket made the score 29-26, and it was 31-28 when Thomas picked off a pass aimed at 6-9 freshman Sam Perkins in the Carolina middle. Wood, the Tar Heels' senior star, cut Thomas off on a drive to the basket, but the Hoosier sophomore glided past him for another lay-up and a 33-28 margin.

"Thomas broke it open," North Carolina coach Dean Smith said. "His two steals were the turning point."

It was 35-30 when Thomas — 1-for-7 in an uncharacteristically chilly first half — swished a shot from the baseline and followed by working free in the low post for a pass from James Thomas and a lay-up that opened a sudden 39-30 lead with 15:23 to play and forced Smith to a time out.

The four-basket blast-off started Thomas toward a 19-point last half and game scoring honors with 23 points — part of the reason he closed out an all-America season by becoming the third Hoosier to win the NCAA's outstanding player award at the Final Four.

Randy Wittman eludes Sam Perkins for lay-up

Isiah's fourth basket was the start of a string of four straight assists by the sophomore who became a national name as IU's "other Thomas" in the tournament, James Thomas. He wound up with eight assists in all and a rarity for a reserve: a spot on the all-Final Four team, along with teammates Thomas and Turner, Carolina's Wood and Jeff Lamp of Virginia's consolation-game winners.

"Maybe it was a bad thing to get (Ted) Kitchel in foul trouble," Smith said wryly. Kitchel started but played only four minutes before drawing three fouls, and Thomas came on to play 29 minutes.

James fed Isiah Thomas for an inside basket and Wittman for a 15-foot jump shot that edged the Hoosier lead to 45-34 with 12:30 left.

The Hoosiers missed a couple chances to add to the lead, and after Wood hit two free throws with 9:37 left to cut the margin to 45-36, Knight went to work on the clock with a spread offense that was in no hurry to get a shot in the air. "That's tough to play," said Smith, who made the four-corner delay game into a late-game trademark.

North Carolina capitalized when IU missed its first scoring try after going to the delay, Wood's rebound basket at 8:00 making it 45-38.

That's the closest the Tar Heels got. IU ran off 30 seconds before James Thomas appeared to be caught in the Heels' half-court trap. He escaped with a pass that got Wittman a lay-up to deflate Carolina hopes that had started to build.

Indiana took a 51-41 lead into the last three minutes and padded it when Isiah Thomas and Wittman made both halves of one-and-one free-throw chances.

North Carolina bit into the 55-41 lead by pressuring the Hoosiers into three turnovers and scoring six straight points. Indiana ran the margin back up by hitting eight of 10 free throws in the last minute and 22 seconds.

Knight tried to get his starters out — for a celebratory exit and an introduction into the box score for some reserves — but the clock never stopped in the last 41 seconds.

The incredible turn-around season wound down with Thomas holding the ball in the back-court. IU's section of the crowd of 18,276 counted down "4 . . . 3 . . . 2 . . . 1" and Isiah Thomas let the season end with the ball high in the air, tossed there with the same show of jubilation that his predecessor as the back-court boss of an NCAA champion at IU, Quinn Buckner, did with a dance in the gold-medal game at the 1976 Olympics — when the U.S. coach was Dean Smith.

Smith had won twice from Knight and IU in a two-year series set up for national TV. The second of the games was last December in Chapel Hill, Carolina winning 65-56.

Smith's 20th season as Tar Heel coach ended with his third championship-game loss. He hasn't won one yet.

"I'm thrilled to be No. 2," Smith said. "But we'd rather be No. 1. I am thrilled as a coach for this year's team."

The Tar Heels finished 29-8, regional winners for the sixth time under Smith.

Indiana closed out 26-9, two more defeats than any previous NCAA champion ever had. It assured a national championship banner that will go alongside ones from 1940, 1953 and 1976 in Assembly Hall's south end. The late Branch McCracken's teams won the first two, both coming over Kansas in final games played in Kansas City — Smith a reserve on the Kansas bench when IU won the '53 title.

Besides the 23 points by Isiah Thomas, Wittman had 16 points and Turner 12. Senior Ray Tolbert scored only five points but led IU to a 33-29 rebounding edge by sweeping off 11, high for both teams.

Wood, who set an NCAA semifinal record with 39 points when North Carolina qualified for the championship try by

Landon Turner powers way to two

117

James Worthy meets Isiah Thomas, Ray Tolbert

beating Virginia, scored 18 against first Turner, then James Thomas.

Perkins scored 11, but both he and James Worthy, who teamed with Wood to form one of the outstanding front-court combinations in college basketball this year, were virtually shut off the last half. Perkins and Worthy combined for only four points in the half, two of those surrendered by IU at the end to avoid a foul. Tolbert and Turner were the match-ups for Worthy and Perkins, till Turner fouled out with 5:33 left. Senior Steve Risley finished the game.

A championship game almost postponed

Conscience pangs tugged at NCAA basketball's ruling gentry. No one has written a Robert's Rules on the order to be followed when presidents are shot, though the growing frequency of such national disgraces may warrant one. The National Football League still blushes over the Sunday of play it let go on when this whole assassination plague got its modern start and John F. Kennedy lay in state in 1963. The NCAA wasn't eager to become another NFL, and when movieland postponed its Oscar night in shocked tribute to the actor-president whose shooting and surgery were uppermost in national concerns, the heat turned up a little higher on the fellows who have that easy, cushy job of running the greatest three-week production in sports: the NCAA tournament.

Less than an hour before the championship game — after Virginia and Louisiana State had played a consolation game that could have been scrapped without anybody noticing — the question was still being debated: To play or not to play?

Within the group that huddled to mull the question — the

INDIANA 63

	M	FG	FT	R	A	BS	St	PF	TP
Turner, f	35	5- 8	2- 2	6	1	0	1	5	12
Kitchel, f	4	0- 1	0- 0	0	0	0	0	3	0
Tolbert, c	40	1- 4	3- 6	11	0	1	2	0	5
I. Thomas, g	40	8-17	7- 8	2	5	0	4	4	23
Wittman, g	40	7-13	2- 2	4	0	0	0	2	16
J. Thomas	29	1- 4	0- 0	4	8	0	1	2	2
Risley	12	1- 1	3- 4	4	0	0	0	1	5
Team				2					
Totals		23-48	17-22	33	14	1	8	17	63

NORTH CAROLINA 50

	M	FG	FT	R	A	BS	St	PF	TP
Wood, f	38	6-13	6- 9	6	2	0	0	4	18
Worthy, f	30	3-11	1- 2	6	2	1	1	5	7
Perkins, c	39	5- 8	1- 2	8	1	1	2	3	11
Black, g	36	3- 4	0- 0	2	6	0	4	5	6
Pepper, g	22	2- 5	2- 2	1	0	0	2	1	6
Doherty	23	1- 2	0- 1	4	0	0	0	4	2
Braddock	5	0- 2	0- 0	0	1	0	0	1	0
Kenny	1	0- 1	0- 0	1	0	0	0	0	0
Brust	5	0- 0	0- 0	0	0	0	0	0	0
Budko	2	0- 1	0- 0	1	0	0	0	0	0
Team				2					
Totals		20-47	10-16	29	12	2	9	23	50

SCORE BY HALVES

Indiana		27	36— 63
North Carolina		26	24— 50

Turnovers—Indiana 14, North Carolina 19.
Technical foul—Turner (grabbing rim).

SHOOTING

	FG	Pct.	FT	Pct.
Indiana	23-48	.479	17-22	.773
North Carolina	20-47	.426	10-16	.625

Officials—Booker Turner (Pac-10), Ken Lauderdale (SEC), Lou Móser (ACC).
Attendance—18,276 (sellout).

Trip to top for Ted Kitchel, Isiah Thomas, Randy Wittman

nine-man NCAA Tournament Committee, plus presidents of the two universities involved and NCAA officers Jim Frank (president) and John Toner (secretary-treasurer) — there even was a suggestion advanced that the final game be called off altogether and Indiana and North Carolina declared co-champions. That, Tournament Committee chairman Wayne Duke said, "received no consideration."

When President Reagan came out of surgery with all signs positive, the NCAA decision was made, Duke said. The choice will be criticized but the marvelous sense of humor that prompted the stricken president to come out of surgery with a paraphrase of the old W.C. Fields line — "All in all, I'd rather be in Philadelphia," Reagan said in a note scratched to aides — was splendidly reflective of what surely would have been Reagan's own vote if he had been in the NCAA's meeting room. Bless ol' Dutch. If only he *had* been in Philadelphia . . .

As conducted, the game may have achieved all that respectful silence would have anyway. There was poignance, and quite surely prayer, in the arena when two high-strung basketball teams and more than 18,000 other people paused in a moment of pregame silence to ponder the matter; when "The Star-Spangled Banner" was played, not at all perfunctorily, and a good many of the 18,000 sang. Take a note back, Mr. President. You may not have been in Philadelphia, but Philadelphia was with you.

The two coaches left the decision to others less passionately involved. Knight and Smith pledged to abide by whatever decision came out. In victory and defeat, they endorsed the one that did. Both clearly wanted to play. "It was a tragic thing," said Smith, after his Tar Heels had lost, "but we heard the president was in stable condition. Had he been near death. . . ."

Knight didn't feel postponement was the proper answer. "I really, honestly don't think so," he said. "I think the Tournament Committee was absolutely right."

Cynicism is not too far from the surface for any of us. When the huddling began, that ol' debbil television was presumed to be a factor. NBC was rumored to be pressing for a postponement, the network theoretically fearing embarrassment if caught going on with life as usual after another network voluntarily called off its Academy Awards. "I didn't want NBC to make the decision," Smith said. "I wanted the NCAA to make it."

Isiah Thomas had just come out of the biggest basketball game — and triumph — of his life when he was asked if the game should have been played.

Thomas, a vibrant and witty conversationalist, groped for words to say nicely that that really wasn't the biggest thing to think about. "We were happy that the president wasn't dead," he said. "We were glad he could still think and use his brain. That's the most important thing."

Wittman called the shooting "a tragic thing — I felt for him and for the other people who were shot. But we had a national championship on the line and we had to go out and play."

And, in a display of the sort of concentration that would improve the performance of anyone in any role, that's what they did. On both sides.

This should have been third NCAA title — Knight

The nets were still affixed to the bright orange rims and photographers, fans and intrepid reporters were knotting around each available personage in red when Indiana coach Bob Knight, architect of a national champion for the second time in six seasons, slipped away to the team dressing room.

He was there for a few brief and euphoric moments with a quiet, weary group: President John Ryan; athletic director Ralph Floyd; assistant coach Jim Crews; two of the early planks in the program 30-year-old Bob Knight came to Bloomington to build, Joby Wright and Steve Downing, and the first really big-name recruit he attracted to his program, Quinn Buckner.

Knight was reminded that five years ago on a similar night, he left The Spectrum long after the cheering and, in a pensive moment, stopped on the steps outside the building to accept congratulations one more time but respond in unexpected somberness: "Thanks, but it should have been two." Not then, not ever will he concede to UCLA nor to the genius of John Wooden and the special aura of Wooden's coaching exit that the 1975 national championship really belonged to anyone but the team he had built and then had shattered by Scott May's broken arm.

"This one," it was suggested, "makes up for the one that got away."

"No," Knight said, grinning widely and feigning gruffness, "it should have been three."

He raised his voice to make sure all targets heard. "And we'd have won one in '73, too, Steve, if we had had any guards." The starting guards on the 1973 Indiana team that started IU down the road to tournament triumph were two freshmen, named Crews and Buckner.

Buckner had come in from Milwaukee, where he captains the Bucks team that won its division and thus got a pass through the opening round of NBA playoffs. He arrived in Philadelphia Sunday and lived with the Hoosiers in their homestretch hours.

119

He spoke to the team before the game, following John Havlicek as a lecturer.

It was the third time in such a role for Havlicek, who soared to triumph in NCAA play with Knight at Ohio State and went on to many more victories and championships as a Boston Celtic. He was still an active player when he went to St. Louis to speak to Knight's first Final Four team in 1973 and when he was at Philadelphia in '76, priming Buckner and friends for their last grab at victory.

"Flashes of all that came back when I heard him speak," Buckner said. "I got all excited." IU's kids heard from the pros, consummate pros.

"It's just absolutely great for you to be here," Knight said to Buckner, several times.

Eventually, the players who had fooled the country trickled in, among the last Ray Tolbert and Isiah Thomas, each wearing a net as a necklace as Buckner and Scott May had when the other Finals Night in Philly reached a similar point.

There were new rounds of hugs and shouts as privacy settled on the group, the huggees of moments before in the midst of excited fans becoming mutual huggers.

Buckner and Thomas embraced for a long moment. Theirs is a special link. They are the two most celebrated guards to come out of Chicago. Ever. The pressure was on them not to do well but to do great, immediately. Together, they have given backcourt direction to six Indiana teams now. All six won Big Ten championships, five went on to the NCAA, three made it to the Final Four, and now two — one apiece — have won national championships.

How sweet it is for Ray Tolbert, Isiah Thomas

"When we were recruiting Isiah," said Buckner, who already was three years out of school and into his pro career by the time mentioned, "I just talked to him about what I enjoyed at Indiana."

That didn't specifically include memories of a championship night in Philadelphia or promises of any for Thomas. "I don't think I could do that," Buckner said. "I just told him there's no question if he goes to Indiana he'll be the best player he can be."

Buckner knows all about leadership. Chances are he was waving the babies at some Chicago hospital into a balanced formation an hour or so after he was born. He saw the signs of it in the sub-par first half Thomas had in the championship game. "He may have been trying to do a little too much," Buckner said. "But he's such a great player. You know he'll straighten that out."

He had no special messages, QB to QB, for Thomas before the game. "The last thing I wanted to do was put any pressure on him," Buckner said. "He knew what he had to do. He just had to play his game."

Pete Newell, whose defensive theories are at the heart of Knight's Hoosier planning, was located in the crowd and brought to the still-private dressing room. "No one has had more to do with the way we play basketball at Indiana than this man," Knight told his team. "Come on up and let him know how you feel about him." Newell was engulfed.

"It's a little different than it was in Hawaii, isn't it?" Newell said later, laughing. "They just hadn't put it together then. I don't know what it was; they were playing tight. But Bobby's teams are always late-comers."

No Knight team, no team put together by anyone, ever came farther later than the current national champions, whose largest strides came after nine defeats. In the record book, they'll look mediocre — in that category.

In another, it will show that their march to the 1981 national championship was about the most crushing since teams have had to play five games to win. This 26-9 Hoosier team whipped its five NCAA opponents by 35, 15, 32, 18 and 13 points — 113 in all, 22.6 per game. They topped the team they most resemble, Michigan State's 1979 champions, whose average margin was 20.8.

That MSU team lost six times and almost got itself eliminated from the Big Ten race before shifting into gear. This IU team was always in the Big Ten race but nearly sank into mediocrity when it lost five of its first 12 games.

For a time, it had a problem winning close games. It solved the problem beautifully, especially in tournament play. It stopped playing them.

"I don't think these kids ever lost sight of the fact that they had a chance to win the whole thing," Knight said.

"I remember even in December, Isiah was quoted several times that we knew we could be a good basketball team but we had to keep working at it.

"I've never seen a group of kids who worked harder to get a goal than these kids have."

It is a championship totally different from the first one won by a Knight-coached team.

"I talked with Quinn on this Sunday, and we both agreed that had we not won in 1976, we would have felt like we had failed. I have always believed we would have won the national championship in 1975 if Scott hadn't been hurt. After that, we felt almost like we had to win in 1976. It was our ultimate objective. When we did win, it was almost a relief.

"Our ultimate objective this year was to be as competitive as possible in the Big Ten and then in the tournament. That's why this is such a joyous feeling for all of us."

That was when he was in public. In private, he simply smiled and hugged a lot, while voices shouted from all around.

No doubts after Philly — Isiah Thomas marks IU's rise to real No. 1

Tolbert convened the players in the middle of the room. "I just want to say one thing," he said. "We worked hard four years for this, and it's worth it."

"Mike only worked one," chirped Mike LaFave, the only freshman on the championship squad.

Knight turned the group loose on Philadelphia for their own celebrations.

"Just remember you're representing Indiana University," he said.

"And you're national champions.

"And you're going to get up at 7 tomorrow morning to fly back home."

Sixth-man Thomas on all-Final Four

Tom Abernethy provided one of the special highlights of Indiana's 1976 rush to the national college basketball championship by waiting until the last round of the last tournament of his last season to make an all-anything team. Abernethy beat out a batch of all-America nominees to make all-Final Four that year, maybe the first ever to debut in all-star consideration at that level.

James Thomas upstaged Abernethy. Records are sketchy, but it appears the sophomore from Fort Lauderdale was the first sub ever to make all-Final Four.

Thomas did it while scoring two points in each game. Still, he was selected on 105 ballots — 15, it might be noted, for every one that a vastly more celebrated sophomore, 7-4 all-American Ralph Sampson of Virginia, received.

Thomas even drew 15½ votes for outstanding player in the field, an honor won by Isiah Thomas with 105 votes.

The one knock against James Thomas as a collegiate player

has been his ball-handling. A front-court player in high school, he still can play that role at IU, though just 6-3. His quick, strong jumping ability was an aspect of his play that stood out, sometimes spectacularly, in his two straight weeks of outstanding play.

In a national championship game against a team noted not only for its defensive strength and skill but also its trickiness, James Thomas moved to the point and ran Indiana's offense.

"It was scary, really," Thomas laughed.

The effect, though, was to move Wittman into a shooting position and to drop Isiah Thomas into an area near the basket where he totally bedeviled the Carolinians in the second half.

Meanwhile, James Thomas shot passes from the point with accuracy and purpose. The ball wound up where the defense wasn't. Cousy never did more than that.

"A couple times after we went to our spread," Knight said, "we were up by 10 or 12 and Jimmy wanted to win by a couple more, I guess." He zipped some passes for baskets rather than security and had them picked off.

"But he handled the ball very well," Knight said.

That wasn't his primary role. He went in to play defense against Wood. "He is a good athlete," Wood said later. "You expect good athletes to be good defensive players."

Wood spun on Thomas and threw in a 15-foot jump shots seconds after he entered the game. "All I knew after that was I had to get there quicker," Thomas said. "He has to be one of the top players in the country. He is really quick and agile with his jump shot."

Thomas gained a certain notability simply by signing at IU, as the first player from out of the Illinois-Ohio-Indiana orbit to be recruited by Knight since his first Hoosier season. Thomas is from Fort Lauderdale, Fla.

"The only goal I had when I came here," he said, "was to be on a championship team."

For Landon Turner, who also made the all-Final Four team as the capstone to an up and down year that was almost all up through the 10-game streak that carried IU to Big Ten and NCAA championships, the national title was staggering.

"I've never done anything like this before," he said. "My teams have never won anything. I'll remember this the rest of my life."

The thought of winning an NCAA title — the actual thought, not a dream — "always was in the back of my mind," he said. "We were definitely thinking championship near the end of the Big Ten season because we were playing pretty well. We always knew we had a chance."

Turner is impressed by the rebounding instincts of James Thomas.

"I'm big, and I really have to work at rebounding," Turner said. "He has a nose for the ball. He just knows where it is going to go and it pays off for him."

Isiah Thomas said James "gave a second dimension to our offense" in the title game. "When Ted got his three quick fouls, they were able to concentrate on Randy and me outside. When James came in and stuck in his first shot, they had to guard him.

"When they went to a man-to-man, I was able to go inside and he got the ball to me."

Isiah Thomas was 1-for-7 shooting the first half, but he said he felt good about the team's victory chances. "We were up one point at the half (27-26) and we had played terrible," he said.

"That's why I said the most important play of the game was the shot Randy hit just before the half. That really helped.

"I think the main difference the second half was we relaxed. We were a little too impatient the first half. And we also shot a little better the second half (12-for-19, .632, after a .379 start)."

Hoosiers get chance to answer: A-C-Who?

At Chapel Hill in December, a national TV audience that included the segment in Bloomington heard a capacity North Carolina crowd celebrate imminent victory over Indiana by chanting loudly and firmly: "A-C-C! A-C-C!"

When a national championship was at stake and Indiana was the one closing in on victory, the Hoosier crowd got its chance to answer and did, booming out: "A-C-Who? A-C-Who?"

There was a distinct lack of bitterness, however, between the combatants. North Carolina went away disappointed, turned back in the championship for the third time under Smith, one of history's most successful coaches. The reason, the Carolinians from Smith on down agreed, primarily was the trademark of Smith's counterpart: Bob Knight defense.

"Defensively, Indiana was more aggressive than at Chapel Hill," Smith said.

"They put good pressure on us. I didn't think it would bother us — it didn't bother us in the first game, but it did at Bloomington a year ago.

"I would have liked to have gotten the ball to Wood more. If we made a mistake, it was trying to get the ball inside too much."

Wood went over the 2,000-point mark in his final collegiate game with 18 points, but the man who scored 39 against Virginia was as impressed with the Hoosier defense as his coach was.

"They took us out of our offense at the beginning of the second half," Wood said.

"We either turned it over or shot it and missed it, and they just kept adding on and adding on. Time just eventually ran out on us."

North Carolina came into the game shooting .548 in tournament play. Against the Hoosiers, their mark was .426.

"We were rushing some of our shots," said Wood, who went 6-for-13 against Turner and Thomas.

"Some of the shots we normally knock in we didn't knock in.

"Their defense puts a lot of pressure on you initially. It's really hard to get into your offense.

"I have to give a lot of credit to their big men. They really make you work for what you get inside. They made us work so hard to get the ball."

Wood also was impressed with the Hoosier offense. "They know each other so well," he said. "You know they're going to go inside to Turner and Tolbert, and Wittman and Isiah are going to hit those jumpers. They have a lot of confidence in each other."

Worthy said IU's defense "was a big factor in the second half. They forced us into some turnovers and they capitalized on

Phil Isenbarger, Chuck Franz, Steve Bouchie, Glen Grunwald — Part of Hoosier bench saluted by starters

them. Their defense is so aggressive they just *makes* you turn the ball over.

"They hound you and make it very difficult to run your offense. We haven't seen a man-to-man like that all season. It's a little difficult to get into your offense when they're picking off the perimeter passes."

Perkins made first-year all-America teams, and he admitted that finishing as a national runnerup in his first try did not leave him disappointed.

He was surprised. The Indiana team he met wasn't the one he and the Tar Heels nailed at Chapel Hill in December.

"They're a new ball club," he said. "They play much better D (defense).

"And they were more patient this time. They've got a guard that's smart and a coach who teaches them well and disciplines them.

"They're the best defensive team we've faced all year. They don't let up in their defense. They're good; they're aggressive. When they come out for the second half, they're still there."

Worthy noted the primary Hoosier defensive pressure is on the guards, and Tar Heel guard Mike Pepper said the Hoosiers exerted exceptional pressure at the start of the second half. "I think for a short span we were slightly flustered," Pepper said.

"Their delay game was excellent. They really controlled the ball game."

IU mark worst of champs, but margin one of best

Indiana's 26-9 record replaced the 27-7 record of Marquette's 1977 NCAA champions as the poorest ever for a winner in the 43-year-old tournament. But the Hoosiers go into the books, nonetheless, as one of the tournament's most authoritative winners. IU's average winning margin of 22.6 points in its championship charge is the third-best ever for an NCAA winner and second-best among teams that didn't have a close game (winning margin under 10) in the tournament. UCLA's unbeaten 1967 team (Lew Alcindor's junior year) had a 22.8 average margin over its four tournament opponents. Other teams high on that list include the Earvin Johnson Michigan State team of 1979, the Jerry Lucas-John Havlicek Ohio State team of 1960, the Alex Groza-Ralph Beard Kentucky team of 1949, the Bill Walton UCLA team of 1973 and the Bill Russell SanFrancisco team of 1956.

NCAA CHAMPS WITH ALL MARGINS 10 OR MORE

	G	Lo	Hi	Av.	W-L
1. UCLA, 1967	4	13	49	22.8	30-0
2. Indiana, 1981	5	13	35	22.6	26-9
3. Michigan State, 1979	5	11	34	20.8	26-6
4. Ohio State, 1960	4	17	22	19.5	25-3
5. UCLA, 1970	5	11	23	18.0	28-1
6. Kentucky, 1949	3	10	29	17.3	32-2
7. Oregon, 1939	3	13	18	15.3	29-5
8. UCLA, 1973	4	11	17	15.3	30-0
9. San Francisco, 1956	3	11	18	14.0	29-0

BIGGEST AVERAGE MARGIN

	G	Lo	Hi	Av.	W-L
1. Loyola, 1963	5	2	69	23.0	29-2
2. UCLA, 1967	4	13	49	22.8	30-0
3. Indiana, 1981	5	13	35	22.6	26-9
4. UCLA, 1968	4	9	32	21.3	29-1
5. Michigan State, 1979	5	11	34	20.8	26-6
6. Ohio State, 1960	4	17	22	19.5	25-3
7. Oklahoma A&M, 1945	3	4	27	18.7	27-4
8. UCLA, 1970	5	11	23	18.0	28-1
UCLA, 1972	4	5	32	18.0	30-0
10. Kentucky, 1958	4	1	33	17.5	23-6
11. Kentucky, 1949	3	10	29	17.3	32-2
12. Indiana, 1940	3	9	24	17.0	21-3

Sagarin had tourney mapped out in advance

Mathematician Jeff Sagarin, who has used a computerized system to rate college, professional and high school football and basketball teams for *The Herald-Telephone*, had a pollsters' dream year in the 1981 NCAA tournament.

When regular-season play ended, Sagarin had eventual national champion Indiana ranked first, runnerup North Carolina second, and the other two members of the Final Four, Virginia and Louisiana State, tops among the teams that made up their regionals.

The coaches who vote in the United Press International poll had Indiana seventh.

Two years ago, Sagarin also differed with the polls when he ranked Michigan State a solid No. 1 at the end of the season.

Last year, neither the polls nor Sagarin liked eventual winner Louisville. Indiana's late-season rush to the Big Ten championship made the 1980 Hoosiers No. 1 at the end for Sagarin that year, too.

UPI PRE-TOURNEY POLL MARCH 10

1. DePaul (35)	27-1	621	11. UCLA	20-6	154
2. Oregon State (6)	26-1	582	12. Iowa	21-6	148
3. Virginia	25-3	470	13. Louisville	21-8	108
4. Louisiana State	28-3	468	14. Wake Forest	22-6	94
5. Arizona State (1)	24-3	467	15. Tennessee	20-7	93
6. North Carolina	25-7	340	16. Wyoming	23-5	76
7. Indiana	21-9	293	17. Brigham Young	22-6	56
8. Kentucky	22-5	289	18. Illinois	20-7	54
9. Notre Dame	22-5	285	19. Kansas	19-7	51
10. Utah	24-4	181	20. Maryland	20-9	42

SAGARIN RATINGS, MARCH 10

1. Indiana	21- 9	94.58	11. Iowa	21- 6	91.27
2. North Carolina	25- 7	93.98	12. Louisville	21- 8	90.68
3. Oregon State	26- 1	93.88	13. Wyoming	23- 5	90.48
4. Virginia	25- 3	93.64	14. Kansas	19- 7	89.97
5. Illinois	20- 7	92.23	15. UCLA	20- 6	89.88
6. Louisiana State	28- 3	91.72	16. Fresno State	25- 3	89.80
7. DePaul	27- 1	91.67	17. Maryland	20- 9	89.78
8. Wake Forest	22- 6	91.53	18. Brigham Young	22- 6	88.62
9. Arizona State	24- 3	91.41	19. Mississippi	16-13	88.53
10. Kentucky	22- 5	91.35	20. Notre Dame	22- 5	88.45

IU goes around UCLA for best tourney record

Indiana's fourth NCAA championship leaves the Hoosiers behind UCLA (10) and Kentucky (5) in national titles, but IU's five victories this year moved the Hoosiers around UCLA into first place in the NCAA's all-time tournament won-lost percentage list. Indiana's 27-7 record is a won-lost average of .794, while UCLA's 60-16 works out to .789.

ALL-TIME NCAA RECORDS
Minimum 10 games won

	W	L	Pct.	1	2	3	4
1. Indiana	27	7	.794	4	0	1	0
2. UCLA	60	16	.789	10	1	2	1
3. Michigan State	10	4	.714	1	0	0	1
4. Cincinnati	20	9	.690	2	1	2	0
5. Ohio State	22	10	.688	1	3	4	0
California	11	5	.688	1	0	1	0
7. Oklahoma State	15	7	.682	2	1	0	1
8. Duke	17	8	.680	0	2	2	0
9. Michigan	15	8	.652	0	2	1	0
10. Kentucky	43	23	.652	5	2	1	0
11. San Francisco	21	12	.636	2	0	1	0
12. North Carolina	27	17	.614	1	4	1	2
13. Kansas	22	14	.611	1	3	0	2
14. Marquette	24	16	.600	1	1	0	0
15. Dartmouth	10	7	.588	0	2	0	0
Illinois	10	7	.588	0	0	3	0

Game drew criticism, but all else went on

In Philadelphia, the morning after the NCAA championship game, the Inquirer *ran two game articles that started with questions whether the game should have been played, and a nationally circulated column censuring the NCAA for letting it go on. Other major columnists joined in the criticism, which included some references to players' answers given to reporters' questions after the game. H-T columnist Bob Hammel's criticism of the criticism ran a day later.*

It has been surprising to me to read in the last two days the widespread and sometimes vitriolic criticism of the NCAA for going ahead with its basketball finals Monday night hours after President Reagan was shot.

It is an absolute outrage to me that some of the critics have used post-game comments by the players involved to build their case of blatant insensitivity at work.

The players' answers were to questions that essentially asked how they could go ahead with business as usual . . . asked by reporters who, in being there to ask the questions, were going ahead with business as usual.

The NCAA is asked how it could run the finals of its tournament, although not one critic I have seen has questioned why the rest of Philadelphia went on with the routine of the day — why, indeed, the rest of the nation did?

It's strange that it somehow was blasphemous to let young athletes go ahead with the peak moment in their lives while no one noticed that *The Best Little Whorehouse in Texas* ran its usual performance on Broadway. As did *The Woman of the Year*, and *Chorus Line*, and *Ain't Misbehavin'*, and *Annie*.

No, said Sandra Hance, special projects coordinator for the League of New York Theaters and Producers, she hasn't seen one word of criticism leveled at Broadway.

In Las Vegas, every house stayed open, every show went on,

Randy Wittman and Isiah Thomas meet the press

except at the darkened operation of that noted sensitivist Frank Sinatra.

NBC was assailed for running a basketball telecast, Bryant Gumbel disowned his own network, and Al McGuire pleaded innocence, though no one said either couldn't forfeit his paycheck that night and walk away if he truly felt business as usual, business as obligated — real or perceived in the extent of that obligation — shouldn't have continued.

It amazes me that it somehow was wrong for NBC to run basketball but acceptable for ABC and CBS to resume their regular programming at roughly the same time NBC did. No one in Bloomington may be able to confirm it, but ABC says it ran a David Frost special on show business, with special features on Marilyn Monroe (subtitled "Suicide or Murder?") and Pat Benatar (subtitled "Hot Queen of Rock") and a John Denver-George Burns special during the time of the basketball telecast. CBS went back to its potent Monday night lineup, with *M*A*S*H* and *Lou Grant*, while Indiana and North Carolina played basketball.

Of course there was a terrible pall cast over the day by the stunning development in Washington. It may be a sickening comment on our age that by the time the national championship was being contested in Philadelphia, there almost was cause for celebration — at the least, there was a sense of profound relief. Yes, the president of the United States had been shot. He also was going to live. We aren't accustomed to having our life-interrupting bulletins turn out with so happy an ending.

Certainly the one that came in November, 1963, didn't. In one horrifying instant, it changed the inconceivable to the all too conceivable. For long hours, days and weeks, the one tragedy in Dallas injected gloom into American life. For years, it has had its effects.

One of those effects was to take the sudden zeal for public service that had been whipped up within young Americans by a vibrant and youthful president and turn it into a cynical distrust with those turn-off words, "What's the use?" at its heart — confirmed and reinforced by the shots that five years later cut down two more American leaders.

It is ironic that the gulf created between youth and its elders began because the kids were telling us about insensitivities, and now it is our generation lecturing to them about playing basketball instead of grieving.

It somehow is read as evil that the NCAA based at least part of its decision on the condition of the president's health. The whole mood of the country swung on exactly those degrees of health. Of course it would have affected mood and activities — yours, mine, the Rockefeller Center janitor's and the cell block occupant's — if the president's condition had been more grave.

It wasn't, and if the critics of the NCAA's activity were not swept away with a flood of relief, perhaps they are blessed with a sensitivity not common to the rest of us.

Please don't cite to me the example of the Motion Picture Academy in delaying its Oscar presentations for a day. Quite obviously, the Oscar people were dealing with a problem that went beyond sensitivity. Johnny Carson had a whole monologue to rewrite.

Otherwise, the show went on across the nation Monday night, and only the NCAA and some 19-, 20- and 21-year-old basketball players were asked to explain why.

Many of those same youngsters — including Isiah Thomas, including Durand Macklin, including Jeff Lamp — were wearing tiny pieces of green while they played, to indicate their concerns for the terrible tragedy that goes on unsolved and unended in Atlanta.

I haven't noticed anyone in my profession wearing green. I don't believe those youngsters, above all, deserve lectures on insensitivity.

North Carolina's Al Wood is hemmed in by Landon Turner and Isiah Thomas

WON 26, LOST 9, NCAA CHAMPIONS

	Playing time			Shooting				Rebounds			Ballhandling				Fouls		Scoring		
	G	S	M	FG	Pct.	FT	Pct.	R	Av.	Hi	A	Bl	St	TO	PF	D	TP	Av.	Hi
Isiah Thomas	34	34	1194	212- 383	.554	121-163	.742	105	3.1	8	197	3	74	107	105	3	545	16.0	39
Ray Tolbert*	35	35	1204	177- 301	.588	74-100	.740	224	6.6	11	50	38	25	71	92	2	428	12.2	26
Randy Wittman	35	32	1202	155- 286	.542	53- 69	.768	79	2.3	5	77	4	27	39	63	2	363	10.4	20
Landon Turner	33	18	709	138- 246	.561	38- 53	.717	122	3.7	9	26	18	15	66	91	5	314	9.5	23
Ted Kitchel	34	27	773	113- 243	.465	88-103	.854	113	3.3	9	46	3	17	43	87	3	314	9.2	40
James Thomas	33	10	495	47- 95	.495	27- 35	.771	105	3.2	9	77	5	24	34	44	2	121	3.7	12
Steve Risley*	31	8	389	33- 73	.452	28- 43	.651	71	2.3	9	21	2	10	14	30	0	94	3.0	12
Tony Brown	28	8	318	38- 83	.458	15- 28	.536	36	1.3	5	34	0	14	30	22	0	91	3.3	18
Glen Grunwald*	27	1	188	21- 41	.512	8- 13	.615	33	1.2	4	16	0	4	17	31	0	50	1.9	10
Steve Bouchie	29	2	211	18- 47	.383	9- 11	.818	35	1.2	4	8	1	4	6	39	2	45	1.6	8
Phil Isenbarger*	26	0	133	15- 25	.600	13- 20	.650	30	1.2	6	15	1	6	12	21	0	43	1.7	6
Chuck Franz	21	0	87	7- 12	.583	14- 16	.875	7	0.3	2	13	0	2	8	14	0	28	1.3	6
Mike LaFave	15	0	33	3- 8	.375	5- 8	.625	13	0.9	5	2	1	2	2	4	0	11	0.7	5
Craig Bardo	4	0	12	1- 3	.333	2- 3	.667	1	0.3	1	0	0	0	2	5	0	4	1.0	2
Indiana	35			978-1846	.530	495-665	.744	1144	32.7	44	582	76	224	450	648	19	2451	70.0	99
Opponents	35			793-1820	.436	462-645	.716	1104	31.5	46	414	72	164	531	665	23	2048	58.5	83

*Seniors

WON 14, LOST 4, CONFERENCE CHAMPIONS

	Playing time			Shooting				Rebounds			Ballhandling				Fouls		Scoring		
	G	S	M	FG	Pct.	FT	Pct.	R	Av.	Hi	A	Bl	St	TO	PF	D	TP	Av.	Hi
Isiah Thomas	18	18	651	107-201	.532	81-103	.786	70	3.9	8	88	2	35	62	58	3	295	16.4	39
Ray Tolbert*	18	18	617	107-171	.626	44- 60	.733	119	6.6	10	29	22	11	42	57	2	258	14.3	19
Randy Wittman	18	15	647	77-137	.562	26- 36	.722	38	2.1	5	36	1	13	21	30	1	180	10.0	18
Ted Kitchel	17	15	435	51-131	.389	59- 70	.843	62	3.7	7	30	1	9	22	43	1	161	9.5	40
Landon Turner	16	5	249	53- 83	.639	14- 16	.875	39	2.4	9	11	4	1	27	43	3	120	7.5	20
Tony Brown	16	7	219	29- 59	.492	9- 16	.563	24	1.5	5	25	0	10	22	15	0	67	4.2	18
Steve Risley*	18	5	259	23- 44	.523	18- 27	.667	48	2.7	9	16	1	7	12	22	0	64	3.6	12
James Thomas	18	7	301	18- 35	.514	21- 25	.840	59	3.5	7	38	3	14	17	24	1	57	3.4	10
Steve Bouchie	14	0	84	9- 16	.563	3- 3	1.000	11	0.8	2	2	0	0	3	12	0	21	1.5	9
Glen Grunwald*	12	1	77	7- 14	.500	5- 7	.714	13	1.1	4	4	0	1	10	13	0	19	1.6	10
Phil Isenbarger*	10	0	38	5- 6	.833	3- 6	.500	9	0.9	3	3	1	1	7	6	0	13	1.3	3
Chuck Franz	11	0	41	3- 4	.750	7- 8	.875	2	0.2	1	6	0	3	3	6	0	13	1.2	5
Mike LaFave	8	0	13	1- 3	.333	2- 2	1.000	3	0.4	2	0	1	1	2	1	0	4	0.5	2
Indiana	18			490-906	.541	292-379	.770	583	32.4	43	289	36	104	255	333	11	1272	70.7	98
Opponents	18			407-962	.423	263-342	.769	554	30.8	46	203	45	86	256	352	14	1077	59.8	83

*Seniors

WON 5, LOST 0, NATIONAL CHAMPIONS

	Playing time			Shooting				Rebounds			Ballhandling				Fouls		Scoring		
	G	S	M	FG	Pct.	FT	Pct.	R	Av.	Hi	A	Bl	St	TO	PF	D	TP	Av.	Hi
Isiah Thomas	5	5	176	33- 56	.589	25- 31	.806	13	2.6	4	43	1	10	13	16	0	91	18.2	27
Ray Tolbert*	5	5	191	28- 44	.636	13- 19	.684	39	7.8	11	10	6	4	8	8	0	69	13.8	26
Landon Turner	5	5	151	28- 51	.549	10- 13	.769	27	5.4	8	5	2	3	8	16	2	66	13.2	20
Randy Wittman	5	5	164	25- 47	.532	12- 13	.923	12	4.0	4	10	0	3	6	3	0	62	12.4	20
Ted Kitchel	5	5	94	12- 32	.375	11- 13	.846	16	3.2	6	5	0	1	6	16	0	35	7.0	13
James Thomas	5	0	103	10- 19	.526	3- 4	.750	22	4.4	9	15	2	2	4	5	0	23	4.6	12
Steve Risley*	5	0	55	4- 9	.444	5- 10	.500	13	2.6	4	3	0	1	1	4	0	13	2.6	5
Phil Isenbarger*	4	0	8	5- 7	.714	0- 0	.000	2	0.5	1	3	0	0	0	3	0	10	2.5	6
Glen Grunwald*	4	0	12	2- 3	.667	3- 4	.750	4	1.0	2	2	2	0	1	2	0	7	1.8	4
Steve Bouchie	4	0	24	3- 10	.300	1- 2	.500	7	1.8	3	3	3	0	1	0	0	7	1.8	5
Chuck Franz	4	0	7	1- 2	.500	2- 2	1.000	0	0.0	0	0	0	0	1	4	0	4	1.0	2
Mike LaFave	3	0	5	1- 1	1.000	0- 0	.000	8	2.7	6	0	0	0	0	1	0	2	0.7	2
Indiana	5			153-284	.539	88-116	.759	189	37.8	43	101	11	25	46	80	2	394	78.8	99
Opponents	5			110-280	.393	61- 84	.726	164	32.8	41	53	7	21	70	111	6	281	56.2	72

*Seniors

Martha Webster and 'Indiana' mop up . . .

Manager Dave Armstrong reads The Good Book . . .

Mary Thomas, mother of Isiah, beams . . .

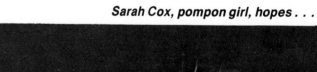

Sarah Cox, pompon girl, hopes . . .

IU recruits John Flowers, Rick Rowray, Dan Dakich, Winston Morgan — All-Stars all

Four Indiana All-Stars recruited for '82 team

Four top players from the 1981 Indiana high school crop comprise the recruiting group that will be added to the returnees from the NCAA champions to form the 1981-82 IU team.

Signing with IU this year were 6-9 John Flowers of Fort Wayne South, 6-6 Rick Rowray of Muncie Central, 6-6 Dan Dakich of Andrean and 6-4 Winston Morgan of Madison Heights. All four were named to the Indiana All-Star team.

Morgan is the third Hoosier recruited from the program of IU letterman Phil Buck at Madison Heights. Others were Bobby Wilkerson and Ray Tolbert. Each played on an NCAA championship team at IU as a senior.

Hoosier starters honor reserves

Plaques honoring the reserves on Indiana's 1981 national champions were presented to them by the five starters at the Hoosiers' awards banquet.

The plaques — to "the toughest team we played in March" — went to seniors Steve Risley, Glen Grunwald and Phil Isenbarger, sophomores Jim Thomas, Steve Bouchie and Chuck Franz and freshman Mike LaFave.

George Washington job to Gimelstob

Gerry Gimelstob, a member of Indiana's basketball coaching staff for five years, became the latest Bob Knight assistant to move into a head coaching role when he was selected by George Washington University.

Gimelstob, 30, joined Knight's staff as a graduate assistant in 1972, after playing at Rhode Island and graduating with honors in economics. He completed work toward his master's in college personnel administration and joined Jerry Pimm's staff at Utah for four years. He returned as an IU aide in 1978.

Previous coaches who have been on Knight's staff at Indiana and gone on to college head coaching roles include Dave Bliss of Southern Methodist, Mike Krzyzewski of Duke, Bob Weltlich of Mississippi, Bob Donewald of Illinois State, Ted Chidester of Brigham Young-Hawaii and Lionel Sinn of Northwest Missouri. Including Knight's six years as head coach at Army, his former assistants in the coaching field include Don DeVoe of Tennessee, Gale Daugherty of Ohio Northern, Bruce Huckle of Miami Dade South Junior College and Mike Schuler, who resigned at Rice this spring to become an assistant coach with the New Jersey Nets.

Jene Davis, who has been serving as a volunteer assistant with the Hoosiers, was named to succeed Gimelstob as a full-time assistant.